a reader's guide to
James
JOYCE

William York Tindall

The Noonday Press
a division of
Farrar, Straus & Giroux
New York

preface

This book is for general readers—for those who, attracted and puzzled by Joyce's books, want to know more about them.

Almost everyone agrees today that Joyce is important. One or another of his works commonly appears in lists of the "hundred best books," along with works of Sophocles, Homer, and Dante. We agree that, like Shakespeare, Joyce was a master of words and that his verbal arrangements, offering ways of accosting reality, increase our awareness and give pleasure. We agree with less enthusiasm that Joyce is a difficult writer, increasingly difficult as, going along, he saw more and more in things and found more ways to say what he saw.

From the comparative simplicity of *Dubliners* and A *Portrait of the Artist* he advanced to the complexity of *Ulysses* and *Finnegans Wake*. Everyone needs help with everyone of these, even the simpler ones, which prove to be less simple than they seem.

Whatever the degree of difficulty, all these books are about the same thing. Indeed, Joyce wrote one great work in several books, each of which is connected with the others. *Dubliners*, an early part of this great work, anticipates *Finnegans Wake*, the last, and *Finnegans Wake* returns to the matter of *Dubliners*. For Joyce, as for Alexander Pope, the proper study was mankind. Mankind in

Dublin, his particular subject, became mankind everywhere at every time. An expanding work of many parts, including everyone and everything, demanded more and more elaborate treatment and a variety of approaches. Joyce is no more difficult than he had to be.

My job, as I see it, is pointing to things in the text: details that might escape notice, relationships among parts and books. My job is asking questions, hazarding guesses, and, sometimes, when almost sure of something, announcing it. Displaying the text, I invite others to go further into it than I. Not as critic here, still less as scholar, I think of myself as teacher.

Centered on the text, this book does not concern Joyce the man, save for incidental reference. He has done his work and here it is before us. Somewhere else, above it or behind it, he is none of our business. Our business is his work alone. Pointing, questioning, and inviting, I do not pretend to have exhausted its possibilities. Like all great literature—like the world itself—his great creation is inexhaustible; and that is part of the fun—for us as for the bums of Samuel Beckett, who find delight and peace in puzzling endlessly. The many-leveled complexities of dancing bees, for example, move Moran of *Molloy* to say: "I was more than ever stupefied by the complexity of this innumerable dance, involving . . . determinants of which I had not the slightest idea. And I said, with rapture, Here is something I can study all my life, and never understand." This goes for intricacies of Joyce as well. We try in vain for last words here.

Some years back I wrote a book called *James Joyce, his Way of Interpreting the Modern World*. By no means supplanting that general introduction and broad survey, the present book is specific introduction and examination of parts.

Intent on texts, I look at the major works in chronological order from *Dubliners* to *Finnegans Wake*. A variety of approaches seemed necessary. *Dubliners* demanded examination story by story. The broader examinations of A *Portrait* and *Exiles* seemed called for by their nature. I consider *Ulysses* and *Finnegans Wake* chapter by chapter, even line by line at times. As for space, I devote most to *Ulysses* because most readers would want to know most about this. Though few may dare to enter the mazes of *Finnegans Wake*, I have provided brief and, I think, useful accounts of the whole and its parts. As I accost the more formidable texts, the apparatus of notes and parenthetical numbers gets more formidable; for if I am to be of use at all, I must take account of pages and details, whatever the cost to appearance. My numbers and notes should bring readers to the text—though not, of course, to all of it. Necessarily I have been selective.

Questioning students have guided me, and I have tried to anticipate further questions. For many years I have taught classes in Joyce. With the texts before us, we have talked, questioned, and pointed out together. My experience with the engineers and executives of the American Telephone and Telegraph Company has been no less helpful. For a number of years I have gone to Philadelphia in the spring to talk with them about Joyce at the Institute of Humanistic Studies for Executives. I am as grateful to them as to my more academic, and less surprising, students for noticing things I should never have noticed without them. They have taught me more than I them. The reading of Joyce, too much for man alone, is necessarily co-operative.

I thank Robert Ryf, Virginia Moseley, Marguerite Warfield, Leo Haas, Jane Coleman, Kevin Sullivan, Leonard Albert, Marvin Magalaner, and Julian Kaye for hints and insights, and, above all others, I thank Nathan Halper, my authority on *Finnegans Wake*. I am indebted for details to Frederick Johnson, Chester Anderson, Lawrence Thompson, Patrick Henchy of Dublin, and Fritz Senn of Zurich.

The editions of Joyce referred to in my clutter of parentheses are *The Portable James Joyce* (Viking Press), which contains *Dubliners, A Portrait of the Artist,* and *Exiles; Ulysses* (Random House); and *Finnegans Wake* (Viking Press).

I am grateful to Mr. B. W. Huebsch and The Viking Press for permission to quote from *Dubliners, A Portrait of the Artist as a Young Man, Exiles, Finnegans Wake,* and *Letters of James Joyce.* I am grateful to Random House for permission to quote from *Ulysses,* and to New Directions for permission to quote a passage from *Stephen Hero.*

W. Y. T.

Columbia University
June 16, 1959

contents

Dubliners

Dubliners consists of fifteen stories about Dubliners. Though each of these stories has a beginning, a middle, and an end, some seem lacking in conventional shape or import; yet, however unlike those in popular magazines, these stories are of a kind more or less familiar since the time of Chekhov. Lacking in obvious action maybe, the stories of *Dubliners* disclose human situations, moments of intensity. Each moves toward a moral, social, or spiritual revelation. To the simple reader, deceived by surfaces, Joyce's stories may seem simple, but they are not so simple as they seem. To the ingenious reader, these stories, though complicated enough, may seem more complicated than they are. Simplicity is the reader's Scylla and ingenuity his Charybdis. Our prudent course lying somewhere betwixt and between, we must try to see these fifteen things exactly as they are.

What holds them together and makes them a book—or one at least of the controlling principles—is a theme or common idea. Hinted on the first page of *Dubliners* and displayed in the last story, this theme is "paralysis" or living death. That paralysis was meant to be the central word and a clue to meaning is confirmed by Joyce himself, who, in a letter of 1904, said he intended *Dubliners* "to betray the soul of that . . . paralysis which many consider a city." His stories, faithful to his intention, betray impo tence, frustration, and death. His city is the heart of paralysis and all the citizens are victims. Eveline, for example, is a girl too moribund to abandon the dust of her native city for the good air of exile; and most of the partygoers in "The Dead," look less alive than the buried.

The paralysis of Joyce's Dubliners is moral, intellectual, and spiritual. In his letters, which provide excellent statements of intention, Joyce calls his book a chapter of the "moral history" of his country and a first step toward its "spiritual liberation." An agent of "civilisation," *Dubliners* affords his countrymen "one good look at themselves" in a "nicely polished looking-glass"; and the mirrors of literary tradition, we recall, are moral devices. Since Joyce was defending his book against the objections of publisher and printer, these letters may exaggerate a little; but it is plain from the text itself that Joyce's aim was moral. Publishers and printers, however, unable to perceive embodied aim and indifferent to his letters, maintained their objections to the immorality of such stories as "An Encounter" and "Two Gallants." With somewhat more justification, they also objected to the indecency of Joyce's diction, to "bloody," for example, a word, harmless to Americans, that leaves no Briton undismayed. Indecency, to be sure, is not the same as immorality. Whatever concerns our fundamental attitudes toward man is the area of morality, whereas decency, temporal and social, is a matter of decorum. Some of the most moral works—those of Rabelais, Moses, and Chaucer—are indecent here and there. Joyce's work, though as moral as he claimed it to be, is often indecent; yet he defended himself against this charge too: "I have written nothing whatever indecent in *Dubliners*." [1] Immoral would have been the just word here.

Paralysis is moral and central. The moral center of *Dubliners*, however, is not paralysis alone but the revelation of paralysis to its victims. Coming to awareness or self-realization marks the climax of these stories or of most at least; for knowing oneself, as the Greeks knew, is a basis of morality if not the thing itself. The

1. For Joyce's remarks about *Dubliners* see *Letters*, pp. 55, 60-64, 70, 72-73; *Finnegans Wake*, pp. 186-87 (Shem is the author).

little boy of "An Encounter" and "Araby" comes to such knowledge; the coming to awareness of Little Chandler and James Duffy
is far bitterer and more terrible because longer delayed; and the
self-realization of Gabriel, the bitterest and most comprehensive
of all, is not only the point and climax of "The Dead" but of
Dubliners. When Joyce's heroes realize their condition, we too, if
alert and sensitive, become aware of a condition so general that
we cannot have escaped it entirely. The revelation of Dublin to
its citizens and of Dubliners to themselves reveals our world and
ourselves. *Dubliners* brings news to everyone today, New Yorkers
and Londoners alike. Maybe that is why Joyce's printer, preferring
to let dead things lie, was unable to recognize or confront what
he was printing. Knowing that and damning his printer's "conscience," Joyce would not change a bloody word.

His attitude and tone may help to account for a general misunderstanding. No longer enjoying the age of enlightenment, we
expect our moralists to be solemn. A common confusion nowadays
is of the solemn with the profound and the moral: a witty can-
didate for public office seems unreliable. Serious to be sure, Joyce
is hardly ever solemn. However moral the purpose revealed in his
letters and his works, his works are never didactic. As for satire,
with which we feel at home when we meet it in George Orwell,
there is none of it in *Dubliners*. There is no sign here of indignation and what, we ask, is morality without this? Examining detestable things, Joyce seems detached and contemplative. His single gesture in the direction of goodness, which hides somewhere
off stage, is irony; and we distrust ironists as we distrust wits.
Moreover, we are puzzled by gaiety. Joyce's most serious stories are
funny at times, and some, however serious and moral, are altogether hilarious. "Ivy Day" is one example of this and "Grace"
another.

This quarrel of sense with feeling and tone reveals a queer mixture of attitudes toward Dublin. The reader who would fix the
meanings of *Dubliners* must keep this mixture in mind. On the
one hand Dublin is a moral and spiritual "dunghill," as Joyce
once put it in a letter. On the other, the streets and houses are

fascinating, if not always beautiful, and the people, whatever their defects, are eloquent and often agreeable. Joyce treats the cheap politicians of "Ivy Day" and the dubious believers of "Grace" with affection as well as contempt; and his horror is tempered with amusement. A kind of genial humanity attends his examination of all those perverts, drunks, and bullies who, after all, are not only monstrous but human and Irish. "Le problème de ma race," Joyce wrote to a French friend, "est tellement compliqué qu'on besoin de tous les moyens d'un art élastique pour l'esquisser—sans le résoudre." (*Letters*, 118) The "elastic art" of *Dubliners*, presenting without solving, is faithful to Joyce's love and hate. Less moral indictment than distant contemplation, his book is a portrait of "dear dirty Dublin" and a compassionate vision of fallen man.[2]

To Joyce, *Dubliners* had a personal application which, though not our immediate concern or even our business, adds another dimension to a many-dimensioned thing and offers another way of getting at it. All but three of the stories were written in exile, and even the original three were written in contemplation of the flight that Eveline could not undertake. To Joyce, I think, *Dubliners* was not only moral censure, ambiguous portrait, and charitable vision, but a statement of his reasons for exile and its justification. Not only a picture of what he had escaped, the book is a picture of what, had he remained, he might have become. In this sense it is a collection of private horrors. Many of the characters are possible Joyces—Joyces who, lacking his enterprise and sharing Eveline's paralysis, have become as corrupt as their city, Joyces who might have been. Two among these frightening possibilities are named James: Father James Flynn, who is what Joyce might have been as parish priest; and James Duffy or what Joyce, confused with his brother Stanislaus, might have been as bank clerk. The green-eyed pervert of "An Encounter," Lenehan of "Two Gallants," and Hynes of "Ivy Day" are projections of parts and potentialities of their creator. But the principal portrait of Joyce as moribund Dubliner is Gabriel Conroy of "The Dead," who is what Joyce,

2. "Dear dirty Dublin," a phrase from Lady Morgan's *Journals*, appears throughout *Finnegans Wake* to suggest Joyce's divided feeling.

married to Gretta-Nora, might have become had he stayed to teach at his University and had he continued to write reviews for the *Daily Express*. Whatever his feeling for Dublin and whatever its complexity, Joyce felt safer away, contemplating his favorite city at a suitable distance. Such distancing proved necessary for life as well as art.

Let us now consider art under its aspects of wholeness and harmony. The question is whether *Dubliners* is fifteen separate things or a single thing that deserves the name of book. We have seen that common themes assure a kind of coherence or togetherness (a word that George Meredith, D. H. Lawrence, and *McCall's* have made respectable). Parts serving the same purpose are parallel at least to one another; and variations on a theme are among the most traditional, if not the tightest, structures. We may grant that much unity, but what about sequence? How within this whole are fifteen parts arranged? Does the first precede the second, the penultimate the ultimate, and the sixth the seventh by accident or design? Could they be arranged in another pattern, if indeed there is pattern at all, without violence to the whole? These are pleasing questions, and though questions are more profitable than answers in matters of this kind, let us survey hypotheses, of which there are an abundance and a variety.

We used to think the thirty-six poems of *Chamber Music* thirty-six trivial and separate lyrics. Now it is plain that these poems, filled with meaning, compose a logical sequence, a narrative, and a suite of moods. It seems likely that *Dubliners,* commenced shortly after the last poems of *Chamber Music,* is as carefully composed—if not more carefully; for Joyce's progress was from the relatively simple to the unmistakably complex. The letters give little help here. One implies a design from which nothing could be omitted and another, offering the omission of several parts, seems a denial of order. Knowing Joyce, however, we may assume a structure. "I have written my book with considerable care," he said, "in accordance with . . . the classical tradition of my art." (*Letters,* 60) And in another letter he spoke of elements that "rivet the book together" without telling what they are.

That much for preparation, this for hypotheses themselves. The first of the three principal guesses is that the fifteen stories proceed from the individual to the general and from youth to an approximation of maturity by degrees. The opening stories are obviously of youth in Dublin, the others, advancing in time and expanding in scope, concern the middle years of the characters and their social, political, or religious affairs. The next guess is that since *Ulysses* is a parody of Homer's *Odyssey, Dubliners* must be one too. According to this hypothesis, the first story shows Telemachus hunting a father and the last the slaughter of suitors. This retroactive hypothesis, now hovering above the text and now descending, demands more ingenuity than the first but is no more certain. The third guess is that since Joyce was a Catholic, however heretical, he must have used the seven deadly sins for frame. A difficulty is that fifteen stories are hard to fit with seven sins; but if we add the virtues, natural and theological, our mystical mathematics can come out right with the aid of ingenuity. This guess is no less accordant with the text than the others. Certainly these stories are about pride, sloth, envy, rage, gluttony, lust, and covetousness; but since several of the deadly seven appear in each story and virtues are rarely more than implicit, it is hard to establish a moral sequence. Whether we accept the temporal, the Homeric, or the moral hypothesis, or, rejecting all, keep on looking, it is fairly clear that some kind of structure assures harmony. It is clear, as well, that although we know a thing or two about *Dubliners,* we know little yet.

There is little agreement among answers to questions of kind and method. Some think the stories naturalistic, some think them symbolist, and others, sitting on a critical fence, look both ways. Each opinion or position has something to commend it. Edmund Wilson, long ago in *Axel's Castle,* found *Dubliners* "a straight work of Naturalistic fiction," different in every way from symbolist *Ulysses.* At the other extreme, recent critics have found the stories symbolist or symbolist in tendency. By naturalism critics mean objective, straightforward work, abounding in external details, and scientifically ordered by the laws of heredity, environment, and gravity. They think of Zola when applying the term or else of Maupassant. By the term symbolist critics mean many things since no term is less certain than this; but most would agree that external details in a symbolist work are there not for their own sake or to demonstrate a scientific point but to embody and suggest something else, preferably a moral or spiritual condition too general, vague, or slippery for tweezer or caliper. The scalpel, too, could adorn this metaphor; for naturalists often put what they called "slices of life" on their microscopic slides. These slices were commonly revolting, at best disagreeable.

Filled as they are with external detail, the stories of *Dubliners* or several at least look straightforward and, if not scientific, objective. Consider "Two Gallants," "Counterparts," and "The Boarding House." If not slices, what shape do they have at all? Some of Joyce's letters lend support to the naturalistic faction. In one Joyce observed that "the odour of ashpits and old weeds and offal hangs round my stories." In another he allowed that at first glance his stories are "somewhat bitter and sordid." (*Letters,* 64, 70) The bitter, the sordid, and stinks of all descriptions, after all, are what we expect of a naturalist. Joyce, who commanded every manner, deliberately chose for *Dubliners* what he called a style of "scrupulous meanness." Surely a style like that is suitable for scientists or even pseudo-scientists like Zola and his rout.

The symbolist faction finds comfort in the images, rhythms, and suggestive actions of *Dubliners,* forgetting that Zola was as good a symbolist as any. The external things of Joyce's sordid and discouraging stories, this faction holds, are other things entirely, there only to disclose or shadow forth one knows not what. Baudelaire, who used the sordid details of Paris streets (the great originals of Eliot's cigar butts and "female smells") for spiritual revelation, seems Joyce's ancestor. Flaubert, whose flower pots and bourgeois furnishings are spiritual revelations, seems another. Both images and sometimes, as in "The Dead," the elaborate recurrence of images in the manner of Wagnerian *leitmotiv,* establish Joyce's musical and suggestive capacity.[3] Music and suggestion are the marks of symbolists. Joyce runs, therefore, with Mallarmé and his rout.

Symbolists find encouragement in the famous theory of epiphany. Like the "objective correlative" or "inscape" or "the destructive element," the term epiphany is useful, centering our sensibilities while displaying them. Not only a respectable word, however, epiphany fits *Dubliners* and, as many have pointed out, offers another hypothesis, this time about method. Most of us owe the word less to the Church, of course, than to Dedalus himself, who employs it in *Ulysses* and expounds it in *Stephen Hero*.

While walking down the street one day, Stephen Dedalus, discouraged by those brown houses that "seem the very incarnation of Irish paralysis," hears an inane and fragmentary conversation of boy and girl on stoop. This "triviality," a detail of Dublin's streets without obvious value, makes him think of putting many such moments together in a book of "epiphanies." By this word he means "a sudden spiritual manifestation," something that random vulgarities, rising above themselves and transfigured, can yield. In such externals of the street he sees, exceeding naturalistic capacity, "the most delicate and evanescent possibilities" for the writer, who must fix them "with extreme care." The most tiresome items of Dublin's "street furniture," he says, expounding his insight to Cranly and pointing to the clock of the Ballast Office, are capable of epiphany. For Stephen, common things—to use Baudelaire's phrase—have "the expansion of infinite things" and all their radiance. Like Baudelaire, then, he thinks this world a storehouse of things as other things, seeing this or that as revelation. Involving the potency of a neutral object and the sensibility of a subject, epiphany is a transaction between object and subject that owes no less to the former than to the latter. Epiphany, he concludes, is identical with the "radiance" of the aesthetic theory he is expounding to Cranly and is to expound to Lynch in *A Portrait of the Artist*. Plainly Stephen's epiphany or radiance, a

3. Many images (of light, dark, Orient, and father, for example) and many significant actions, recurring frequently, link the stories.

shining out or showing forth, is what we call symbolism and his radiant object a symbol.

Fussy about terms, Stephen prefers epiphany to symbol because the radiance of epiphany is ecclesiastical, that of symbol more secular nowadays, and Stephen, though far from innocent of literary tradition, is centered in the church and country he rejected. The feast of the Epiphany, which occurs on January 6, celebrates the arrival of three kings at a manger, where, though they saw nothing more than baby, saw something more. This Baby, now apprehended and showing forth, is the radiant body. It is from this that Stephen gets his way of looking at the inconsiderable but revelatory objects of Dublin. Of the thing, made potent by insight, by wholeness, and by harmonious relation of parts, he continues: "We recognise that it is *that* thing which it is. Its soul, its whatness, leaps to us from the vestment of its appearance. The soul of the commonest object, the structure of which is so adjusted, seems to us radiant. The object achieves its epiphany." (*Stephen Hero*, 210-11, 213)

Stephen speaks of gathering some into a book; and Joyce himself made a collection of twenty-two epiphanies, some of them fragments of trivial conversation, like Stephen's sample, others dreams or prose poems. Oliver Gogarty tells how at a party Joyce would suddenly leave the room to put an epiphany down in his tablets or so Gogarty guessed. However that may be, we have the collection of twenty-two, set down from time to time between 1901 and 1904. This manuscript, now at the University of Buffalo, was published in 1956. It is less important in itself than for what it implies.

Stephen's theory and this manuscript give us a profitable way of approaching Joyce's works, all of which, as Theodore Spencer observed in his Introduction to *Stephen Hero*, may be thought of as epiphanies, *Dubliners* especially. Each story of this sequence, which Joyce commenced as he was writing the last items in that manuscript, may be thought of as a great epiphany and the container of little epiphanies, an epiphany of epiphanies. We know that Joyce, apparently regarding his collection of twenty-two fragments as a kind of storehouse of material, adapted several for his later works. What better way of conceiving *Dubliners* than as an elaborate extension of these radiant fragments, a more formidable work of the same design? According to this guess the common-place things of Dublin, becoming more than setting or example or stimulus to action, are embodiments or symbols.

Of what, we may ask? That is a good question, and the answers are questions too. Is the radiance of *Dubliners* an idea of paralysis, a feeling of paralysis, or a sinking sensation such as Stephen seems to have felt that day on Eccles Street when he overhears the inane triviality? All we know for sure is that such ideas, feelings, or sensations seem more immediate and authentic when embodied and presented to our sensibilities than when stated or described. Symbol does more, and something else, than statement can and, though radiance evades precise definition, more precisely. Without radiant body *Dubliners* would be a diminished book. We might get the idea, but we should miss the quality and lack the experience; for experienced things are juicier than abstractions—as a dinner seems more authentic than a vitamin pill. This is simile, and simile, like metaphor, is illogical, approximate, inaccurate; but a work of art is also a kind of metaphor, somewhere beyond logic, yet accurate in its domain. *Dubliners* as epiphany is a metaphor for something unstated and unknown, for which *Dubliners* experienced is the only equivalent. Our guesses about it, ultimately beyond demonstration, will be enlarged and limited by the text, by our capacity, and our experience. *Dubliners*, not only a thing, is what we make of it. Cranly, unable to see what Stephen sees and points out, finds the Ballast Office clock inscrutable. What would he make of Waterhouse's clock on Dame Street?

Descending now or maybe ascending, let us abandon figures for facts. Joyce wrote works that are essentially the same, each a part of the great whole to which he devoted himself. *Dubliners*, assuming its part in this grand design, has clear connections with other parts, with A *Portrait* and *Ulysses* in particular. In a letter (83) Joyce called *Ulysses* a "continuation" of A *Portrait* and *Dubliners*. This works the other way as well, and we can look at *Dubliners* as preface to these works, both of which are as firmly rooted in Dublin. *Dubliners* establishes the cause of the exile attempted in A *Portrait*. *Ulysses*, in a sense, is *Dubliners* enlarged. Each episode— the Wandering Rocks or the Cyclops—recalls something of *Dubliners*. The differences of method that seem to separate these three books are not so great as they seem; for each develops from the others or from *Chamber Music*, their general predecessor. Most of the characters of *Dubliners* reappear in *Ulysses*: Bob Doran, Lenehan, Corley, Hynes, Cunningham, Kernan, and many others, having developed, play their parts; and others like Gretta, Mrs. Sinico, and the toddling Morkans are alluded to. Dublin, its people, and a creator's vision are what connect these books.

Before publication, *Dubliners* displeased, and after publication, failed to please. According to Joyce's letters, two hundred copies were sold in the first half year, twenty-six, in the second, and seven in the third. Like Cranly confronted with that clock, first readers must have found the book inscrutable or tedious.

THE SISTERS

One of the most complex and disturbing in the sequence, this story is a riddle. Nothing comes quite clear. The nameless boy who tells the story is "puzzled" by hints and "intricate questions," and so are we. Raising such questions, teasing us with possibilities, the story provides no answers. The key sentence, "There was something gone wrong with him," comes last. We may guess what has gone wrong and with what and with whom but we never know, and that seems the point of the story. Fascinated with the unanswerable question, Joyce put riddles into all his major works, which, to be sure, seem riddles too. Stephen Dedalus and Shem confront them, and Mr. Bloom's day ends with the enigma of M'Intosh. It is proper that Joyce, for whom riddle became obsessive theme, began with a riddle that seems designed in part to establish the idea of riddle.

"The Sisters" opens simply enough with night, paralysis, and death, which, as we have seen, point toward the final story. The word "paralysis" is accompanied by two others, "gnomon" and "simony." These three fascinate the boy, sensitive to words, as we too must be, accosting Joyce. Expert in words, he used them for all they are worth; and we, following at a suitable distance, must use the dictionary, of which his talking boy was also amorous. Gnomon, a figure from geometry, carries a suggestion of Euclid, hence of intellect. Simony, an ecclesiastical sin, has moral and religious bearing. A gnomon is an imperfect figure, however, and simony is an imperfection. These words, neighbors of paralysis, are there to define it. The paralysis in question, though literally a physical imperfection, is also intellectual, moral, and spiritual. Poor James Flynn is the victim and embodiment of this syndrome.

Never there in person, poor Father Flynn is talked about by old Cotter and the sisters and thought about or remembered by the boy. Almost nothing happens. The boy inspects the death notice on the door, and, feeling free at last, crosses to the sunny side of the street; later he visits the corpse with his aunt and, having tasted sherry, retires to a chair. All the rest is talk and memory, from which, by a gradual and almost static process of disclosure, we learn that Father Flynn, a kindly man, who taught the boy much about ritual, tradition, and the sacraments, was a queer one, untidy, ambiguously smiling, torpid, and probably perverse, a priest whose duties "was too much for him." Unable to face his inadequacies and imperfections, he went mad, laughing to himself in the dark of his confession box, before yielding to paralysis and death.

Taken literally, this disclosure is case history; taken symbolically, it means or can mean many things, all of them doubtful. Only the latter possibility detains us. Who or what is Father Flynn, literally a parish priest, potentially more? Since a priest is a father, the Rev. James Flynn, ascending from his parish, may be *the* father, a kind of archetype of fatherhood or the father principle. In this capacity, suggesting all that the image affords, he could include the idea of God, of the Pope, of fatherland, or of ecclesiastical tradition, a fatherly hand-me-down. If we may take him so, his incapacity, madness, paralysis, and death leave Great Britain Street and environs[4] without fatherly assurance. The boy and the sisters, equally at a loss, attempt to supply his abandoned functions. A pseudo-priest, the boy hears confession in a dream and, waking, sips wine, declining the congregational biscuit; and the sisters, though plainly incapable of fatherhood, attempt to carry on by offering wine and biscuits, which, by parodying the sacrament, maintain tradition. They are doing their best; but one is deaf and both, though they beckon and invite, are ignorant and senile. Fatherhood, so maintained, is in a bad way here.

Those sisters, who enjoy (without seeming to deserve) the title role, are even more puzzling than their clerical brother. Are their names, Nannie and Eliza, significant? Why are there two of them?[5] I should find it easier if there were only one. A poor old woman (the traditional figure) could serve as an image of Ireland or of Ireland's Church, attempting to preserve a dead tradition; but two seem one too many unless one is Ireland, the other the Church or unless the word sister implies nurse or nun. This is dubious. Whatever the number, these survivors and Father Flynn, far from being allegorical signs with a definite meaning, are unassigned symbols, without certain import. We cannot call them this or that. That they offer feelings and ideas associated with religion and country is all we can prudently guess. The encounter of the boy with the priest and his survivors is that of a boy, at once dutiful and uneasy, with what surrounds him in Ireland.

This "Rosicrucian" boy[6] brings up another problem: who or what is central in the story, the boy, the priest, the sisters, or an idea? Since the boy tells us the story in first person, it is tempting to think him central and his mind our theater. If so, he is to the priest as Marlow to Kurtz in Conrad's *Heart of Darkness*. Kurtz or Father Flynn is the enigmatic ostensible object of an inquirer

4. This is really Great Denmark Street where Belvedere is located.
5. Compare the two Morkan sisters in "The Dead," the two women in Stephen's Parable of the Plums, (*Ulysses*, p .143) the two washerwomen of *Finnegans Wake* (196), and the two girls near the magazine wall. (8)
6. Does his uncle call him a Rosicrucian because, trained by the priest, the boy (like Rosicrucian Yeats) is an amateur in an elaborate mystery? Rose and Cross, implying the Church, also imply occult heresy in this context.

whose real concern is himself. Like Marlow, the boy is uneasy and no more than partly aware of the mystery he is approaching. From his account, however, we learn more than he seems to know. At the end, Marlow is almost fully aware, but the boy, implying much, displaying little, is content to report. If this is a story of sudden awareness, like many of the others in the book, the awareness is successfully concealed. Doubt alone is well established. Our knowledge, such as it is, comes from three conflicts: the first within old Cotter between suspicion and prudence, the second within the boy between affection and uneasiness, and the third that of the sisters, at once defensive and anxious. Never was subjective drama more ambiguous.

The methods by which Joyce establishes this ambiguity are various and appropriate, ranging in kind from the expressive dots of old Cotter's monologue ("I puzzled my head to extract meaning from his unfinished sentences.") to conversation, image, rhythm, and dream. That none of these devices was present in the first version (published in the *Irish Homestead* in 1904) proves them deliberate. Two devices from Joyce's twenty-two epiphanies reappear here: the objectively reported, desolating conversation (Eliza's in this case) and the dream. The boy's nightmare of Father Flynn's heavy grey face, feebly smiling, and of his murmured confession is one of the most terrible epiphanies of the story—equal in horror to the boy's waking memory of Flynn: "When he smiled he used to uncover his big discoloured teeth and let his tongue lie upon his lower lip—a habit which . . . made me feel uneasy." The dream, like all else here, is incomplete: "I could not remember the end of the dream." There is nothing of "scrupulous meanness" about the hypnotic rhythm or the diction of this dream.

Two carefully elaborated themes, one of confession, the other of communion, control the imagery. Confession, which begins with that dream, ends with the confession box where poor mad Father Flynn sits laughing to himself. The chalice is the principal image of the more important of these themes. Father Flynn incompetently drops a chalice; for he was "crossed." When dead, he "loosely" holds a chalice; and the glass of wine received by the boy at the table (altar) brings this sequence to its climax. His communion (and we must take this word literally as well as ecclesiastically) is reluctant and, since the congregation takes the biscuit, uncongregational. Are we to take this glass of wine as a kind of Protestant rebellion, as a priestly gesture, or as partial rejection of communion with Ireland and its Church? [7] All we can be sure of is that father's gone.

AN ENCOUNTER

Somewhat less enigmatic, "An Encounter" seems nevertheless a continuation of "The Sisters." There are evident connections between these stories. Both are told in first person by the same boy, who, a little older now, is a student at Belvedere of Great Denmark Street. Both stories are archetypal. The first employs the image of the father, lost, missed, but not yet sought. The second employs the more active archetype of the journey or, rather, of the quest, a journey with a goal. Homer's *Odyssey*, Dante's *Comedy*, Bunyan's *Pilgrim's Progress*, Melville's *Moby Dick*, and many other works owe something of their power, if Jung and Maud Bodkin are right, [8] to this symbolic action.

The present quest is for the Pigeon House, Dublin's electric light and power station on the breakwater in the bay. Light and power suggest God; and the traditional icon of the Holy Ghost is the Pigeon, as we could infer from the first and third chapters of *Ulysses*, where Pigeon and Pigeon House reappear. The quest, therefore, can be taken as a search for the third member of the Trinity or, since Father, Son, and Holy Ghost are one, as that hunt for the father which was to become a theme of *Ulysses*. The questing boys, significantly "mitching" or playing truant, never get to the Pigeon House. Their quest (which only truancy allows) ends

7. Answers to small questions: "High Toast," literally a brand of snuff, may imply the Eucharist administered by the boy as pseudo-priest. "Faints and worms" pertain to a distillery, where spirit is made.
8. See Maud Bodkin, *Archetypal Patterns in Poetry*, available in paperback

in frustration—as such quests must in Dublin. But maybe they find an approximation of the lost father and discover his nature.

The queer old man whom they encounter near the bank of the Dodder at Ringsend resembles Father Flynn in clothing, teeth, perversity, and preoccupation with ritual. Obsessed with hair and whips, his mind, "as if unfolding some elaborate mystery," moves slowly "round and round" like the goats of Stephen's nightmare vision in A *Portrait*. Never having read Krafft-Ebing and not yet aware of what he has encountered, the boy is uneasy at first, as in the presence of Father Flynn, and at last frightened. The pervert's one action is so extraordinary that even insensitive Mahony, the boy's companion, calls the ritualist a "queer old josser." Nothing in Joyce is unconsidered or accidental. Josser, according to Webster, can be English slang for a simpleton, which hardly seems to apply; but the word can also be Pidgin English for a devotee of a joss or a god. (Compare "Lord Joss," *Finnegans Wake*, 611.) Probably not God, as some have thought, the pervert may imply what men, unable to reach the Pigeon House, find in place of Him. Pidgin, a suppressed pun, may be to Pigeon as perversion or a defect of love to love itself. In this sense the old josser with his ritual and his desire to initiate others into the mystery could suggest the Church, burner of Irish joss sticks. However possible, there is nothing certain about this interpretation or, indeed, about any other, whatever the assurance of those whose delight is making molehills of mountains.

Whatever these uncertainties, it is plain that Joyce's intention was partly ironic, even sardonic, and plain that he had the Church in mind. Joe Dillon, playing Indian, yells, " 'Ya! yaka, yaka, yaka, yaka!' Everyone was incredulous when it was reported that he had a vocation for the priesthood." The irony of this juxtaposition recurs in Mahony's question: "What would Father Butler be doing out at the Pigeon House?" That the pervert himself embodies another irony of the kind is made more likely by this context.

Joe Dillon's Indian dance introduces a second theme, that of illusion and disillusionment. Desiring relief from the tedium of school and Dublin, the boy centers his notions of escape and adventure in "green eyes," a private symbol of his romantic ideal. His quest for green eyes is disappointed twice, first by the green-eyed Norwegian sailor, who, shouting, "All right! All right!" seems commonplace, and next by the pervert with his bottle-green eyes. The romantic quest, encountering ignoble reality, proves to be as discouraging as that of the Pigeon House and, though more nearly final, no less frustrating. Paralyzing Dublin, destructive of all ideals, has intervened again.

The third theme, and perhaps the most important, is moral. Pride is the sin, the virtue charity. This boy, feeling superior to Mahony, despises him as crude, obvious, and illiterate, with no interests beyond games and the chasing of birds, cats, and girls. But the boy's pride is shaken by the discovery that he has much in common with the horrible josser and that despised Mahony, their opposite, is normal, human, and solicitous. The last sentence, proving self-realization, expresses an awareness that he too, suffering from pride, suffers from a defect of love. Mahony and the pervert, enabling the narrator to see himself, have shown him charity and humanity. "He ran as if to bring me aid. And I was penitent; for in my heart I had always despised him a little."

Clearly this story is neither naturalistic nor psychopathic. The news that perverts are around is no news at all. Case history is there to reveal something else, something at once theological, ecclesiastical, and moral. What is more, the encounter, involving these, is less with something else or someone else than with self. Meeting himself for the first time, the boy suddenly knows himself, his sin, and his folly—and maybe the nature of Dublin.

Smith, his pseudonym, anticipates Stephen's smithy?

ARABY

The third and simplest part of the opening trilogy is another story of illusion, disillusionment, and coming to awareness. Here again we have a disappointed quest, not for God this time but, plainly, for Ireland's Church. The boy's present quest, like that of Eliot's shadowy Parsifal in *The Waste Land*, is directed by a degenerate Sibyl.

That North Richmond Street, where the boy lives and Joyce once lived, is a "blind end" (dead end to us) is not without significance. A priest has died in the back parlor of the boy's "brown" house, leaving some yellowing books of a romantic sort, and in the back garden, which, like the place of man's fall, has a central apple tree, a rusty bicycle pump. This two-handed engine at the back door (not unlike A.E.'s theosophical bicycle pump in the Circe episode of *Ulysses*) is an instrument of inflation—abandoned now. There are odors of ashpits and stables there.

But in this brown street (brown and yellow are Joyce's colors of paralysis and decay) is the brown but exciting figure of Mangan's sister. Though she keeps the light behind her, the boy's heart leaps up; for he fails as yet to see the meaning of light and dark and of their relative positions. Since Mangan, one of Joyce's favorite poets, dedicated "Dark Rosaleen," his most famous poem, to his country, it seems likely that Mangan's sister is Ireland herself, beckoning and inviting like the sisters of Father Flynn. This Sibyl, commending Araby, starts the boy on his quest.

A bazaar, Araby promises "Eastern enchantment" of the sort that surrounds Father Flynn in the boy's dream. The Church, after all, is a more or less Oriental foundation, and the ecclesiastical suggestion of Araby ("not some Freemason affair") is supported by metaphor. The boy, hearing "litanies" and "chanting" in the secular street, bears his "chalice" safely through the crowd, unlike poor Father Flynn. The boy's distant devotion to Mangan's sister is not unlike that of Dante to his Beatrice.

Delay with mounting suspense, however, puts Araby off. "I'm afraid you may put off your bazaar," says his aunt, implying more than she intends, "for this night of Our Lord." Provided with his florin at last and going into that night, the boy arrives at the building displaying the "magical name," but it is too late: "Nearly all the stalls were closed and the greater part of the hall was in darkness." At this point the ecclesiastical tropes, fixing the implication, resume. The silence is "like that which pervades a church after a service," and at a Café Chantant, two men are counting money "on a salver."

The inane conversation of a young lady with two young gentlemen, a typical epiphany, shows forth emptiness and provides the sinking sensation. To her question the boy replies: "No, thank you." The promise of enchantment has been followed by disenchantment: "the light was out. The upper part of the hall was now completely dark." The final sentence, like that of "An Encounter," records the moment of realization—of Church and self alike—the moment of truth: "Gazing up into the darkness I saw myself as a creature driven and derided by vanity."

EVELINE

One of the earliest of the stories, "Eveline" may have set the theme and tone of the book. Many of the later stories seem elaborate variations upon it or its extensions. I think of this story first when thinking of *Dubliners* not because it is the best story in the book but because it is the most nearly straightforward expression of paralysis and one of the most moving. Though many like to place value in the high region of complexity and obscurity, "Eveline" offers proof that value, not permanently established there, can visit the lowlands too.

The plot is simple. This girl, fretting at a dull job and leading a life of quiet desperation with a brutal father, is offered escape by a sailor. Marriage and flight across the sea promise life and "perhaps love too." But Irish paralysis frustrates her bold design. The end is not a coming to awareness but an animal experience of inability.

In this horror story, which proceeds with great economy of means, every part is functional, even items that at first reading seem casually introduced, the Italian organ grinders, for example, and the visit to the opera. Those organ grinders seem at once messengers from abroad, offering hints of a happier land, and Roman invaders, suggesting Ireland's Church. "Damned Italians! coming over here!" says Eveline's father. As for Balfe's *Bohemian*

Girl, this Irish opera seems there, as in "Clay," to suggest a dream of riches and marble halls, all that is opposite to brown, dusty Dublin.

Images, though less abundant than in the first three stories, are never insignificant. Less nearly central, images serve this story as assistants, supporting and giving immediacy to what is attended to by more discursive means. The chief images, however, include life and death. Dust, which occurs at the opening and recurs during the course of the story, finds its opposites in the good air promised by Buenos Aires and in the sea, the penultimate image of the story. Not unlike Conrad's "destructive element," Joyce's sea, while offering escape and life, threatens death. Unable to swim or walk a gangplank, Eveline fears what alone could save her: "All the seas of the world tumbled about her heart. . . . he would drown her." This terrible living sea, embodying opposites, revealing her dilemma and concentrating it, is what critics would call ambivalent. The iron railing of the dock becomes a cage for this non-amphibious "animal."

The themes of escape and frustration link this story with others, "A Little Cloud," for example, and "An Encounter." Buenos Aires, never reached, is Eveline's Pigeon House. There are other connections too. In "Eveline," as in each of the first three stories, there is a missing priest, represented here by a "yellowing" photograph in the parlor. (Among such priests I count Father Butler, missing from the Pigeon House.) In the stories so far the father image has been important. Eveline's father is as worthless as her fatherland. Her mother, who, like Father Flynn, goes mad before dying, enigmatically exclaims, "Derevaun Seraun!" [9]

Joyce, we recall, described the style of *Dubliners* as one of "scrupulous meanness." Passages such as the boy's dream in "The Sisters" and the final pages of "The Dead," though scrupulous, are far from mean. In "Eveline," however, the style—barren, flat, and scrupulously mean—suits her desolating history and all the living dead.

9. Patrick Henchy of the National Library in Kildare Street thinks this mad and puzzling ejaculation corrupt Gaelic for "the end of pleasure is pain."

AFTER THE RACE

A companion piece to "Eveline," this story, written at about the same time, was also published during 1904 in the *Irish Homestead*. Romantic illusion, disenchantment, and frustrated escape, by now familiar, affirm the place of this story in the general structure. But, plainly prentice work, "After the Race" seems meager by comparison with the rest.

The trouble seems Joyce's unfamiliarity with the subject. Expert in the lower middle class and the upper lower, he had little knowledge of the upper or of the lower upper, the *nouveaux riches*, his present concern. The Shelbourne Hotel was outside his area. What Joyce knew about cars, yachts, and triumphant butchers was nothing at all or less. Such ignorance may excuse the failure of this story but not its unfortunate inclusion.

It is a fact that Joyce had interviewed a French racing driver and published the result in the *Irish Times*, but this brief encounter was not enough to establish insight. Jimmy may owe his name to Joyce's temporary infatuation with speed, elegance, and machine. A first study for Buck Mulligan maybe, Jimmy is less convincing because less lived with.

Nothing alien is alien to romantic, socially-climbing Jimmy. Enamored of Frenchmen and Hungarians, even Englishmen and Americans, he finds their cars and yachts his Pigeon and his Buenos Aires. Bitter realization of his "folly" comes with the grey light of day.

The image of the race, occurring here for the first time, recurs in *Ulysses*. There it is for a Gold Cup; here it probably goes round and round and, like something on the circular track of *A Portrait*, gets nowhere.

TWO GALLANTS

Joyce felt more at home with these two bums. The story of Corley and Lenehan, who reappear in *Ulysses*, was one of Joyce's favorites.

His admiration seems justified. In every way this is a more considerable thing than "After the Race."

Nevertheless "Two Gallants" opens awkwardly with character sketches, traditional devices that the later, economical, and more allusive Joyce would never have allowed. The statement that Lenehan is nimble-witted, good at "limericks and riddles," is unsupported by demonstration here, though abundantly demonstrated in *Ulysses*. Later in the story, however, statement and description yield to image and action.

Lenehan's actions, three in number, are not without possible significance: he looks, eats a mess of peas, and wanders around the city. The emphasis placed on looking makes him seem the neutral, uncommitted observer, attentive to the moral horrors around him, but indifferent—as if his interests were purely aesthetic. As Corley's capital sin seems covetousness, so Lenehan's seems sloth. His dish of peas could imply the mess of pottage for which he has sold his birthright; for, according to the dictionary, pottage is a dish of vegetables, as Joyce expert in Bible and dictionary knew. Jacob and Esau, like Cain and Abel, are generally lurking in his works or behind them. Nothing less than speculation of this sort can account for the emphasis placed on Lenehan's inconsiderable supper. As for his wandering around the city: a map of Dublin shows his course to be almost circular, like that of the racing cars or of the pervert's mind.

Noticing Lenehan's circular movement and all those frustrated journeys toward the east in the preceding stories, Brewster Ghiselin finds a pattern of significant action in *Dubliners*, connecting parts. Eastward movement toward escape and some place of Oriental or Continental enchantment in the earlier stories is balanced by westward movement, toward death, in the later ones. Circular movement, that of Lenehan or of Gabriel Conroy in the Morkans' hall, suggests hopeless acceptance. Applauding this insight, I agree that Joyce used symbolic action as he used image, parallel, and allusion.

Significantly-moving Lenehan sponges on Corley as Corley on the servant girl he met under Waterhouse's clock on Dame Street.

Not that clock but the piece of gold he receives from her constitutes an epiphany. Since jesting Lenehan calls Corley a "base
betrayer," it seems probable that Joyce, continuing his Biblical
allusions, takes this goldpiece as an equivalent of thirty pieces of
silver. It is certain that betrayal, one of Joyce's central themes, is
involved—betrayal in this case of love, humanity, and, I think, of
Ireland herself. That this servant girl, more than literally significant
as she would be in a work of naturalistic fiction, is also the traditional figure of Ireland is all but established by the episode of the
harpist, who plays a mournful melody by Tom Moore, Ireland's
national poet.[10] If we keep Joyce's love of parallels or analogies in
mind, this harpist of Kildare Street suggests Corley and his harp
the girl: "His harp, too, heedless that her coverings had fallen
about her knees, seemed weary alike of the eyes of strangers and of
her master's hands." Corley's connection with the police fits him
for the role of Ireland's "conqueror." In fancy Lenehan becomes
the harpist too as he trails his fingers along the railings of the
Duke's Lawn to Moore's remembered melody.

Not only dressed like Joyce, Lenehan is also eloquent and witty.
To some degree a pitiless self portrait, Lenehan seems Joyce's own
epiphany—or one of them. If this bum is a projection of one aspect
of Joyce or of one of his potentialities, we must consider the identity of Corley. However close their association, Lenehan and Corley are opposites, one the introvert and the other the extrovert.
Their strange relationship, developing into one of Joyce's major
themes, was to produce the equally strange relationships of Stephen
and Mulligan, Shem and Shaun. Corley is the prototype of Shaun.

THE BOARDING HOUSE

Compared with "Two Gallants," this story seems simple—simple
maybe but admirably handled. The style is fittingly ignoble, the

10. Moore's "Silent, O Moyle" includes this line: "Yet still in her darkness
doth Erin lie sleeping." Stephen's "Lir's loneliest daughter" (*Ulysses*, 190) refers to this poem. Two mysterious images recur in "Two Gallants": the veiled
moon, related to both girl and coin; and Lenehan's biscuit. Three times, praising his host, this parasite says: "That takes the biscuit."

revelation of human nature disheartening and funny. We are confronted here with a butcher's daughter, who solves moral problems with a cleaver, with her somewhat common daughter, Polly, and with their conspiracy against poor Bob Doran, whose subsequent decline is recounted in *Ulysses*. For a plot at once so full of guile and so guileless comment seems unnecessary. It is as plain to us as to poor Bob Doran that "he was being had." That all men and all women are implied adds to the fun.

Our interest, aside from pity, fear, and laughter, must be with kind. For the first time in *Dubliners* we encounter a story that can be called naturalistic—more or less. Even with this qualification, "The Boarding House" affords comfort to those who think Joyce loyal to Zola. Never was pressure of environment more obviously displayed. Bob Doran's fall, determined by Dublin's moral conventions and hypocrisies, seems exemplary. The theme, like that of any naturalistic story, is this pressure, within which the "Madam" and her daughter work.

Yet "The Boarding House" lacks the overabundance of observed detail that Zola delighted in; and the end, with action off stage or interior, seems more or other than naturalistic. What links this story with the earlier stories of *Dubliners* is the yielding of Polly's absence of mind to awareness. A difference is that this awareness is less of self (though at her moment of truth she looks at self in mirror) than of conquest. Polly is Corley's female counterpart.

A LITTLE CLOUD

Dense and tightly constructed, "A Little Cloud" is more akin to "Two Gallants" than to its immediate predecessor—as if Joyce's structural principle were slipping doubtful items between strong ones. The pathetic story of Little Chandler and Gallaher is another approach to the affairs of Shem and Shaun.

The title comes from 1 Kings, 18:44. Here, Elijah makes rain to relieve the drought in a literal and moral wasteland. (Elijah "Is coming! Is coming!! Is coming!!!" as we discover in *Ulysses*.) The first sign of rain is a little cloud (also apparent in *Ulysses*), no bigger than a man's hand; and general darkness precedes the down-pour. This seems clear enough, but its application to the case of Little Chandler is uncertain. What is his little cloud, precisely, and what does it portend: increasing darkness or saving rain? Does it promise, after darkness, an end to Chandler's private drought or, through a general enlightenment, to Dublin's? Five or six little clouds are possible, but do not be too sure of yours.

Gallaher, the Shaun of this story, is brighter and more articulate than Corley though, like him, crude, aggressive, and extroverted. Enterprising enough to have escaped, he returns to patronize his unenterprising friend and to condescend to dear, dirty Dublin. His sin is pride. Chandler, our Shem, is an introvert and, as many refer-ences to children and size suggest, both little and childish, however refined. That this timid soul thinks of himself, in a moment of daring, as T. Malone Chandler makes him seem Prufrock's ances-tor. Gallaher is a successful journalist, Chandler a frustrated poet. His sin is envy, complicated by sloth.

"If you wanted to succeed," thinks Little Chandler, "you had to go away." Supporting his friend's conviction and a central theme of *Dubliners*, Gallaher boasts of Continental elegance, of gilded vice, and of the Oriental voluptuousness offered by rich Jewesses. Gallaher, having gone away, has lived. A Dubliner no more, he is man of the world. Though aware of this exile's vulgarity and of his own superiority in certain directions, Little Chandler is impressed. A single attempt at asserting his manhood is necessarily uncon-vincing.

Little Chandler's poetic yearnings are at once pathetic and funny. The poor, stunted houses along the Liffey inspire a simile, which, elaborated, might become a poem. Not sure of what idea to express, he cherishes nevertheless "an infant hope." Maybe he could compose a slender volume of melancholy, unpopular verses (like *Chamber Music* perhaps): "he would put in allusions." Suc-cess assured by such devices, he proceeds to quote imaginary review-ers. That this portrait of the artist has sardonic reference to what Joyce might have become is confirmed by a parallel passage in the third chapter of *Ulysses*, where Stephen, another frustrated artist, also imagines reviews of books he has not written. " 'Ay very like a whale' " concludes his fantasy—this whale, of course, the little cloud of Polonius, by whose aid Stephen becomes another Little Chandler. All three are under little clouds.

Back, like Eveline, in his dull, loveless home, one of many images of enclosure in these stories, Little Chandler has his moment of truth, his showing forth: "He was a prisoner for life." Lord Byron, on the other hand, was real poet, real exile. Minding the baby, Little Chandler gets his Byron out and, thinking of his wife, reads a poem about Margaret's "clay." It may be that Little Chandler's wife is Annie, not Margaret, but Byron's poem on her tomb flatters Little Chandler's less conscious wishes. When, on her return, unburied Annie rebukes her husband, he feels "shame" and "remorse," immediately perhaps for his failure to mind the baby but ultimately for his wasted life.

Rays emanating from the curious complex of Byron, baby, Annie, and Gallaher, converge at last. Their focal point is Little Chandler's epiphany. For the alert reader the showing forth came earlier. As in most of these stories, there are two epiphanies, similar but not identical: one for the reader, the other for the hero or victim. For both reader and victim the details of the story compose the harmonious whole that produces radiance; but although reader and victim respond to much the same materials, the reader, aided by Joyce's selection and arrangement, responds sooner than the victim. The details of the story, consciously followed by the reader, constitute the victim's unconscious until their sudden emergence into light.

COUNTERPARTS

"Counterparts," a good word for analogies, probably refers to the symmetry of structure that sets this story apart. Mr. Alleyne is to dirty-eyed Farrington as he to his son. Father has gone wrong again.

A disclosure of sloth, gluttony, and wrath, this story includes bullying, boasting, frustration, and humiliation. There are excellent scenes in Dublin's pubs, with their snugs, curates, and treating drunks. Nosey Flynn sits and drips in Davy Byrne's as he will sit and drip there in *Ulysses*. Everything in this all but naturalistic story is evident until the boy's desperate cry in the kitchen at the end. A "Hail Mary," manifestly preferable under the circumstances to an "Our Father," is a good prayer for an emergency; but this prayer could also serve as a kind of preface to Maria in the next story—as a kind of transition from inadequate, perverse, or missing fathers to inadequate mothers. The Joyce of *Ulysses* and *Finnegans Wake* was always solicitous of such transitions from part to part.

CLAY

The story of virginal, old Maria, taken at face value, seems naturalistic; for she works in a laundry, and naturalists, delighting in whatever is ignoble, find laundry workers almost as congenial as drunken servant maids with illegitimate children. Maria's daily life and even her night out are tedious enough for naturalistic purposes. Her environment is indicated, if not displayed. If we take her story literally, it has little point beyond the exhibition of pointlessness. There seems more to it, however, than this. Symbolic devices indicate that Joyce intended something beyond a memorial to a frustrated, futile, and uninteresting life. There are allusions—such as Little Chandler esteems; and there are counterparts.

Maria's night out is on Halloween, a night when witches are out. The tip of her nose almost touches her chin, and this is the case with all the witches I have known. The copper boilers among which she works are a witch's equipment. But, far from proving Maria a witch, these circumstances only suggest that she is witchlike; for analogy or parallel does not establish identity. Maria remains Maria, witch, witch. That Maria is also like the Blessed Virgin Mary is suggested by her name and by the reactions of those around her. The matron hails her as a "peace-maker";[11] and, though she is not his actual mother, Joe hails her as his "proper mother." That she presides over a little garden in the wilderness and that she distributes tea and cakes add the possibility that she is also like the Church, often represented as a woman. No more than parallel to one another, these three parallels do not mean that the Virgin is a witch or that the Church is identical with the Virgin. The three parallels, agreeing as they can, make Maria seem more than a particular old woman.

These enlarging parallels seem subordinate to another, which, though less explicitly established, seems more important. Not only a poor old woman, Maria is like the Poor Old Woman or Ireland herself. That her particular figure serves as the traditional figure of Ireland is suggested by other circumstances. Like most in Ireland in her day, she works for the Protestants who control Ireland's purse. (Maria's purse is from Protestant Belfast.) Shopkeepers condescend to her; and when a British colonel is polite to her on the tram, she loses her cake. Distracted by colonels and conde-scended to by a nation of shopkeepers, Ireland had been losing her cake for several centuries. Moreover, Mother Ireland's sons, commonly drunk, were always quarreling among themselves. Alphy and Joe, Maria's "proper" sons, are always quarreling; and Joe, who is not altogether unlike Farrington, is certainly a drinker. As peace-maker, Maria seems ineffectual.

At Joe's Halloween party, they play the traditional game of saucers. Failing to pick the ring (marriage), Maria picks clay (death), and then, given another chance, the prayer book. Her choice of death and prayer suits Joyce's idea of his moribund, pious country.

As we have been prepared for a meaning of "clay" by a refer-ence in "A Little Cloud," so we have been prepared for Maria's song from *The Bohemian Girl* by a reference in "Eveline." Maria's conscious or unconscious omission of the second stanza, which

11. "Peace-maker," which occurs in the Mass for All Saints' Day (the day after Halloween) is ultimately from the Beatitudes of the Sermon on the Mount (Matthew 5: 1-12). "Blessed" (the recurrent word of the Beatitudes) is the Virgin's adjective.

concerns love and suitors, suits one who, lacking love and avoiding fertility, has chosen prayer and death.

Joe detects the meaning of her omission. "Very much moved" by it, he calls for the missing corkscrew (one of many lost or misplaced things in this story) and presumably for another bottle in which to drown his understanding. The epiphany, not Maria's but Joe's, is one of barrenness, lovelessness, disorder, and loss. Not even Balfe, thoughts of "the long ago," or drink itself can hide the bitterness.

A PAINFUL CASE

As if taking off from Maria's omitted stanza, "A Painful Case" pursues the theme of lovelessness. James Duffy, paralyzed by Dublin, less living than dead, may be a portrait of Stanislaus Joyce, as this unlovable brother claims; but probably a composite figure, James Duffy seems to owe almost as much to his creator, with whom he translates Hauptmann and with whom he shares the "odd autobiographical habit" of composing sentences about himself in third person and past tense. Like Joyce himself, James Duffy lives "at a little distance" from his own image.

The story of this ascetic man, whose only rage is for order, begins with a character sketch. Like Heyst on his island in Conrad's *Victory*, Duffy keeps himself aloof from the vulgar confusion of the world around him. Without friends, church, or creed, he lives— if one can call it that—"without any communion with others." "Communion" is the important word. Little wonder that the face of this unconnected man, who denies life, love, feeling, and humanity, wears the "brown tint" of Dublin's streets.

As Lena, offering love, intrudes upon Heyst's insulation, so Mrs. Sinico, promising love, upon Duffy's insular solitude. Trouble and ambiguous victory follow in both cases, a victory of a sort for love maybe, certainly a victory for awareness.

However serious the account of Duffy's relationship with Mrs. Sinico, it is hilarious. She is ready, he unready. She knows; but innocent and egocentric, he fails to understand: "He lent her books, provided her with ideas, shared his intellectual life with her. She listened to all." (Meditate here, when through smiling, on some men, all women.) As Duffy, mistaking sofa for platform, lectures her one day on the "soul's incurable loneliness," Mrs. Sinico, who knows what this is all about, touches his hand. Dismayed at this misconception, the lecturer recoils, stops lecturing, and withdraws to his lonely bed in Chapelizod.

When, four years later, he discovers in the paper that his "soul's companion," having taken to drink, has fallen under a train on the Kingstown line, he feels nothing but disgust.[12] How right he was to break relations off with that degrading person. But this reaction is only the first of a series which, as the light fails, ends with enlightenment. Never was epiphany more gradual. Disgust is followed by guilt (Was he to blame for her death?), and guilt by knowledge. Withholding love, he has betrayed her and, what is worse, himself. Betrayer, furthermore, of humanity, an "outcast from life's feast," he is alone. Not Mrs. Sinico but Mr. Duffy is the painful case. The beast, as Henry James puts it, has sprung from the jungle—and the Tyger from Blake's forest.

Mr. Duffy's deadly sin is pride or, as Freud puts it, ego. Mrs. Sinico's virtue is charity or, as Lawrence puts it, love. A choice of words reveals this virtue and that sin. As "communion" is the important word of the first part, so "touch" and "alone" are the important words of the last. These words, thematically recurrent, carry feeling and idea with hypnotic effect. "Touch" and "alone," together with "love," were to become the key words of A *Portrait*, as "communion" was to become climactic in *Ulysses*. "A Painful Case" is Joyce's first considerable statement of a great theme. Here, as in his larger works, Joyce is the celebrant of charity and communion with mankind.

The innovation here is a rhythm or pattern of important words, but images and allusions of the sort we have come to expect are

12. Mrs. Sinico, according to this story, died in November; yet, according to Mr. Bloom, who attended her funeral, she died October 14, 1903. (*Ulysses*, 680)

here as well. It is fitting, for example, that Mr. Duffy lives or exists near a "disused distillery" and a "shallow river." But the impressive images are his room at the beginning and the railroad train at the end. This sterile room is the outward and visible sign of an inner state. The wormlike train, leaving Kingsbridge for Cork, not only recalls Mrs. Sinico's train but unites intimations of life and death—like all those worms of Dylan Thomas.

It seems worth noting that Mr. Duffy, living where Tristan visited Isolde, misses the meaning of Chapelizod; as he misses the meaning of almost everything else until too late. That his epiphany occurs in Phoenix Park, however, may bear another significance. Awareness under these circumstances could promise a renewal like that of the fabulous bird, however unlikely the hope of it must seem. Yet this story, not only our introduction to Phoenix Park and to Earwicker's Chapelizod, is the eleventh in the sequence; and to Joyce, attentive to such matters, eleven was the number of renewal.

There is an unpublished letter, I am told, in which Joyce rates this story among his lesser things. I cannot accept that estimate. Not only an elegant form, "A Painful Case" concerns our concerns—and that is what we are after.

IVY DAY IN THE COMMITTEE ROOM

It is easy to see why of these fifteen stories this was Joyce's favorite; for here is Dublin entirely. Nowhere else, save in the Cyclops episode of *Ulysses*, did Joyce find a form so appropriate for his love and contempt of the place; and nowhere else did he capture so well its authentic tone and quality. Clearly the product of Joyce's notebook or of a remarkable memory, this conversational interchange among Dubliners, who, representing the whole, are less individuals than types, also anticipates the episode of the Wandering Rocks as Dublin's summary—and Dublin, for Joyce, was the microcosm or the epitome of everywhere. It is easy to see how Hynes and Crofton, conspicuous here, find their way into Dublin's great novel. Still a "sponger," Hynes owes Bloom money, and Crofton, still a conservative Orangeman, tags along with Martin Cunningham. Though moral Mr. Lyons is not the Bantam Lyons of Mrs. Mooney's boarding house and Mr. Bloom's acquaintance, he too is an essential Dubliner. Composed of such, "Ivy Day" is Joyce's vision of his "gallant venal" city. People, rhythm, movement, and texture, working together, produce Dublin's epiphany.

Like John Donne's world, Joyce's Dublin seems "all in pieces, all coherence gone," lacking all just relation between father and son, priest and church, master and disciple. Looking at a "sick World, yea, dead, yea petrified," Donne also found it lacking that moral "cement" which once "did faithfully compact and glue all virtues." Joyce's covetous or amoral Dubliners have lost loyalty and principle. Theirs is a world without faith, hope, or charity. Even Mr. Hynes' poem, the most faithful and hopeful sign, is a little shoddy.

The day is October 6 when Parnell is brought to mind by a sprig of ivy in the buttonhole. For some of Joyce's generation Parnell, who almost led Ireland and Parliament out of confusion ("He was the only man that could keep that bag of cats in order," says Mr. Henchy), remained a heroic figure—as Franklin Roosevelt remains for some Democrats or (since we must go back a little here) Abraham Lincoln for some Republicans. "Parnell is dead," says Mr. Henchy. That is manifestly true in Joyce's story; yet the dead hero is the center of value. Everything acquires meaning by analogy with Parnell or by reference to him, even the seemingly casual remarks about sons, priests, and visiting Edward. By their attitudes toward Parnell Joyce's boys in the back room expose themselves and his idea of Ireland's soul. Whether nationalist or conservative, whether moral, neutral, or sentimental, these unprincipled politicians agree in nothing but disloyalty. Holding noble Parnell's ignoble successors up to their dead chief and missing center for estimate, Joyce approaches satire.

Concerning analogy: old Jack and his disloyal son are not unlike Parnell and his disloyal followers. That King Edward, whose visit dismays the patriotic heart, is not unlike Parnell, the "un-

crowned King," is implied by Mr. Lyons. "In the name of God,"
asks Mr. Henchy, "where's the analogy between the two cases?"
But it is clear to us at least that Mr. Lyon's moral objection to
King Edward and his alleged mistresses is no different from Ireland's moral objection to Parnell and his Kitty O'Shea. A third
analogy, not apparent until Mr. Hynes' poem at the end, is with
betrayed Christ. Dubious Father Keon, off to discuss business in
his "discreet, indulgent, velvety voice" with a politician, may represent those "fawning priests" to whom and by whom Christlike
Parnell was betrayed.

Whether or not Father Keon serves in this capacity, he does link
this story to those about missing, incompetent, or imperfect fathers.
The theme of betrayal, here as in "Two Gallants," also helps establish the coherence of *Dubliners*, and so does the less apparent
motif of the Phoenix. This singular bird, following Christ in Mr.
Hynes' poem, promises renewal, however unlikely the prospect
may seem for dead Parnell and his moribund disciples. The rejection and death of Parnell figure in *A Portrait* and his possible
return in *Ulysses*; but the Phoenix motif, generally there by reference to Dublin's happily named park, occurs not only in "A Painful Case" and in "The Dead" but throughout *Finnegans Wake*,
Joyce's novel of resurrection.

Mr. Hynes' Phoenix, rising from his flames, takes its place among
many references to fire. The story opens with the attempt of old
Jack to encourage the reluctant fire.[13] Although some critics have
found Jack's fire an intimation of Hell, to which all of Joyce's
Dubliners seem committed, there is little in the immediate context to support this opinion. No devil, old Jack is a "caretaker,"
trying to keep the feeble flame alive; and this flame, far from
torturing, seems rather the flame of life, dying in dying Dublin in
spite of care. This sinking fire, which fails to dispel darkness and
hardly seems sufficient for the requirements of Mr. Hynes' firebird, has a more immediate function. Serving to expel the corks

13. Old Jack may refer to Joyce's father and the disloyal son to Joyce, who
liked to call himself Jackson: "J. A. Jackson." (*Ulysses*, 234) "Jacqueson's
Island" (*Finnegans Wake*, 245) is Huck Finn's island in the Mississippi and
Ireland, which, says Stephen, "belongs to me." (*Ulysses*, 629)

from three bottles of stout on the hob, it produces three expressive poks—lest the epiphany lack its point. Pok, the *mot juste*, says much more than pop.

Stout, the wine of the country and its essence, requires a corkscrew, but this instrument (as in "Clay") is missing. Called into service as a corkscrew, the caretaker's fire releases the gas of Dublin's peculiar beverage, and the epitome of all her political gases. The first "pok," an apologetic one, is from Mr. Lyons' bottle, the second from Mr. Crofton's, and the third, aligning his with theirs, from Mr. Hynes'. Following his recitation, this final pok shows him a sentimentalist, as gaseous and empty as the rest, and supplies the suitable comment. Dublin's eloquence of whatever sort is gas from a bottle.

Mr. Hynes' tawdry, well-meant poem, which may resemble one Joyce wrote at the age of nine, has several functions. Plainly ironic and supporting the main idea of windy emptiness, it also gathers the themes together, stating what has been implicit. Had Joyce remained in Dublin, he might have been another Hynes. He too might have cherished Parnell, "now that he's dead and gone," in Hynes' manner, and he too might have worn a sprig of ivy in his buttonhole. After all, however, ivy is a tree of life, associated with Bacchus, who, like the Phoenix himself, died and rose again.

A MOTHER

This story occupies the middle place in a trilogy about Dublin's more or less adult social interests, a trilogy which balances the opening trilogy about youth. "Ivy Day," the first of the second trilogy, concerns political life, and "Grace," the third, concerns religious life. "A Mother" displays Dublin's cultural interests and pretensions. The third-rate concert of *"artistes"* in the Antient Concert Rooms is as desolating as the meeting of third-rate politicians in Wicklow Street. Plainly Dublin suffers from cultural as well as political paralysis.

The characters, somewhat more elegant than those in the committee room, belong not only to Dublin's middle class but to its nationalistic faction. Kathleen, who bears the name Ireland takes for herself when assuming body for allegorical purposes, has studied Gaelic, and knows a few words of it. Her friends, also participants in the "language movement" (which Joyce, good European, thought provincial), sing local songs and recite patriotic pieces.

Not about Kathleen, however, but about her terrible mother, this story is essentially a portrait of this lady. Our problem is whether to take her literally or figuratively or both. If, in consideration of her name, Kathleen can be taken for Ireland in one of its aspects, can we or should we take her mother and manager as something equally important—Ireland's Church maybe? We seem invited to dare this hypothesis. Like the Church, Mrs. Kearney slips "the doubtful items in between the old favourites." Like the Church, she offers wine and biscuits to the visitors whom she dominates. Like the Church, she insists on being paid; and like the Church, she futilely excommunicates those who displease her.

These possibilities—and they are no more than that since Joyce was not writing allegory—expand the meaning of one who, however surrounded with implications of something almost general and abstract, remains a particular woman nevertheless. But that this particular, solidly-presented woman carries suggestions beyond her apparent capacity seems an obvious improvement. If we take her not only as an obnoxious Dubliner but as an unassigned symbol—that is as a meaningful thing of uncertain meaning—we must admit that she is more narrowly assigned by the context than Mr. O'Madden Burke's mysterious umbrella, which occupies the middle and end of this story, as Stein's butterfly occupies the middle and end of *Lord Jim*. Guessing the significance of butterfly or umbrella, trying our ingenuity on the scrutinized text, we remain blameless until dogmatic about our guesses and our scrutiny.

Aside from this shady object and Mrs. Kearney herself, Joyce's story of the concert offers a simple and agreeable surface for our enjoyment. People, we conclude, are odd and this story funny. Far from bare and scrupulously mean, the manner is one of polished irony, as urbane as the matter is provincial. The deadly sins encountered here are pride, wrath, and covetousness. (Mrs. Kearney's demand for payment is even louder than that of the politicians in "Ivy Day.") The virtues, save for a kind of ignominious fortitude, are hardly there at all.

GRACE

The fall, repentance, and rehabilitation of Thomas Kernan follow the progress of Dante through Hell, Purgatory, and Heaven. That, we are assured by Stanislaus Joyce, was his brother's intention, and there is little reason for doubt. Parody and parallel, which were to become favorite methods, serve a comic purpose here as later in A Portrait and Ulysses, in both of which the parallel of Dante's Comedy is employed. There are many points of resemblance to Dante in "Grace," but the disparity between Dante's progress from Hell to Heaven in The Divine Comedy and Tom Kernan's progress from the filth and ooze of the lavatory to his bed and thence to the Gardiner Street Church fixes the tone of Joyce's human comedy, while increasing the volume. But the casual reader is unaware of this parody. For him the tone of irony is fixed and the quality of the text established by the character sketches, which, however old fashioned in appearance, are functional. Take, for example, the account of Mrs. Kernan's piety in which every word is loaded: "Her beliefs were not extravagant. She believed steadily in the Sacred Heart as the most generally useful of all Catholic devotions and approved of the sacraments. . . . if she was put to it, she could believe also in the banshee and in the Holy Ghost." (172)

This woman puts fallen Tom Kernan to bed, but his spiritual welfare is taken in hand by Mr. Power, Mr. M'Coy, and Mr. Cunningham, whose conversation around that purgatorial bed, an epiphany like the conversation in "Ivy Day," discloses a union of piety, kindliness, and ignorance peculiar to Joyce's Dublin. Martin

Cunningham's infallible pronouncements on Papal infallibility[14] and his dogmatic assurance (his unenlightened insistence, for example, upon "*Lux upon Lux*"), though hilarious and relevant are less immediately relevant to the theme than his remarks about the Jesuits, who "cater for the upper classes." (I know a Jesuit who thinks this story the funniest in the world.) For washing the upper-class pot, Father Purdon, S.J. is eminently suitable, for "He's a man of the world like ourselves." This observation, the key sentence of the story, complements the masterly opening: "Two gentlemen who were in the lavatory at the time tried to lift him up." (I am lost in admiration of such elegant economy.) All are "gentlemen" here, whether in lavatory, pew, or pulpit; and the lifting up of gentleman Tom Kernan is a gentleman's job. Undertaking it, Martin Cunningham proposes making "a good holy pious and Godfearing Roman Catholic" out of his fallen friend, an ex-Protestant and bad Catholic, whose rejection of candles may imply Protestant habit, capricious humor, or loathing of light. Imagery of light is present throughout—as in most of these stories and in Dante too.

The respectable and "decorous" congregation in the Gardiner Street Church (also attended by the parents of Joe Dillon) includes a usurer, an unprincipled politician, and a pawnbroker. Mr. Harford, the usurer, is one of the drinkers who abandoned Kernan on the lavatory floor; and Mr. Fanning, the politician, who reappears in *Ulysses*, is Father Keon's "business" associate. Among these gentlemen our retreating four, joined by Mr. Fogarty, grocer, take their places in the shape of a "quincunx," whether, recalling the five wounds of Christ, to crucify Him again by their presence or merely to remind the literate reader of Sir Thomas Browne's obsession with the figure five we cannot be sure. It is notable that the tiny red light over the altar, signifying the Real Presence and recalling Dante's Heaven, seems "distant."

14. Cunningham's Cardinal Dowling is Johann Döllinger, excommunicated in 1871 for opposing the dogma of infallibility. Note Fogarty's misquotation of John Dryden in a Papal context. A reference to Leo XIII, who died in 1903, places this story in the time of Pius X, his successor. Other matters that may puzzle: a "curate" is a bartender and an "outsider" a jaunting car.

Father Purdon[15] rears his burly figure and massive face above the pulpit rail, a man of the world, about to address men of the world, man to man. As he admits, his text (Luke 16: 8-9) is one of the most difficult to interpret properly; for when taken out of context as he takes it, it seems "at variance with the lofty morality" and unworldliness of Jesus. Most preachers would avoid this curious passage from the parable of the unjust steward, but not Father Purdon, who, speaking, like his Jesus, as man of the world to businessmen "in a business way," finds it splendidly adapted to the interests and needs of his congregation. The Lord's surprising advice to make friends with "the mammon of iniquity" leads the ingenious Jesuit to a metaphor of accounting that anticipates Stephen's spiritual "cash register" in A *Portrait*. Thanks to Father Purdon's elaborate metaphor, God's grace becomes the period of grace accorded in financial circles to debtors.

Another epiphany, corroborating the conversation round the bed, this sermon, which proves Dublin's religion—or that of its gentry, at least—to be as worldly as the world, is presented by indirect discourse for greater concentration and more desolating impact. There is no comment, for none is needed; but there is a parallel. Martin Cunningham's story of "65, catch your cabbage" [16] suggests Father Purdon's congregation and his approach. That Tom Kernan failed to catch Father Purdon's spiritual cabbage or else that he caught it only too well is evident from the graveyard episode of *Ulysses*, where he seems as unregenerate as before this elegant retreat.

Tom Kernan's hat and his connection with tea inaugurate motifs that were to recur and expand throughout *Ulysses* and *Finnegans Wake*. Having bitten off the tip of his tea-tasting tongue, Kernan is temporarily separated from that important beverage; but in *Ulysses* Kernan's tea (like Keyes' keys) becomes the goal of one of

---

15. Actually Father Bernard Vaughan, mentioned in *Ulysses* (216) and a fellow seminarian of Gerard Manley Hopkins, an authority, as the "Deutschland" proves, on the quincunx and those five wounds.
16. A Constable 65 appears in *Ulysses* (571).

Bloom's frustrated quests. There as here, tea, often but not always, occurs in association with hat. Content to present, Joyce almost never explains. Tea and hat are unassigned symbols, and we should defer our guesses until we have encountered them again and again in the greater works, where more elaborate contexts may be helpful. Kernan's high silk hat, an obvious sign of his commercial integrity and gentlemanly aspiration, lies dented on the lavatory floor. Carried at his wedding, this hat, "rehabilitated" by Mrs. Kernan, reappears on Mr. Kernan's knee during his retreat.

The connection of "Grace" with *Ulysses* is affirmed by the reappearance there of Power, M'Coy, and Cunningham, a good "practical" Catholic, who also reappears in *Finnegans Wake*. (387) M'Coy, a canvasser for advertisements, whose wife is a soprano, is an obvious anticipation of Bloom. Like him, M'Coy is generally snubbed. In *Ulysses*, where Bloom meets this shadow of himself, M'Coy is still borrowing valises. Such interconnections help to assure the unity of Joyce's works, making them seem parts of one great work, as similar interconnections help to assure the unity of these fifteen stories. Kernan of this story, for example, knows Crofton of "Ivy Day," as Lenehan of "Two Gallants" knows Holohan of "A Mother." Not only of service as links, these references reveal the compactness, indeed the microscopic character of Joyce's microcosm, where everyone knows everyone else.

Though discovering divine justification for covetousness, "Grace" is not altogether without signs of virtue. Power and Cunningham are charitable, and so is the mysterious stranger in the cycling suit, who first lifts Kernan up. As for Father Purdon: he may justify covetousness, but, meaning well and paving a broad road with his intentions, he does his best according to his lights. That there is a light, however "distant," above the altar assures divinity behind local darkness and human aberration. Fallen men are men after all, and God, though somewhere else, is somewhere. According to Stanislaus Joyce—and I see no reason to disbelieve him here—his brother, an idealist who saw things as they are, never faltered in his love of father, fatherland, and God the Father.

THE DEAD

This fiction stands out from its fourteen companions because, however similar in theme, it seems denser, more elaborate, and by every common standard greater. Written apparently after the others[17] and improved by experiment, "The Dead" is at once the summary and climax of *Dubliners*. Of intermediate length, neither story nor novel, it claims a place beside Conrad's "Heart of Darkness," Mann's *Death in Venice*, and other fictions of a kind which, by subtlety, seems suited to an age that Gabriel calls "thought-tormented" and, by form, to an age neither here nor there.

Moral again, the theme involves the sins of pride, envy, lust, wrath, and the virtue of charity. From conflicts of death and life, lust and love, taking and giving, past and present, self and selflessness knowledge emerges at last and with it the triumph of love. The dead and the living dead lie uncovered for our inspection, but the story of Gabriel is not altogether desperate; for awareness promises renewal. His New Year may be new indeed. Fixing this moral theme and its implications is important since character, structure, image, and the other elements work together in its service, and to know the many we must know the one. All the parts (even pictures on the wall or Mr. d'Arcy's cold in the head) seem as functional as the parts of something by Mozart. Wholeness, harmony, and radiance, Stephen's requirements for any work of art, were never more evident. Like music, but not music, this radiant harmony is both absolute and referential. "The Dead" is a structure of references or meanings which, like those of all great literature, are human—not all but superhuman like those of Mozart.

At his crisis of realization, Gabriel, who has been shown to be a sensitive introvert, at once superior to his environment and faithful to it, knows himself and those at the party to be deader (if that is possible) than the dead boy in Galway. Whatever his resemblance to the little boy in "An Encounter" and James Duffy

17. *Letters*, 60, 61. In 1906 the fourteenth story was last.

in "A Painful Case," who seem preliminary sketches now, Gabriel finds himself guilty not of withholding love but of lacking it entirely. Pride or that complacent concentration upon self which seems a cause of his incapacity for loving yields to a kind of generous impersonality, accompanied by pity and sympathy, not for himself this time but for others. His self destroyed, his identity gone, he becomes one with all the living and the dead. This dramatic extinction of personality could be another hopeful sign. No longer Gabriel alone but one with everyone, he may be ready to accept, give, and participate.

The other characters, like those in *A Portrait*, are less important in themselves than in relation to the hero for whom they provide irritant and setting. A first study for Bertha of *Exiles*, a more provincial Mrs. Sinico, and a friend of Molly Bloom's, Gretta is little more than an object, a presence, an agency. Gabriel's aunts,[18] like Father Flynn's sisters, are fixed in the past, which they try to maintain. The annual dance of the Morkans is a dance of death, as Gabriel's graceful tribute, a funeral oration. Mr. Browne, uniting the browns of Joyce's Dublin, is "all brown," and, as one of the aunts acutely observes, seems "everywhere." Only Miss Ivors and Mr. d'Arcy, refusing complete participation, are reluctant guests. Mr. d'Arcy prefers the present to the past, and Miss Ivors leaves the party for the Aran Islands, where the air, like that of Buenos Aires, is fresher.

At the party and afterwards Gabriel's experience follows a course of emotional ups and downs and ups and downs again. His plump complacency is injured at the party by three rebuffs: Lily's remarks about men, Gretta's about "goloshes," and Miss Ivors' about politics. These small embarrassments, menacing his superiority, leave him increasingly ill at ease. But the triumph of his speech, bringing complacency back, restores habitual adjustment. Joy and desire, leaving his big head, crowd his little heart. After the party, however, a series of compulsory readjustments composes a climax more intricate than that of "A Painful Case," but not unlike it in structure and meaning. As his lust is disconcerted by

18. Cf. *Ulysses* (654): Kate Morkan is Stephen's godmother.

Gretta's abstraction at the Gresham Hotel, so his defensive irony by her simplicity. He has a rival. His rival is dead. Though employed in the gasworks, his rival was capable of love. These successive disclosures, shattering habits and defenses, prepare him for epiphany.

This structural rhythm of rising and falling co-operates with character to establish theme. Such elements are as immediately apparent as in common fiction, but what detains a reader familiar with the earlier stories or with stories by Mann or Conrad is the imagery. Less apparent but no less functional than character or structure, the images of "The Dead," more nearly central than those of the earlier stories, embody so much of that meaning that, missing them, the careless reader misses almost all. Of several kinds, these figures are simple and single at times and at others elaborate, developing into clusters and systems. There are two principal clusters in "The Dead," that of light and fire and that of cold and snow. But let us consider some of the incidental and unsystematic images first.

Take, for example, the "brown" roast goose provided by the sisters and carved by Gabriel. Necessarily brown, since roasted, this important bird displays nevertheless the color of Dublin, like Mr. Browne himself. Why goose? Turkey, as we know from *A Portrait*, is more customary in Ireland during the Christmas season, but goose serves Joyce's purpose better here; for "wild geese" are those Irishmen who, unlike Little Chandler, have escaped from Ireland to become Napoleonic marshals or, like three-star Hennessy, makers of brandy. The flights of Gabriel's tame goose,[19] like those of Mallarmé's swan, are unflown. Moreover, Gabriel's goose is cooked. When he offers a wing to a guest, she significantly refuses it, preferring breast or something nearer the heart of the matter. This brown goose (inspired, no doubt, by two common sayings) is simple enough, but there are two more difficult birds around, the crow and the Phoenix, the first mysterious, the second shadowy, implied by Gabriel's wish to go walking in the Park, which faces the windows of Usher's Island. This hopeful bird, tra-

19. Stephen calls Davin "tame goose." (*Portrait*, 442, 466)

ditionally associated with fire but here with snow, may modify our idea of Gabriel's future. Since, as we should be ready to agree by now, nothing in Joyce is accidental, the crow must be important too. This ill-omened bird, mentioned by Miss Ivors and Mr. d'Arcy, the reluctant guests, serves to link them—but why crow? Let your ingenuity work prudently on what still baffles mine. I think it enough sometimes to point things out and question them. Providing answers, pretending assurance where none is justified, could be of disservice to text and reader alike. The text is not a system of mathematical equations but a flexible relationship of possibilities. The reader, whether common or critical, is no business machine.

Unworried by crow, I point to other things: the metaphorical beast, for example, that like Henry James' beast in the jungle or James Duffy's in the Park, pounces on its victim: "A vague terror seized Gabriel . . . as if, at that hour when he hoped to triumph, some palpable and vindictive being was coming against him." (238) Other images rival those of Joyce's bestiary. That picture of the balcony scene from *Romeo and Juliet*, hanging on the Morkans' wall, seems there to anticipate Gretta at the window and her lover in the rain. What else would Romeo and Juliet be doing at the Morkans' house, unless promising death? The Trappist monks, sleeping in their coffins at Melleray, seem more suitable for that party. Mary Jane's "academy piece" is sterile; but the songs, though no doubt as significant as Maria's in "Clay," remain as "distant" as Gabriel's "thought-tormented music." Directions and seasons (east and west, Christmas and New Year's), though less distant, are not wholly unambiguous. The sisters' dance of death occurs during the twelve days of Christmas, but whether before New Year's Day or after it we cannot be sure. Though Christmas means birth (as well as cold) and New Year's means renewal, are we to take these meanings literally or ironically? A possible date for the party, as an ingenious critic has announced, is January 6, the twelfth day of Christmas or the Epiphany; and we must welcome so happy a possibility. As for directions: Gabriel takes his vacation on the Continent, to the east, and Miss Ivors (a friend of Kathleen Kearney's, with equal command of rudimentary Gaelic) takes hers in the west, where Michael loved Gretta and caught his death of cold. Gazing at the snow, Gabriel feels the time has come to "set out on his journey westward." Traditionally, going west means dying and to Joyce nationalism was little better than death; yet Gretta and Michael, who lived and loved in Galway, represent the reality that must be faced. Gabriel's westward journey, which includes these implications, remains ambiguous—not, I think, to tease us with choices but to offer two meanings at once; for Gabriel, facing reality at last, goes westward to encounter life and death.

This encounter is attended and its nature disclosed by the two systems of images I have spoken of. Those of fire and light[20] commence when, after an overabundance of good-nights, Gabriel goes out into the yellowish dark. As his lust burns, he appropriately recalls a bottle maker at his roaring furnace. Tedium of life with Gretta has almost "quenched" their "souls' tender fire," though fires of lust keep hot enough. Enlightenment, despite, or maybe because of, those fires, is difficult. The electric light at the Gresham has failed, but whether the trouble is local or at the Pigeon House is unclear. Preferring the dark anyway, Gabriel refuses the porter's candle (as if Tom Kernan) and contents himself with the "ghastly light" of a lamp, possibly a gas lamp, in the street. He consistently keeps his back to the light, like Mangan's sister, as the "dull fires of his lust" glow within him; but Gretta comes towards him "along the shaft of light," then looks "away from him along the shaft of light towards the window in silence." The dark is light enough for Gabriel to see his image by in mirror.[21] Not entirely from physical reflection, Gabriel's enlighten-

20. Compare the images of fire and light in "Ivy Day," "Grace," and "Araby." Chandler's name means candle maker—one candle power?
21. Mirrors fascinate all of Joyce's more egocentric heroes and heroines: e.g. Stephen, Gerty MacDowell, Isabel, and the girl of *Chamber Music*. A Gabriel Conroy, lost in the snow, is one of Bret Harte's heroes. Michael and Gabriel are great angels, the first, Satan's militant adversary, the second, blower of the Last Trump. But Gabriel, whose emblem is the lily (the first word of "The Dead"), presides over renewal as well as end. It is he who announced the coming of

ment is at Gretta's window by the light of that lamp in the street and the snow's light. The first of these lights is common, the second general. That Michael's job was in the gasworks is plainly of more than social or ironic import.

This imagistic process, attending Gabriel's moral process and expanding, while deepening, our sense of it, is connected, as we have noticed, with the more considerable system of cold and snow. Like Hans Castorp's in *The Magic Mountain*, Gabriel's enlargement is centered in the snow. His goloshes, like the brown macintosh of *Ulysses*, reveal his dislike, even fear, of the snow that covers his shoulders. Liking snow, Gretta dislikes goloshes. Many at the party suffer from colds, yet, as the stuffiness increases, Gabriel imagines the refreshing coldness of Phoenix Park outside the windows and the cap of snow on the Wellington Monument, plainly visible from the windows. Phallic in shape, yet a memorial to the dead, this monument in the Park is as ambiguous as the snow that caps it, flashing "westward." Snow is frozen water, and water a traditional image of life. Accepting snow (without goloshes) is accepting life and death; for in snow there is prospect of thaw, especially in the snow of Phoenix Park, home of the firebird. But Michael catches cold in the rain; for water, as well as frozen water, means death and life. That snow cloaks the statue of Dan O'Connell is far from casual, since O'Connell (after whom the street where the Gresham is located was to be renamed) is the "Liberator."

The tremendous final page of "The Dead" gathers these meanings into rhythm and image. Never was page, even in Joyce, more masterly. But "Lily," the first word of the story, is a greater and more astonishing concentration. Taken literally, Lily is the name of a bitter servant; but a lily, white as snow, serves at funerals and at the ceremony of resurrection at Easter. And, as we have seen, the lily is Gabriel's emblem. Constantly amazing us, Joyce anticipates with this brilliant concentrate his disclosure of reality

---

Christ to Mary, and he who will announce the Second Coming. The Angelus, which celebrates his Annunciation, becomes a motif in *Finnegans Wake*.

in all its kinds. In this word is all the story. Yet discovering what this word contains means reading the story again and again and coming back for more. Let readers and critics, too, do what they can, there is always more.

However serious, "The Dead" is lightened by humor as well as irony. The brown goose is moderately funny and so is Michael in the gasworks; but Gabriel's story of Mr. Morkan's horse is funnier. This animal, fascinated with the conqueror (like Ireland herself), circles around King Billy's statue in College Green.[22] Illustrating his story and placing it for us among images of snow, Gabriel walks round and round the hall in his goloshes.

So much for images, which I do not pretend to have exhausted; but other things of interest remain. From these I single out the device of the repeated word that we noticed in "A Painful Case." The word "touch" reappears significantly (as it will in *A Portrait*); but "tender," far more important here, recurs rhythmically throughout the latter part of the story to bring promise maybe of humanity and love.

Involving the triumph of dramatic impersonality and the radiance of "distant" harmony, "The Dead" is both human and personal. Gabriel, who teaches in Joyce's University and writes reviews for Joyce's newspaper, is an aspect of Joyce as he might have been, and Gretta seems Nora as she probably was. The very personal poems of *Pomes Penyeach* prove the personal references. "A Memory of the Players in a Mirror at Midnight" is about Gabriel-Joyce consulting that mirror. "She Weeps over Rahoon," on Nora lamenting her dead lover, is Gretta lamenting her delicate boy again. Although Rahoon[23] is the cemetery of Galway and Gretta's Michael is buried at Oughterard, a town in the Joyce Country of Connemara, the connection is plain. Even the rhythms of "She Weeps over Rahoon" are those of the final page of "The Dead," where Gabriel hears snow "falling faintly . . . faintly falling":

22. For many Irishmen King Billy (William of Orange), who won the Battle of the Boyne and put wild geese to flight, approaches Cromwell's infamy. King Billy's statue (now gone) seems to balance Dan O'Connell's statue (still there), passed by another horse.
23. For Nora and Rahoon see Joyce's Notes to *Exiles* (New York, 1951).

Rain on Rahoon falls softly, softly falling,
Where my dark lover lies. (650)

Looking into his heart and Nora's too, Joyce depersonalized, generalized, and distanced what he found. Looking there, he kept finding the same thing: the conflict of pride with love, of ego with humanity. "The Dead," his first major presentation of what obsessed him, is not only the epitome of *Dubliners,* but a preface to A *Portrait, Exiles,* and *Ulysses.*

A Portrait of the Artist as a Young Man

Of a kind with "The Dead," though more elaborate and even more admirable, A Portrait of the Artist as a Young Man makes that ultimate story seem preliminary sketch. Story and novel alike portray man alone—alone yet surrounded by shades. These shades, whether actual people, ideas, or shades themselves, leave that man —man or boy—by himself, loving himself alone. A defect of love is the moral center of both fictions; and both involve epiphany. A difference, however, is that Gabriel's moment of awareness is complete and terrible, whereas Stephen, though enjoying epiphanies of one kind or another, never sees himself entirely. His trouble here is failure to realize himself; but this is attended to in Ulysses, which makes A Portrait seem preliminary sketch.

What detains the most casual eye is an abundance of brilliant scenes and episodes, not only immediate in effect but persistent in memory. No eye could be more casual or innocent than mine when I first picked this great novel up, and I cannot forget my impression of the first two pages, which by selection, tone, and rhythm create a child's world. The scene of the wading girl is memorable; and there are the unforgettable sermons on hell, which emerge from their Catholic setting to inflame the infidel, or even the Protestant, heart. But most striking of all is the Christmas dinner, which might have found a place beside the first three stories of

Dubliners. For masterly storytelling nothing in *A Portrait* surpasses this little drama of Dante and the spit and these portraits in miniature of Mr. Casey and wonderful Simon Dedalus. Yet each of these emergent scenes, falling into place, is a working part in the apparatus. None could be done without. Each, moreover, is an epiphany for Stephen and reader alike, but the reader with the casual, innocent eye, ignorant of epiphanies and design, is detained by compelling surfaces. A good story, *A Portrait* is composed of good stories.

A story, what is more, of a familiar kind—and most of us feel more at home with things of this kind than with other things; for we are less adventurous than we think, and, however daring we think him, so was Joyce. For a hundred years or more before *A Portrait* appeared (in 1916) writers had found the "novel of adolescence" (or the *"Bildungsroman,"* development novel, as the Germans name it) a congenial form. The subject is convenient since every writer, like the rest of us, was first a child and then an adolescent, developing and struggling toward maturity. The subject is also agreeable since it is agreeable, as the poet said, to look back at troubles escaped or overcome. Mature at last, the writer, looking into his heart and at his past with all its trials and horrors, finds it easy to celebrate heart, past, and present maturity. "Look! We have come through," he seems proudly to exclaim with D. H. Lawrence. Lawrence's *Sons and Lovers,* Mann's *Magic Mountain* and *Tonio Kröger,* Maugham's *Of Human Bondage,* and Wolfe's *Look Homeward, Angel* are outstanding among innumerable twentieth-century examples of a kind for which Goethe's *Wilhelm Meister,* Meredith's *Richard Feverel,* and Butler's *Way of All Flesh* had set the pattern. Joyce was familiar with Butler, Meredith, and Goethe.[1] Whether deliberately based on this pattern or not, *A Portrait* generally conforms to it. In Joyce's *Bildungsroman,* as in most of the others, both before and after his, we find a sensitive youth shaped by his surroundings, feeling their pressure, and rebelling against them to become himself.

1. For references to *The Way of All Flesh* see *Finnegans Wake,* 234, 621; for *Richard Feverel* and *Wilhelm Meister* see *Ulysses,* 182, 197.

Since these surroundings and the pressures of tradition are commonly represented by a father or uncle, the theme of these books is not only the process of growing up but the revolt against father that every son must undertake in order to become something like him. This is one of Joyce's great themes, not only here but in the later books. Here, Stephen Dedalus, created by Simon Dedalus (who represents the fatherland), rebels against father in order to become Stephen Dedalus, a proclaimed enemy of the fatherland and a better creator than father. The novel ends at this point, but we may infer from Joyce's subsequent works, that Stephen, becoming himself, will become a kind of Simon, in exile maybe, but no less faithful to the fatherland. Fathers and sons, like T. S. Eliot's circling boarhound and his boar "pursue their pattern as before" to be reconciled at last—not among Eliot's stars but here in Joyce's sublunary region.

Naturally, these novels of father and son, with son as hero and father as author, fondly or ironically looking back, are more or less autobiographical. Stephen Dedalus, the son who wants to become creative father or artist, says that every artist uses "his image." (480) [2] Though this could mean an image made by him or an image of himself, the second alternative seems more applicable here; for this artist as a young man is more or less Joyce's image of himself when young. We know that Joyce signed early letters and stories "Stephen Daedalus." But more or less is not altogether. God created Adam in his image; yet Adam is not God. We must be careful to separate created image from creator. Like young Joyce in many ways, Stephen is no more Joyce than Gabriel Conroy is or Lenehan for that matter. Stephen's home is something like Joyce's own, and his father a little like Joyce's own. Stephen goes to Joyce's schools and shares many of Joyce's friends, disguised by other names; but it becomes plain, the more we know of Joyce, that A *Portrait* is not autobiography. Events and characters are distorted, rearranged, and invented to serve a novelist's purpose. A *Portrait* is less record than invention. It is

2. Parenthetical numbers in the text refer to pages in *The Portable James Joyce*, Viking Press.

the artist's image now in the sense of something he has made.

Whatever his inventive power, an artist must get his materials somewhere, where he can. Preferring to write about what he knew about, Joyce took his materials from himself and his experience. These, however, were things to be selected, shaped, and, however personal, to be depersonalized. A few examples should make this clear. However much Simon Dedalus owes to Joyce's father, he is not that man nor is Stephen's attitude toward his father Joyce's toward his. Intending a story of son rebelling against father, Joyce changed the father whom he loved to Stephen's irresponsible and contemptible old man. Intending a story of an unhappy egoist and a romantic rebel, Joyce, who was commonly (though not always) gay and witty,[3] made Stephen solemn. That gloomy boy, like Gabriel Conroy, is no more than an aspect of Joyce or Joyce as he might have been. Not autobiography, *A Portrait* is work of art. The word *Portrait* in the title is significant; and it is no less significant that the article preceding this word is A, not *The*. This novel, like a painter's work, is one of several possible interpretations of a subject. Not representational, the distortions and arrangements, like those on canvas, are expressive.

Novels of this kind are all, or almost all, portraits of an artist since the hero grows up to be something like his creator, who is, of course, something of an artist. This raises a question. Why should ordinary readers like ourselves, not artists in the sense of painting pictures, composing music, or writing books, be interested in a portrait of an artist or of something like one? Ordinary readers, we are interested ordinarily in our own business and the artist's business seems none of ours; yet the popularity of these novels about his business proves it somehow ours or, at least, not altogether alien. This needs looking into.

At this time when the ideals of our *élite*, centered in Madison Avenue and adjacent suburb, or rather "exurb," seem to be "to-

---

3. Joyce's classmates at University College called him "Jocax" or jokester. According to Joyce, Joyce means *"joyeux."* Of the twins Tristopher (sad) and Hilary (gay) in *Finnegans Wake* (21) Joyce seems closer to the latter, Stephen to the former. Cf. "pseudojocax," *Finnegans Wake* (63).

getherness" and "other-directedness," and working in "teams" (as the Madison Avenue sociologists maintain), the artist is little better than a maverick unless he works for an advertising concern or a magazine. A lonely outsider, rejecting team, he is a kind of exile at home or, if abroad, abroad. He is often a Democrat or worse. The last of romantic outlaws, praising individual values, condemning group values, he rejects Avenue and suburb as he is rejected by them. Why then, I repeat, should portraits of that man please?

Maybe his portrait pleases the young, who, however conventional their demeanor (when not "beat" or delinquent), are young in heart and like to see themselves as they might be in other circumstances. Still at school and still excited by books, some of the young still open them. But the popularity of the *Bildungsroman* suggests a wider and older audience as well. The problem is what literate elders—and many are still around—find in portraits of the lonely outsider, whose image must satisfy some general need. Can it be a conviction that despite togetherness, we too are all alone? Have we a suppressed and probably unconscious desire for rebellion against suburb and Avenue? Can it be that a desire for making things is flattered by dreams of creative youth? Hardly if we are engineers, maybe if brokers or account executives. Is a frustrated desire for daring flattered (as in Westerns) by pictures of youthful daring, however aesthetic, moral, or spiritual? Or, since the young rebel represents freedom as well as enterprise, does he serve us as an embodiment of the free enterprise our fathers esteemed and politicians still commend in the teeth of togetherness? I answer my question by questions which, however rhetorical, accost possibilities.

Whatever the uncalled-for answers, the artist as hero has taken his place beside other favorites: the cuckold, the bum, and the betrayed man. Dr. Bovary, Mr. Bloom, Waugh's Tony Last, Huckleberry Finn, Kerouac's Kerouac, and Beckett's waiters for Godot are suitable examples. If the philosopher Vico is right in assuming that our deepest selves are projected and revealed in our heroes, as in our myths and dreams, it may be that we see ourselves in cuckold, bum, and lonely artist, as an earlier generation saw itself in the figure of George Washington or Prince Albert—or as madmen see themselves in the figure of Napoleon. Maybe the outsider, fulfilling our deepest fears and wishes, is our chosen image. But neither psychologist nor sociologist, I abandon these tempting speculations for other uncertainties. These, however, are literary.

Example: I said awhile ago, when talking of *Dubliners*, that the first thing to determine in considering a book is theme, whether we take this slippery word in the sense of central idea or general movement; for it is in the service of theme that elements operate. Still maintaining this, I modify it nevertheless, a little, here. In A *Portrait* there are ideas, both moral and social, and there is narrative movement, but what seems central here is character. Since A *Portrait* is portrait indeed, character takes the place of idea or movement, conducting, as visitor, the concert of elements. Before looking at structure, parallel, image, and other subsidiaries, we must look at character again—at character as theme.

A gifted young man, with greater promise than James Duffy or Gabriel Conroy, Stephen resembles those sensitive introverts in proud isolation. Superiority protects him from communion with others, whom he regards with contempt, weary indifference, or, at best, with "desolating pity." (453) Yet these inferiors, who surround him at a suitable distance, see him more clearly than he sees himself. As each looks out, he in. McCann says: "Dedalus, you're an antisocial being, wrapped up in yourself." (438) Davin, who alone dares call Stephen familiarly by his first name, says: "You're a terrible man, Stevie, . . . always alone." (466) "Try to be one of us," he continues a little later. "In your heart you are an Irishman but your pride is too powerful." (467) Cranly, closest to Stephen and most searching of all, asks: "Have you never loved anyone?" (510) Such questions and comments, justifiable and accurate on the whole, make it plain that Stephen, having developed through four chapters, lacks humanity in the fifth. Given this inhumanity, all else follows: all of Stephen's triumphs and troubles, all the matters from which Joyce composes his portrait of an unhappy egoist, and all the methods.

The action, centered upon developing Stephen, shows him becoming what he becomes in the eyes of those friends. In the sense of narrative movement the theme is this: shaped by home, religion, and country ("This race and this country and this life produced me." 467), Stephen, increasingly impatient with what has shaped him, resolves at last upon escape and exile. Unlike Eveline and Little Chandler, fellow creatures of Dublin, he has the enterprise to act on his resolve.

Until near the end of his schooling at Belvedere, "habits of quiet obedience" (332) persist. He heeds the voices of father and masters, urging him to be a gentleman, an athlete, a patriot, and, above all, a Catholic. A little "hollowsounding" perhaps, these voices, abetted by his faith and trust, make him attempt the conformity they urge on him. The playing-fields of Clongowes[4] are the epitome of his relation with Ireland. This scene, the first we encounter after his infancy, reveals Stephen attempting togetherness with what he finds alien: the heavy boots, the flashing eyes of careless extroverts, the terrible scrimmage in the mud. "He kept on the fringe of his line," going obediently through the motions, pretending to be a member of the team.

Faith and the habit of obedience, defeated in the social game, gradually decline, and Stephen feels "betrayed" by what he has trusted. When unjustly beaten by Father Dolan, Stephen flies to Father Conmee and the "castle" for refuge—as Gerard Manley Hopkins once fled from God to God; for Stephen's faith in Jesuits survives the injustice of a Jesuit. Later, however, Father Conmee's laughter, reported by Simon Dedalus ("Father Dolan and I . . . had a hearty laugh together over it. Ha! Ha! Ha!" 320), proves this refuge imperfect. As the Dean of Studies fails to conform to the pattern set by "knightly" Loyola, founder of the Society of Jesus, so the Irish Church, becoming for Stephen "the scullerymaid

4. Elegant Clongowes Wood is an Irish approximation of Eton. Belvedere is a day school. Before taking final vows Jesuits are called Mister, not Father. For Joyce's schooling see Kevin Sullivan, *Joyce Among the Jesuits*.

of christendom," fails to conform to his idea of what a church should be. His own father, increasingly like the priests with whom he is hand-in-glove, joins discarded Father Conmee and the Dean. It is not until the visit to Cork, however, that Stephen finally gives that drinking, philandering, sentimental gentleman up— that "storyteller, somebody's secretary, something in a distillery." (511) No father, actual, ecclesiastical or even divine, seems fatherly or reliable. Anticipating these rejections, the Christmas dinner has proved home and politics no less unreliable to the "terrorstricken" boy, whose companions—one can hardly call them friends—betray him one by one, from Heron to Cranly. As for the city where these disenchantments and betrayals occur, Stephen finds it the city known to us from *Dubliners*, a place of squalor, insincerity, and corruption. Even the tidal Liffey bears a "yellow scum": for yellow is Stephen's (as it is Lynch's) equivalent for Dublin brown. The "order and elegance" within him are insufficient to dam or clear the "sordid tide" of life around him and within him. (349) Discouraged at last and let down, he resolves to "communicate" no more, whether the "communion" (and this is the important word) be religious or secular. Serving others no more, he will serve himself alone, abroad: "I will not serve that in which I no longer believe, whether it call itself my home, my fatherland, or my church." (518) Society has betrayed him, not he it. He has found the trouble with Dublin, if not with self.

Escape has three aspects: negative or getting away from an intolerable situation; positive, for freedom to create; and romantic or a kind of Byronic expansiveness and exploratory enlargement. Stephen, an impatient romantic and potential creator, is moved by all three. Fascinated with words, as a man of letters must be, he finds the necessity for escape in a series of terrible verbs, all imperative in mood: *apologize, admit, submit, obey, confess, commune, conform*. The eagle of authority, threatening his eyes unless he apologize, shows all these imperatives forth. Indeed, that demanding bird with his hypnotic rhyme first appears in Joyce's little book of epiphanies. Heron's "admit," supported by cane and cabbage stump, is the second of these radiant imperatives for Byronic Stephen, a proclaimed "heretic," and later an "outlaw." "Obey," "confess," and "commune" are the burden of the retreat in the school chapel; and "conform," though unspoken, is implicit in the final interview with Cranly. As for "submit," like Mr. Browne of *Dubliners*, it is everywhere.

These imperatives are the "nets" which the outlawed heretic and self-proclaimed creator must fly above in order to find the "unfettered freedom" that creation demands. In exile, with a creator's cunning, "I will try to express myself," he says, "in some mode of life or art as freely as I can and as wholly as I can." (518) As Cranly observes, the penalty of escape, whether positive, negative, or romantic, is loneliness, not only man's general condition in our time, if we believe Conrad, Kafka, and many others, but a particular improvement on it: "Alone, quite alone. . . . And you know what that word means? Not only to be separate from all others but to have not even one friend." (519) It may be, as John Donne affirms, that no man is an island, but the daring young man wants to be one and leave his.

Escape, despite Stephen's idea of it, is not the creator's necessary condition. Wallace Stevens, our great poet, remained in Hartford, selling insurance. In England, Henry Green managed to write novels while managing a foundry. And T. S. Eliot, an exile from St. Louis, Missouri, but less of an exile than he seems, has spent his life hunting the traditions and limitations that Stephen endeavors to avoid. Nets, pressures, and imperatives may be good for art or, at least, not bad. Maybe Stephen is to find this out.

In any case, his first attempt at exile is unsuccessful. The first chapter of *Ulysses* shows him back in Ireland, still silent, with cunning unimpaired. At the end of *Ulysses* he tries again, more successfully maybe, though we never know. If for the moment we may confuse Stephen's undisclosed but implied future with Joyce's past, Stephen is to remain obsessed with what he has rejected. He only thinks he has given up being lover of the place he is lover of. Physically abroad, he never leaves home; for exile fails to diminish his concern with Ireland and her traditions. Indeed, coming to terms with Ireland (at a distance) seems to be Stephen-Joyce's success. Though this success is implicit in *Ulysses*, it is altogether absent in *A Portrait*, which ends with the artist's beginning. However improper the confusion of Stephen with his creator, the future of this future artist, however hypothetical, cannot be avoided. The suggestions are inescapable.

The making of an exile determines structure, an important part of form or the harmony of parts. Each of the five chapters, faithful to Stephen's nature, reveals a stage of its development. The first chapter concerns infancy at Bray, a town to the south of Dublin, and childhood at Clongowes Wood. The second, which includes childhood at Blackrock (also to the south, but less remote), the removal to Dublin, the first years at Belvedere, the visit to Cork, and, subsequently to the whorehouse, shows childhood becoming adolescence. The third chapter, exploring the troubles of adolescence, concerns sin, guilt, confession, and communion. The sermons are central to this difficult period. A very short one, the fourth chapter is nonetheless climactic. Starting with repentance and austerity, this chapter proceeds through rejection of one priesthood for another—of Catholic priesthood for that of the more or less secular imagination. Stephen's encounter with the wading girl, the climax of this climactic chapter, is the climax of the book. The last chapter, though a kind of diminuendo, recapitulating while it resolves, shows the inevitable consequences of his vision. The University, the aesthetic theory, the poem, and the last interview with Cranly are the major materials of this long, important chapter, where Stephen stands fully revealed. Fragments from a diary may disappoint our expectation of a strong ending; but, as we shall see, these fragments, functional, necessary, and less feeble than they seem, provide the final revelation.

This five-part structure, with climax in the fourth and resolution in the fifth, is that of classical drama, Joyce's model maybe. Uncommon in the novel, where customary shapelessness yields at times to three-part division (as in *Nostromo*, *A Passage to India*, or *To the Lighthouse*), this veritable quincunx was anticipated by Conrad's *Nigger of the Narcissus*. Other analogies suggest themselves, the classical symphony, for example, or the poem. Though its major parts, like those of the symphony, are four, not five, T. S. Eliot's *Four Quartets* provide adequate parallel; for in this poem each of the developing parts is intricately composed. Structure is not only the sequence of large, related parts but of smaller parts within them. Chapters three and four of A *Portrait* are almost as straightforward as chapters of a common novel, but chapters one, two, and five, intricate in structure, puzzle many readers. The symphony or the poem affords a good analogy for such structures, but the cinema a better.

The first chapter consists of four parts, connected by idea and theme, but separated by gaps without transitions. The first and shortest of these parts is Stephen's infancy. Suddenly, skipping years, we find Stephen at school, on playground, in classroom, dormitory, and infirmary. The third part finds him back at home for that Christmas dinner. He suddenly reappears on playground and in refectory, complains in the rector's study, and, on playground again, enjoys social success.

Although the gaps that separate these matters give some readers trouble, they are what we are accustomed to in movies, where flashbacks abound and where we pass without the aid of transitional devices or explanations from one scene to the next. Interested in movies at the time he wrote this book, Joyce may have availed himself of their method. At any rate, the sudden juxtaposition of apparently unrelated things is like that with which the moviegoer is familiar. D. W. Griffith was master of this method, which Eisenstein, his successor, called "montage" or the placing of unlikely things together for the effect of their union. The juxtaposition of home and school—alike in some respects, different in others—is the principal montage of Joyce's first chapter. By no means peculiar to movies, lack of transition should bother no reader of T. S. Eliot's poems, which also proceed by a kind of montage. In one of his essays Eliot says that the difficulty some readers find with his poems is the absence of what they expect: transitions, for example, and supporting explanations. Such unimportant assistants, he continues, have been omitted by the poet in the interests of condensation and intensity, values in all the arts. Working according to this principle, discarding padding, Joyce concentrates on moments of intensity and puts them suggestively together, letting the reader detect their radiance as best he can. The practice is justifiable; for most readers require less help than they think.

Selection, which determines the four matters of the first chapter, also operates within them. The first, less than two pages long, is a selection from the memorable experiences of infancy to reveal infancy. But each experience, centered upon one or more of the five senses, also suggests a direction of Stephen's future development. Together, though Stephen and reader alike are unaware of this, they anticipate most of what is to follow. For Stephen these moments are as immediately significant as they should be for us —or as they are for us, if alert. Each is an epiphany for him and us. Never was selection for a harmony of purposes more economical or more admirable. Soon we shall see what these selections suggest.

The second part of the first chapter, showing Stephen at school, is an intricate pattern of actual experience, memory, and thought, connected by free association, parallelism or antithesis, and recurrent images. Typical in structure, the opening scene begins with Stephen on the playground. Bodily there but hardly there at all, he attends to memories of father and mother, the square ditch, and mother again. After a momentary return to the playground, his mind wanders by way of words like "belt" and "suck" to the drain at the Wicklow Hotel and the lavatory at school. This cross-section of a mind (combining sensation, memory, and thought) anticipates the stream of consciousness that Joyce was to perfect in *Ulysses*. The square ditch, to which Stephen recurs, suggests mother in two ways; by a similarity of which he is unconscious and by an obvious difference. Wetness, coldness, and whiteness connect other items of memory and experience—as the theme of sickness, beginning with the ditch, continuing through the jingle of "cancer" and "canker," and ending in the infirmary, is to connect subsequent experiences at school. Nothing less than an explication as long as the passage itself, if not longer, and as intricate could display the intricacy of this structure or the play of meanings; but hints should do as much for the alert as tedium can. It seems enough to say that the rest of the first chapter and all of chapters two and five, equally formidable, are of similar pattern, selective, passing readily from outer to inner or from present to past. However dissociated in appearance at first encounter, the materials are firmly arranged and linked by many devices. Always in the interests of epiphany, selection shows Ireland forth for Stephen and for us the nature of Stephen. Everything, in short, is determined by Stephen or for him. In the most economical way and with the greatest intensity, everything is designed for his discovery.

Although I do not understand the function of every part, I am sure from what I understand of Joyce that no part could be omitted or placed elsewhere without injuring the great design. Uncle Charles in the garden house at the beginning of Chapter Two must be important because all of Joyce's openings are important; yet Uncle Charles remains mysterious though plainly representing the tradition from which Stephen must escape and curiously anticipating, by burlesque, the exiled artist. Sitting, creating,[5] he smokes and sings, but sings traditional songs. The old lady's confusion of Napoleonic Stephen with Josephine[6] takes its place with pretty Bertie Tallon and the *"jupes"* of Capuchins in a queer series suggesting sexual confusion. I cannot altogether account for this theme, which recurs in *Ulysses* and *Finnegans Wake*, unless we are to conclude that the creator must have both male and female elements. Pretty Bertie fills Josephine-Stephen with greater impatience than the occasion seems to require. The visit to Cork, entertaining enough to seem there for its own sake, is an essential step in Stephen's development; for it is here that he aban-

---

5. Defecation becomes a symbol of creation in *Finnegans Wake*. (E.g. 17, 23, 185) In the outhouse Mr. Bloom brings fertility to his infertile back yard.
6. The Josephine episode is one of a series of three boyhood experiences, presented without explanation or transition. (313-16) The others concern Mabel Hunter (a remote and unattainable actress) and the party where Stephen meets E. C. For Stephen all three experiences seem epiphanies (of the nature of women?).

dons his father, and, seeing that carving on the desk, sees his own monstrosity. The tiresome conversations of the students at the University are harder to account for; but their inanity, presenting what Stephen must escape, develops into the pointed conversation with Cranly, who concentrates all that his foolish fellows have implied.

Like selection and arrangement, the point of view is determined by the nature of central Stephen. A point of view is where the author stands to see his subject. His point is necessarily ours as well. To display self-centered Stephen, Joyce chose a point of view at once subjective and objective. Telling his story in third person—at a suitable distance from his subject—Joyce takes his stand nonetheless within his subject, limiting his disclosures to what that boy notices and what affects him. We see him, therefore, from within and without at once. Since all that Joyce selects has passed through Stephen's eyes and they commonly turn inward, externals are increasingly vague as Stephen's egocentricity improves. His friends, unsupported by character sketches, like those in *Dubliners*, are there only as he sees them—little more than shadows, provocations or stimuli. Details of environment, having passed through the subjective process, are hardly there at all unless summoned into service as epiphanies. Take, for example, his walk across Dublin from home to school at the beginning of the fifth chapter. The "sloblands," Talbot Place, the statue of Tom Moore over his urinal, and St. Stephen's Green are no more than occasions for memory or thought. Yet, though all is centered in Stephen, Joyce remains in charge, selecting and arranging. This subjective-objective method is the invention of Henry James, who employs it in *The Ambassadors*, for example. Often called "impressionism," the Jamesian point of view allows the author, at once within his subject and somewhere between it and the audience, to control as he presents the impressions of an observer. Not what he observes but the observer observing is the subject and his mind our theater. Chad and his affair may be what Strether observes in *The Ambassadors*, but Strether and his expanding awareness crowd the boards of James' stage. Adapted by Joyce to the portrayal of his egoist, this point of view is no less suitable to the purpose than Meredith's comic objectivity.[7]

Joyce's attitude toward Stephen and the tone by which he is presented to us are what, knowing Joyce and Stephen, we might expect. The tone demanded of Joyce by the nature of Stephen is also a consequence of the chosen point of view and maybe among the reasons for choosing it. Stephen is as solemn as Meredith's Sir Willoughby or as Molière's Tartuffe. Taking any of these on their own terms, though possible, is neither rational nor civilized. But the civilized comedy of Meredith and Molière requires an objectivity beyond the limits of impressionism, which is at best an uncertain mixture, half out, half in. Taking a stand within a subject may forbid comedy, but a virtue of impressionism is that it allows the author to stand alongside his subject as well—at a little distance. Not enough for comedy, this distance is suitable for irony, as civilized and critical as comedy and far more disagreeable. Distance lends disenchantment to the view. A value of Joyce's method is that Stephen exposes himself while Joyce, at that little distance, exposes Stephen. The difference between their views of the same thing constitutes an irony so quiet that it escapes many readers, who, reducing two to one, take Stephen at his own estimate. To miss Joyce's estimate, however, is to miss half the meaning and all the fun.[8]

That Stephen, less admirable than he thinks, is not Joyce seems proved again by Joyce's irony. "I have been rather hard on that young man," Joyce told his friend Frank Budgen, emphasizing the last words of his title. Young man no more, Joyce looks at a young man with compassion, to be sure, but with mocking eye. The first word of his title, that indefinite article, also seems significant in this connection. Meaning not only one of several possible portraits, the article may imply a portrait of a particular kind, ironic perhaps. The kind of irony tenderly lavished upon one's self

7. Adapting Meredith's *Feverel* and *Egoist* to his purposes, Joyce drew upon Richard and Sir Willoughby for the portrait of Stephen.
8. In Chapter VII of *Finnegans Wake*, (169) which reviews the material of *A Portrait* with Shem as another Stephen, the irony is more obvious, the indictment plainer, and the defense, though mostly implicit, more personal.

to enhance it may not be altogether absent; for though not Stephen, Joyce had been young. He was humane moreover and a creature of his romantic time. But his tone, generally more distant than sentiment prefers, seems the real thing, not its sentimental substitute. There is room, of course, for disagreement here. Rebecca West and Frank O'Connor think ironic Joyce sentimental; but she is English and O'Connor Irish. I am unable to share their detestable opinion. In judging Joyce national differences sometimes make all the difference; but there are texts to base my difference on.

Irony of the better sort is established by action, idea, juxtaposition, and inflation deflated. After composing a poem on "E—C—" (or Emma Clery), the girl on the step of the tram,[9] Stephen, lost in wonder at his accomplishment, gazes "at his face for a long time in the mirror" of his mother's dressing table,[10] taking his face at more than its face value. Joyce is there as well, holding a nature up to mirror. So held, the young poet becomes a figure of fun like Meredith's Sir Willoughby before the mirrors that line his walls to reflect patterns of perfection. Then, there is Stephen's repentant piety:

His life seemed to have drawn near to eternity; every thought, word and deed, every instance of consciousness could be made to revibrate radiantly in heaven; and at times his sense of such immediate repercussion was so lively that he seemed to feel his soul in devotion pressing like fingers the keyboard of a great cash register and to see the amount of his purchase start forth immediately in heaven, not as a number but as a frail column of incense or as a slender flower. (405)

As for juxtaposition and deflation by juxtaposition: Stephen, approaching the wading girl, hears inner music:

then the music seemed to recede, to recede, to recede: and from each receding trail of nebulous music there fell always one long-

9. For Emma Clery, shadowy in *A Portrait,* see *Stephen Hero.*
10. A. M. D. G., preceding Stephen's verses, (317-18) is the Jesuit motto: *Ad maiorem Dei gloriam.* L. D. S., following them, is *Laus Deo semper.* These initials commonly appear on themes in Jesuit schools. Cf. "*Ad majorem l.s.d.*" (*Finnegans Wake,* 418)

drawn calling note, piercing like a star the dusk of silence. Again!
Again! Again! A voice from beyond the world was calling.
—Hello Stephanos!
—Here comes The Dedalus! (427)

Mixing its figures in an ecstasy of rhythm, absurdly lyrical, this
juicy prose encounters the prose of reality and Stephen's inflation, improved and mocked by Joyce, deflates, leaving behind
a little doubt, increased by two more inflations and two defla-
tions. That this devastating sequence occurs at the climax of the
book invites questions. Plainly young, is Stephen also a fraud,
deceiving himself at his moment of truth? Turning to the second
parody of romantic ecstasy, consider particularly the repetition of
"radiant," a word that is to become central in Stephen's aesthetic. After this preparation, what are we to make of radiance
there?

His soul was soaring in an air beyond the world and the body he
knew was purified in a breath and delivered of incertitude and
made radiant and commingled with the element of the spirit. An
ecstasy of flight made radiant his eyes and wild his breath and
tremulous and wild and radiant his windswept limbs.
—One! Two! . . . Look out!
—O, Cripes, I'm drownded! (429)

He sees that wading girl shortly after this second deflation, and,
inflated again, soars heavenward, his soul swooning amid heavenly flowers. Suddenly down, he is back in the kitchen, where,
drinking watery tea, he sops his crusts in "yellow dripping."

There is more than one way of taking these ironies as there
is more than one way of taking Lynch's irreverent interruptions
of Stephen's aesthetic discourse. Are these interruptions no more
than necessary relief to what might otherwise have been tedious
or are they further ways of deflating Stephen's pretensions—or
both together? There is irony again in the conjunction of Stephen's brilliant aesthetic with the mediocre poem that immediately follows it—a little better than Hynes' in "Ivy Day" maybe,
but not much. Are such unimportant verses the result of such

exalted intentions and the best a cunning priest of the eternal imagination can do? "Cunning indeed! . . . You poor poet, you!" says Cranly, ambiguously. (516) That Joyce's principal ironies attend Stephen's attempts at art, his theories of art, and his aesthetic ecstasies is notable. For just what kind of "artist" are we to take the boy or, as the Irish ask, what sort of artist is he at all?

Indeed, the word *Artist* in the title may be the irony of ironies and the prime ambiguity of an ironic, ambiguous portrait. Oliver Gogarty, Joyce's Mulligan, wanting to run Joyce down, says that Stephen is no artist at all; for in Ireland the word "artist" means deceiver or faker. Maybe, without intending to, Gogarty has hit upon what Joyce intended. Also aware of this meaning, Joyce may have implied it with all the others. He seems to have included all of them in the word "forge," among the last, and surely one of the most important, words of the book. "To forge in the smithy of my soul" (525) is Stephen's ultimate intention. Plainly what Stephen means is to create things in the manner of Daedalus, the Grecian smith, his "fabulous artificer." But "to forge" has another, less creditable meaning, of which Joyce was conscious, as we know from Shem the Penman of *Finnegans Wake.* This penman, Stephen's successor, is not only a writer but a forger in the sense of forging checks. In this sense, the forger, like Gogarty's "artist," is a deceiver or faker; and Stephen gives himself away again. His heavy word combines his own idea of what he is doing with Joyce's less flattering idea of it. In the sense that art is artifice, hence unnatural, all art is deception.[11] And in Aristotle's sense all art is imitation. But Joyce, far from condemning art, seems to have Stephen's kind of art in mind, as later he had Shem's. As forger, then, one thing to himself, another to Joyce, Stephen is ambiguous at best. Deceiving himself maybe and the

11. Joyce called himself a "trickster." (*Letters,* 409) Homer's Ulysses is a trickster. Shem the Penman, Stephen's equivalent, is a sham, a forger, a fraud, a bilker, and a fake. (*Finnegans Wake,* 170-72, 181, 182, 185) Jim the Penman, Shem's original, was a notorious forger; but a penman is a writer and an artist. Cf. "Jameymock farceson . . . the cribibber like an ambitrickster." (*Finnegans Wake,* 423)

simpler reader, he does not deceive ironic Joyce—or envious Gogarty for that matter.

Aside from his weekly essay at school and the verses composed in bed with creator's ardor to an accompaniment more seraphic than the occasion warrants, Stephen's forgery is less practical than theoretic: "he was striving to forge out an esthetic philosophy." (440) From the evidence before us and whatever the title, Stephen is less artist than aesthetic philosopher—aesthete, in short, or man of letters. His interests, not only personal, are literary. Even in infancy he is fascinated by words ("belt" and "suck," for example); and his adolescence is detained by the words "detain" and "tundish." Fascinated by rhythm, he esteems it whether in the supple periods of Newman or in nonsense verses of his own composition. However internal his concerns and whatever the weakness of his eyes, each of his five senses is keen, a cause of trouble or delight. These are hopeful signs. The extent of his reading, displayed by quotation and allusion, is also impressive. If no artist yet, Stephen has some of the equipment. Potential or future artist perhaps, he has some of the matter from which an artist could be forged, in whatever sense we take this pleasing and useful ambiguity. But, plainly, something is lacking there.

Since this "artist" fails to become an artist or a complete forger, his portrait is not a story of success. In this respect it differs from most novels of adolescence, which show a creative hero becoming his creator or the next best thing. *The Way of All Flesh*, which established the pattern for our time, ends with old Samuel Butler, in the person of Overton, embracing young Butler, in the person of Ernest, while Butler himself looks benignly on. Hugging himself and applauding, Butler, raised to the third power, becomes the very image of solipsism. Irony and distance—and irony is a distancing device—prevented such triumph for Joyce or Stephen. Triumphant Ernest, becoming Butler, is heroic, but Stephen is not Stephen hero.

If further proof of that is needed, consider the curious ending of Joyce's book. Fragments from a diary, no form for triumph, are a form for disorder and despair—like the fragments from literature that end *The Waste Land*. Always aware of what he was about, Joyce chose this significant form to suggest his solipsist's condition: all in pieces, all coherence gone, at loose ends at last—his diary not unlike the "pok" from a bottle that ends "Ivy Day." This feeble ending, the very form for Stephen, shows what he lacks. To become more than diarist the "artist" must have not only a forger's cunning but humanity and love. Stephen gets away, but he does not know himself or all mankind as an artist must.

Though determined, like irony and point of view, by the character of Stephen, which is complex enough, the moral idea of *A Portrait* is simple. Joyce condemns pride, the greatest of the seven sins, and commends charity, the greatest of the three virtues.[12] The trouble with Stephen is pride, the greatest of sins. Pride is a defect of charity or love. Secular Andrew Marvell defined love in terms of solid geometry; but Joyce, like Stephen, whose mind is "supersaturated" with the religion in which he says he disbelieves, (510) preferred ecclesiastical terms for everything. A psychologist, prejudiced by his past and suspecting Stephen's, might call his pride inflated ego.[13] Whether we name the trouble this or that, it is plain that a man in love with himself can love no others. However natural, loving oneself is no love at all. The chief words of the conversation with Cranly are "love" and "alone." (510-11, 518-19) These words, condensing the moral theme, fix Stephen's incapacity and his state. Corroborating them, the diary that follows this conversation with Cranly and ends the book has a meaning besides things going to pieces. Fragments may suggest failure, but a diary is certainly a form for suggesting egocentricity. A man in love with himself keeps a diary.

In the conversation with Cranly, "love" and "alone" are accompanied by "touch," a word almost equally loaded. Frank O'Connor has acquired merit through its discovery:

12. For the seven sins see pp. 357, 378; for the three theological virtues see p. 405. The greatest of these is charity; and charity is love—of God and mankind.
13. Shem, an "egoarch" and "supreme prig," "self exiled in upon his own ego," sails off on the S. S. *Pridewin*. (*Finnegans Wake*, 171, 173, 184, 188)

The soft beauty of the Latin word touched with an enchanting touch the dark of the evening, with a touch fainter and more persuading than the touch of music or of a woman's hand. . . . And all hearts were touched. . . . (515)

This great word, having accumulated meanings from previous contexts,[14] implies at last not only the human necessity of contact and companionship but Stephen's lack. That untouchable is out of touch.

During his moral crisis, Stephen all but realizes his condition. "What," he asks, "had come of the pride of his spirit which always made him conceive himself as a being apart in every order?" (420) He would try to be "meek and humble," like Jesus, who followed "a lowly trade." (398) "He would be at one with others and with God. He would love his neighbor." (399) However worthy of praise this resolve, it proves vain. His penitential piety, "intricate" and formal, fails to bring "humility," as brooding over "the great mystery of love" fails to bring comprehension. "To merge his life in the common tide of other lives was harder for him than any fasting or prayer." (406-09) Exile, coming more easily, demonstrates his inability to master self and confront mankind. Stephen's exile is running away from both.

Stephen attempts "communion," however—and one must take the word literally—in chapel and kitchen. When the ciborium comes to him and he takes the biscuit, Stephen, full of God, is one with man, temporarily. When, after private ecstasies on the beach, he returns to the kitchen and joins the "choir" of voices there, he is at home, in harmony with others. That kitchen, not only a device for deflation, is also a place of temporary togetherness. It is in Bloom's kitchen that Stephen will discover real community. In his own home—kitchen or parlor—Stephen makes his most elaborate attempt at communion, after the award of prize money. Yet the family "commonwealth," with himself as leader, is a failure more pathetic than the rest, and he relapses into "futile isolation." (347, 349, 403, 423) Shelley's moon, providing a fitting image of his state, is a barren shell, " 'wander-

14. E.g. pp. 331, 380. Cf. "A Painful Case," "The Dead," and *Ulysses*. (49)

ing companionless.' " (354) But moral abstraction seems more
accurate than Stephen's analogy. Like Gabriel Conroy before
him, Stephen sees himself the victim of "loveless lust." (346)
This realization of self, no more than partial and passing, is complicated by the sermons at Belvedere: "Every word . . . for
him." (368)

Father Arnall's tremendous sermons, cold and lucid (if not
altogether consistent or logical), appeal to conscience through the
five senses. We smell, feel, see, hear, and taste our likely future
and contemplate it systematically. Made according to St. Ignatius
Loyola's "composition of place," (382) yet prudently adapted to
the minds of boys, these spiritual exercises intend moral improvement through terror, the readiest means. The text, from Ecclesi-
astes 7:40 by way of the catechism, is the "four last things:
death, judgment, hell, and heaven." (362) That Father Arnall
omits the last of these accords with his intention; for what has
scaring little boys to do with heaven? Some readers, amazed at
discourse so remote from their experience, have thought these
sermons parodies or even burlesques; but their like, uncommon
now, was common enough in Stephen's day and had been for
four hundred years. Even the imagery is traditional. Not the
product of Joyce's imagination, these sermons are the product of
memory, selection, and leafing old sermons through.

The occasion is a "retreat" from worldly concerns for the examination of conscience. (361) As Joyce takes the word "communion" literally as well as theologically, so he takes the word
"retreat." For Stephen proceeding on his dubious way, these
sermons mean regression. That the preacher is Father Arnall
from Clongowes Wood makes Stephen, remembering the pandybat, feel a little boy again. "I will go back," (335) he says ambiguously, fleeing a present too formidable to cope with, before
visiting his father's past at Cork. The sweating boy, confronted
with Father Arnall's grander past and a more dangerous present,
goes back.

Reported partly by indirect discourse (as in "Grace") but
mostly by direct, these sermons come to us through Stephen's

ears, which, distorting and giving emphasis, no doubt improve them. Accounting for his Catholic-crowded hell, Father Arnall impartially surveys the seven sins, from Lucifer's "intellectual pride" to simple goatishness, maybe the least of all. Each, of course, involves the others, and to be guilty of one is to be guilty of all. To selective Stephen, however, lust, the immediate cause of his guilt, is there alone and his hell the one reserved for goats. Lucifer means nothing yet, but even when Stephen proudly identifies himself with him later on, it is not that great angel's pride but his glorious rebellion that appeals—and his blazing fall. Self-realization is difficult. Yet these sermons are a kind of epiphany for Stephen, though partial at best; for the enormity they reveal to him is not his true enormity. Recollected in tranquillity, these sermons show forth the Church and all he must escape. For readers there is epiphany too, but for each according to his past and his capacity.

Whatever Stephen's opinion of the Church, then or later, and whatever Joyce's, it is clear that Joyce is moral. Disapproving of the Church's morality, he approves of the morality that the Church approves of and professes. No wonder that Thomas Merton, the Trappist, was helped on his way to holiness by Joyce. No wonder that Catholics, despite original dismay, are turning more and more to Joyce. Let F. R. Leavis say what he can, morality is still a value, one among many in the great design, guaranteeing nothing maybe, but active in most good books.

Joyce's morality is general and, like his irony, distancing. In his endeavor to make Stephen a particular young man yet more than a particular young man, something touching us all, both morality and irony were useful. Stephen himself, recollecting in tranquillity his experience with E. C. at the tram, shares this endeavor when he comes to write:

During this process all those elements which he deemed common and insignificant fell out of the scene. There remained no trace of the tram itself nor of the trammen nor of the horses: nor did he and she appear vividly. The verses told only of the night and the balmy breeze and the maiden lustre of the moon. (317)

Pretty bad no doubt, those verses seem general. The process of generalization when Joyce came to write is helped by other devices too. To make Stephen every young man, every proud, young egoist with creative pretensions, Joyce called upon parallel and analogy, which, like morality and irony, make things distant and general.

Since analogy is the more formidable device, let us put it off while attending to parallel, a kind of analogy, to be sure, but distinguishable for convenience. Stephen is compared or else compares himself with a multitude of important figures—mythical, fictional, and historical—ranging from God Almighty to Charles Stewart Parnell. Impressed by these resemblances, which certainly improve as they generalize, we are moved to shout when Stephen comes: Here comes Everybody himself or, since Stephen is no H. C. Earwicker, Here comes almost Everybody. Axiom: a thing compared with many things begins to seem their sum, and, if not altogether general, more nearly general than before.

Joyce's problem, then, was not only how to make a work of art from moral matter but, making the particular universal, how to suggest all youth, all loneliness, all desire. Stephen's inscription on the flyleaf of his geography book provides a clue: "Stephen Dedalus" it begins, then proceeding through class, school, town, county, country, continent, it ends with "The World, The Universe." (255) Joyce told a friend: "If I can get to the heart of Dublin, I can get to the heart of all the cities of the world. In the particular is contained the universal." This applies to Stephen in his degree. The definite article in Joyce's title, which seems periodically to detain us, may imply generality as well as irony. Not *The Portrait of an Artist*, his title is A *Portrait of the Artist*, and whatever meaning we assign to *Artist*, we cannot miss the general *the* without missing something. When the swimming boys hail soaring Stephen, deflating him, they also inflate him a little. "Here comes The Dedalus!" (427) they shout. Although they have The O'Reilly in mind or the head of any Irish clan, and although joking, the implication of their "The" is wider than they know. So distinguished, Stephen becomes at once comic, local, and mythical. Not Daedalus entirely, nor even the chairman of an Irish clan of Dedaluses (or Dedali), Stephen, The Dedalus, becomes a provincial parody of the fabulous artificer, suffering from the comparison as well as gaining by it—as, a few years later, Mr. Bloom was to gain and suffer by comparison with Ulysses, a fabulous voyager.

Comic and general, such parodies of myth served Joyce's purpose well. The most important of these counterparts in A *Portrait* is Daedalus, of course, as the epigraph (no less functional than that of Eliot's *Waste Land*) lets us know. Ovid's Daedalus, who bends his mind to "unknown arts," is inventor and creator, an artist in short. It was he who made an artificial cow for the convenience of Queen Pasiphaë, the cow that Stephen, in *Ulysses*, (554) calls her "confessionbox." To contain the ambiguous result of his assistance, Daedalus made a labyrinth, intricate, formal, endless, yet niding and revealing bull. Certainly Joyce's pattern and maybe Stephen's, a labyrinth seems what modern artists try for. But Daedalus did more. Inventor and craftsman, creator of ambiguities, he made wings, handy for exiles like himself to fly with above obstacles and away. These parallels to his own condition and aims before him, Stephen follows, however parochially, his famous namesake, becoming according to his capacity, artist, craftsman, inventor, victim, flier, and exile, too.

But Daedalus made something more than Dedalus seems aware of. Before inventing the flying machine, the Cretan exile invented the robot. This mobile thinking machine, named Talos after one of Daedalus' sons, was made of bronze with jointed limbs. Moved by a tube of "ichor" up his back—atomic fuel maybe—Talos ran round the shores of Crete to keep invaders off, and, having found some, hugged them with sardonic grin. One day, however, Medea, returning from Colchis with Jason, invaded that shore. While Talos hugged an Argonaut or two, she got behind him, pulled the plug, and let the ichor out. This was the end of Talos, defeated, as if man, by woman. If aware at all of this invention, Joyce found it irrelevant to his design; but it seems a pity that nothing in Stephen's experience invited comparison

with Talos and his end. Everyone to his taste. Joyce preferred
the labyrinth and wings for flying above it, at a considerable
altitude. Picasso likes the Minotaur.

Named as he is, Stephen naturally identifies himself with
Daedalus. As the boys shout *"Bous"* (ox) at him on his way along
the Bull Wall,[15] he thinks of the strange, prophetic name he
shares with one who once made walls for the Minotaur, a bullier
bull than Stephen's:

Now, at the name of the fabulous artificer, he seemed . . . to see
a winged form flying above the waves . . . a hawklike man flying
sunward above the sea, a prophecy of the end he had been born to
serve . . . a symbol of the artist forging anew in his workshop out
of the sluggish matter of the earth a new soaring impalpable im-
perishable being. (429)

Soaring in fancy, the young forger is suddenly brought down by
those boys: "O, Cripes, I'm drownded!" Daedalus no more, he is
Icarus now, the son of Daedalus who, trying to fly on father's
wings, went too near the sun and fell into the sea. Not the product of his own fancy there, Stephen as Icarus is the product of
Joyce's ironic juxtaposition; but on the last page, about to fly off
over the waves, Stephen himself, as if unconsciously, calls upon
Daedalus as father: "Old father, old artificer, stand me now and
ever in good stead." (525) Stephen Icarus, a forger in one sense if
not the other, is looking for a fall, which, according to the opening of *Ulysses*, he takes, unready as yet for the wings of art, or flying too near the sun too soon. Down to earth in *Ulysses*, (208)
yet all at sea, he sees himself as "lapwing" Icarus. But that is another story, no more than implied by the parallel here.

Other major parallels assist Stephen's disclosure, but before we
take the great ones up, let us glance at some minor assistants.
When Stephen at play thinks of himself as Napoleon, (309) his
self-identification with the type of egocentricity and the mad-

15. The Bull Wall, where the girl wades, is not to be confused with Sandy
mount Strand and the Pigeon House breakwater where Stephen walks in
Ulysses. The Bull Wall is the northern breakwater of Dublin harbor; the
Pigeon House breakwater is the southern. Consider Lynch's "Bull's eye!"
(478-79)

man's delight has more than literal significance. To be sure, it is what any boy at play might fancy; but in Stephen's case, it points to an egocentric future. Imagining death in the infirmary at school, Stephen identifies himself with dead Parnell, a "betrayed" patriot. (268) Hence much of Stephen's discomfort at the Christmas dinner. Betrayal also commends the Count of Monte Cristo, "dark avenger" and lover of an unattainable Mercedes. (308-09) Defending Byron, (329-30) Stephen becomes one with a heretic, a romantic outlaw, and, as poet, creator of *Cain*.[16]

The parallel of Dante, which we encountered in "Grace," also functions here before reappearing more elaborately in *Ulysses*. When Stephen turns on the "spiritual-heroic refrigerating apparatus, invented and patented in all countries by Dante Alighieri," (524) the reference, which makes E. C. seem frigid Beatrice and Stephen her Dante, makes it likelier that Stephen's progress parodies Dante's. The sermons now seem Dante's hell, Stephen's period of repentance and austerity seems purgatorial, and his experience of the wading girl, attended by a vision of roses, approximates Dante's heaven. Though exile and poet, Dante is far less secular than Byron. In Dante's company we ascend to spiritual regions occupied by St. Stephen, Lucifer, Jesus, and God, with all of whom Stephen compares himself.

Not only generalizing Stephen, such parallels serve other purposes as well: psychological, moral, social, and comic. When making a boy one with creators, rebels, fallers, exiles, and questers, the parallels are more or less serious; but when a boy finds his counterpart in Jesus Christ, for example, or even in a Seraph, that boy becomes absurd. Egocentricity and pride were never more fittingly displayed. Detained by Joyce's serious demeanor and by Stephen's solemnity, we may forget that Joyce is most comic when most serious.

Some of his comic devices are concealed so well, however, that

16. Before making his decision, Stephen walks significantly back and forth between Byron's pub and the Clontarf chapel. (423) The meaning of Byron and pub is apparent. Clontarf, scene of an Irish victory, and the chapel combine nation and religion. Stephen is weighing a choice between poetry and piety, exile and nation, world and Church. Byron's *Cain* was one of Joyce's favorites

the reader without special knowledge cannot be blamed for missing them. Stephen's admiration of Claude Melnotte is a case in point. Thinking of Mercedes, Stephen abandons the role of Monte Cristo for a moment as "the soft speeches" of Claude Melnotte rise to his lips. (350) This romantic figure is the hero of Bulwer-Lytton's *Lady of Lyons*, a play to which Stephen has taken his parents. (348) Apparently casual, the reference to Bulwer-Lytton's hero conspires with other trivialities to reveal unheroic Stephen. He is able to identify himself with Claude Melnotte because this hero is an outsider and an artist, who writes verses to an ideal lady. But that Stephen misses Bulwer-Lytton's moral point is ironic and comic too. The full title of his play is *The Lady of Lyons or Love and Pride*. Melnotte, declaiming against pride, represents love; and his eventual triumph is that of love over pride. Misled by Melnotte's accidental qualities, proud, loveless Stephen absurdly identifies himself with his moral opposite.

The more evident identification with St. Stephen, the first martyr, is no less brief. Crossing St. Stephen's Green or thinking of it, Stephen refers to "my green." (521) And to whom if not that martyr does martyred Stephen owe his name? The identification with Lucifer is elaborate, however, and more important.

In his sermons on the four last things Father Arnall brings that fallen angel up twice, both times in connection with Adam and Eve, who fell from disobedience, tempted by eloquent Lucifer, who fell from pride. Once "radiant," that bad angel, victim of "rebellious pride of the intellect," fell into darkness and became Satan, the "foul fiend" in serpent's shape. "*Non serviam: I will not serve*," said Father Arnall's Lucifer. Thus far, Father Arnall; but Stephen, a good Latinist, meditating radiance, is aware that the name Lucifer means "Light Bringer." Familiar with Shelley, Stephen must have connected Lucifer with Prometheus, romantic outcast and bringer of fire from heaven to mankind. Familiar with Milton (as we know from *Ulysses*), Stephen must have been aware of the heroic rebel of *Paradise Lost*. It is easy to understand how, after immediate terror passes, Stephen, whose sin is also pride and whose desire is also bringing light, finds Lucifer congenial. The radiant rebel against traditional authority, denying service to the Father, fell from glorious daring, like Icarus, but farther and more gloriously. "I will not serve," says Stephen, echoing his splendid prototype. "I will not serve that in which I no longer believe." [17]

This announcement, which constitutes identification, occurs during the conversation with Cranly. It is at the Bull, however, after the epiphany of the wading girl, that Stephen first finds Lucifer agreeable. Becoming "a wild angel . . . of mortal youth and beauty," this girl throws wide the gates of "error and glory. On and on and on and on!" In the "holy silence of his ecstasy," Stephen resolves "to live, to err, to fall, to triumph, to recreate life out of life." (432-33) Lucifer, the bringer of light, has become patron of life and letters, and Stephen his disciple if not that radiant being himself. To fall from spirit to matter, to bring radiance to dull earth, is the creative act. Lucifer's creative fall, like that of Milton's Adam, becomes the happy fall, the *felix culpa*, and Stephen, like H. C. Earwicker, who also falls to rise again, becomes the "foenix culprit."

Happily fallen and creative at last, Stephen writes a poem in a "seraphic" ecstasy: "the choirs of the seraphim were falling from heaven." The Seraph Gabriel, who has managed a literary annunciation, makes way for Lucifer, and E. C., taking the place of the wading girl, becomes "Lure of the fallen seraphim." Since Gabriel did not fall, the plural here must include Lucifer and Stephen, fittingly haunted by Nashe's "Brightness falls from the air" and by all bright, falling bodies, even of lice. (484, 503)

Though a Seraph is one step lower in the celestial hierarchy than Jesus and God the Father, fallen Stephen, ascending a little, takes the step and dares these awful identifications too. The surprise is his neglect of the Holy Ghost, whose "august incomprehensibility," (406) however, may have deterred him. It is bad enough to think oneself Napoleon, worse to think oneself Lucifer;

17. Pp. 370-71, 389, 509, 518. Cf. *"Non serviam," Ulysses.* (567) In *Stephen Hero*, Stephen calls Satan the "romantic youth of Christ." For Prometheus see *Finnegans Wake.* (297)

but what are we to think of one who thinks himself Jesus and Almighty God?

Stephen becomes Jesus when, thinking of Cranly's "severed head" and his figs (for which "read locusts and wild honey"), he confuses his friend with John the Baptist—Stephen's "precursor." (520) If Cranly is precursory John, Stephen is Jesus, another betrayed martyr to add to the confusion of identities. Jesus is the body of believers, hence everyman. In this sense He is the best parallel for Stephen as every young man.

But as Icarus is the son of Daedalus, Jesus is the Son of God. Being God the Son may be more or less justifiable; but Stephen wants to be God the Father, creator of Heaven and Earth and all the Seraphim. Stephen is an artist, he thinks, and the artist is godlike, distant, and alone. "The artist, like the God of the creation," says Stephen, "remains within or behind or beyond or above his handiwork, invisible, refined out of existence, indifferent. . . ." (481-82) Having given up God's world, the godlike artist will create its aesthetic counterpart, round, solid, and crammed with everything. "It was very big to think of everything and everywhere," thinks young Stephen. "Only God could do that. . . . God was God's name just as his name was Stephen." (255)

The distinction is soon attended to by Stephen-god, but a difficulty remains since the world is "one vast symmetrical expression of God's power and love." (407) What kind of world can a loveless, powerless creator create? Something like his bedwritten villanelle maybe, "an ellipsoidal ball," but this queer substitute for the real thing, as Stephen admits, is more seraphic than divine. (484-85)

For word-loving Joyce, God and dog, verbal mirrors, were closely related. The black mass in the Circe episode of *Ulysses*, where God is impiously echoed by dog, makes their connection plain. Thinking himself god, Stephen fears dogs; (514) yet there is a running suggestion that, fearing dogs, he fears himself, and that his portrait, as if reflected in a mirror, is that of the artist as a young dog. (Word-loving Dylan Thomas, fond of Joyce, seems to have apprehended this.) Simon Dedalus calls his son "a little

puppy," and confusing sexes, a "lazy bitch." Even on his way to
becoming god at the Bull, Stephen fears "his father's shrill whistle
might call him back." Heron calls Stephen "a sly dog." (270, 324,
424, 435) But Nasty Roche's "dog-in-the-blanket" for Friday pud-
ding at school seems to combine suggestions of the Infant Jesus
and of infant Stephen. (247) Closely related by appearance, God
and dog remain opposites, and Stephen, desiring to be one, remains the other.[18]

So much for parallels, serious and ironic at once. Not parallels,
however, but other kinds of analogy, images in particular, were
Joyce's main reliance here. As in *Ulysses*, for which *A Portrait*
seems a technical study, parallel, image, and other kinds of analogy abound. All are symbolic devices, embodying suggestions beyond their apparent capacity and, often, carrying the principal
meanings.

Inexact and far from logical, an analogy—whether parallel,
image, allegory, metaphor, or simile—is at once like and unlike
the thing to which it corresponds.[19] Yet sometimes, when the
thing is evasive, analogy is the only way of getting at it. Analogy
is not unlike those ritualistic acts of the priesthood that pleased
Stephen "by reason of their semblance of reality and of their distance from it." (417) Citing St. Anselm's book on "similitudes,"
(373) Father Arnall employs analogy to make eternity clear to
boys. "Try to imagine," he says, calling upon the images of bird
and grains of sand. Evading our apprehension, eternity can be
presented only by the simile of time. St. Thomas Aquinas com-
mended analogy and Dante used it. Jesus used parables. Like Stephen, Joyce was familiar with this Christian method.

A writer who wanted his readers to be no less conscious than he
of what he was about, Joyce seems to have provided clues to his
analogical method, among them the algebraic equations that fascinate Stephen. The more than casual emphasis that falls upon

18. Shem, a "dogpoet" with any "dog's quantity" of lowness, thinks himself a
"god in the manger." (*Finnegans Wake*, 171, 177, 188)
19. For an account of analogies see Tindall, *The Literary Symbol*, available in
paperback.

these mathematical exercises, claiming our notice, raises questions of function and meaning. (354, 454) Proudly spreading a peacock's tail, then folding itself together again, Stephen's first equation, like the vast cycle of stars, bears his mind outward and inward to the accompaniment of "distant music." To Stephen, the equation seems an analogy for his soul going out to encounter experience. To us, the equation, suggesting peacock's pride, may also seem an analogy for analogy.

If taken so, it is no more than approximate, partly like and partly unlike what it suggests. What an algebraic equation has in common with metaphor is the equation sign, balancing things; but there is difference too. The mathematical equation is more nearly definite and limited. For example: in algebra, $x = 3$ (with some margin, when applied, for probability). In literature, metaphorical equation is both like and unlike, both limited and unlimited. For example: $x = 3 + ?$ The figure 3 is that part of the analogy that is like its object. The question mark is that part which, unlike its object, sends the imagination outward yet brings it home to the embodiment (or the metaphor) that sent it forth. A literary analogy has both definite and indefinite meanings. Both accurate and uncertain, it owes its power to the suggestive union of resemblance and difference.

Metaphor for literature maybe, Stephen's equations, like mathematics itself, may be applied to other things. By position, character, and structure his two equations introduce and anticipate by parody the cold, intricate sermons of Father Arnall and, later, the cold, intricate aesthetics of Stephen. His equations suggestively unite or compare these apparently alien and incomparable structures. Literature—even sermon and critical theory—is not mathematics, however, and what I say about these suggestive equations lacks mathematical assurance. A critic, eyes on text, can never be sure.

But there are other, less ambiguous clues to analogical method. Their context is literary; for they occur when, on the steps of the library, after the composition of verses, Stephen contemplates symbolic birds. It is then and here that he thinks of Swedenborg,

a philosopher of correspondences, and of Thoth, their inventor
and patron. A scholar, one eye on text and one eye off, may be
pretty sure of meanings here.

It is likely that Joyce—and Stephen too—encountered the literary correspondence in Baudelaire's famous sonnet "Correspond-
ances," a kind of manifesto of poetic method. Magical in origin,
the correspondence, whether magical or literary, is an evocative
agreement among things, one more or less related to others. "Evocative" because this arrangement of things shows another forth.
Epiphany, correspondence, symbol, image, metaphor—call it what
you will—this happy combination of things came down to men of
letters from the magicians. Baudelaire got it from Swedenborg
and he from Thoth.

There on the steps of the library, like an "augur," inspecting
symbolic birds ("Symbol of departure or loneliness?"), Stephen
quotes Yeats on birds[20] and thinks of Swedenborg "on the correspondence of birds to things of the intellect." (491-94) Stephen
thinks of Cornelius Agrippa, the alchemist, another follower of
Thoth, and then of Thoth himself: "Thoth, the god of writers."
Commonly called Hermes Trismegistus, Egyptian Thoth, inventor of magic, alchemy, astrology, and writing, discovered the correspondence among all things that is the basis of these arts.[21] "As
above, so below," said Hermes-Thoth. Calling on this god, Stephen becomes one with all the Hermetists, both magical and literary—with Agrippa, Swedenborg, and Yeats. There seems little
doubt that Joyce intended this scene as clue to his method of correspondence, analogy, or symbol. Thoth, "god of writers," was
Joyce's god of images.

Imagination fascinates Stephen, who, like Gabriel now, pro-

20. The verses on Oona and Aleel (493) are from Yeats' *Countess Cathleen*,
at the opening night of which Stephen's fellow students rioted. (494)
21. Hermes-Thoth (who also figures in Mann's *Magic Mountain*) reappears
in *Ulysses*. (191, 499) Augury reappears in *Ulysses*. (214-15) "The tasks above
are as the flasks below, saith the emerald canticle of Hermes." (*Finnegans
Wake*, 263) "Eliphas Magistrodontos" (*Finnegans Wake*, 244) may be a
reference to Eliphas Lévi, the great Magus or occultist. For Joyce and Hermes-
Thoth see Tindall, *The Literary Symbol*. For Joyce on Swedenborg's correspondences see *Critical Writings*, 222.

claims word becoming flesh in the "virgin womb of the imagination." (484; cf. *Ulysses*, 385) When, composing his third-rate
verses, he announces himself "priest of eternal imagination," we
must take this in its context, suitably impressed with his power of
"transmuting the daily bread of experience into the radiant body
of everliving life," (488) or doubting it. By imagination Stephen
may mean the creative or shaping spirit, celebrated by Shakespeare and Coleridge, or else—and this is no less likely—the
image-making power. Sharply distinguishing himself from his
creature, Joyce denied having imagination;[22] but this denial is not
so astonishing as it sounds; for by imagination he may mean
image-making power alone. It is a fact that he never, or hardly
ever, invented an image; but he discovered plenty, and, pene-
trating their possibilities, made context put them to work. Lacking
imagination in the sense of image-making maybe, Joyce had
image-finding and image-transmuting power, the power of picking
trivia from city streets to show moral or spiritual significance forth.
What the commonplace embodies he alone could see, but now the
reader sees it too. Why Joyce denied this enviable power, that he
shared with Baudelaire, the name of imagination is strange, and
why he denied it to his power of transmuting is stranger. When
Stephen says "transmuting," he has in mind not only what priests
achieve, making bread God in the morning, but what Hermetists
achieve by night, making baser metals gold by correspondence.
Surely these accomplishments are work of the creative imagination. Denying himself this faculty, Joyce used a word too narrowly
and modestly for once, but he was only writing letters at the time.

Consider an example—and a very good one too—of image-finding and image-transmuting in *A Portrait*. After walking back and
forth between Byron's public house and Clontarf Chapel, Stephen reaches a decision and sets off for the Bull and the Bull
Wall. To reach the Bull (a small island on which the wall or
breakwater is based) he has to cross a wooden bridge. Crossing it,
he meets a squad of Christian Brothers, going home. (425) Here

22. *Letters*, 101, 113, 243. Joyce praises the "magical powers" of the imagination, *Critical Writings*, 101, 220.

is the trivial detail and here the trivial action to be raised by Joyce to radiant image and symbolic action. "As above, so below," said Hermes-Thoth, but correspondence works other ways as well: as below on that bridge, so above in moral or spiritual regions—or as out, so in—or as here, so there. The trivial detail becomes the given term of a correspondence or metaphorical equation. The other term, inviting our guesses, is nonetheless embodied in and suggested by what is given. Aware of it, Joyce offers it to our awareness. He was commonly disappointed; for if we take Stephen's action literally, as common readers do, it is casual and meaningless, like things in common books. There is an actual bridge, of course, on which one day perhaps Joyce met someone. When Stephen meets the Brothers there, the actual, transmuted, corresponds to his spiritual and moral condition.

Our guesses about the correspondence are guided, expanded, and limited by context and detail. Stephen has crossed a bridge before—over the river Tolka, at a moment of decision—as Caesar once crossed his Rubicon. (421) Bridges lead from one place to another and across something by their nature—and, as we shall see, there is a significantly "disappointed bridge" in *Ulysses*, that gives the present bridge by retrospect another meaning. Crossing his second bridge, after escaping father's dog-whistle, Stephen approaches a positive decision, to be embodied in the wading girl. Crossing this second bridge, Stephen is heading out to sea, the way to life and exile, away from living death. The Christian Brothers, however, are headed back to the shore he is escaping. He is alone. They march two by two in a kind of squad or team, proved respectable by top hats and Irish by uncouth faces and clumping boots. It becomes more and more evident that in this encounter Joyce discovered and presented, if not the epitome of his book, something nearly that; for there is more here than we have noticed yet. To discover it in our turn we must ask why Joyce picked Christian Brothers for this encounter of the self-centered with the other-directed.

Stephen has been reared by Jesuits, not Christian Brothers, who conduct a school conveniently on the corner of North Richmond

Street, across the way from one of his homes and that of the young hero of "Araby." The Jesuits of Clongowes and Belvedere, like those of the Gardiner Street Church in "Grace," cater to the upper classes, to sons of magistrates and their like. When the director offers Stephen the chance of joining the order, he appeals to Stephen's social ambition and his pride. The Rev. S. Dedalus, S. J. would be a very superior priest indeed, his knowledge of the most mysterious of sins and his power of transmuting bread improved by social distinction. (416-18) Sending Stephen to the Jesuits, Simon Dedalus observes: "Christian brothers be damned! Is it with Paddy Stink and Micky Mud? Let him go to the jesuits in God's name. . . . Those are the fellows that can get you a position." (318) So conditioned, Stephen, meeting Brother Hickey, Brother Quaid, and the rest on that bridge, finds them socially and intellectually beneath him—not only going the wrong way, but the wrong sort entirely—not even priests. "Their piety would be like their names, like their faces, like their clothes," inelegant, unjesuitical, lower-class. Stephen tries to be human, but it is idle for him to tell himself that these humble Christians have the charity he lacks, that "if he ever came to their gates, stripped of his pride, beaten and in beggar's weeds, they would be generous towards him, loving him as themselves." (426) The crossing of that bridge, therefore, shows Stephen morally forth: on one hand the daring nonconformist and exile, on the other the victim of pride, loveless and inhumane. The irony, here as elsewhere, lies in the difference between what Stephen exhibits and Joyce exposes.

This compendious correspondence, a thing gathering up and offering many things, is one among many of its kind but not the only kind. Another is the recurrent image. Unobtrusive, escaping notice at first appearance and even at second or third, it gains power through reappearance. Bringing meaning from one place to another, it deposits some there and, acquiring more, brings it along. We have met these accumulators and depositors of meaning in *Dubliners*, especially in "The Dead," where the snow, peripheral and no more than natural fact at first, becomes central and moral at last through reappearance in many contexts. Shakespeare used recurrent imagery of this kind, but twentieth-century writers seem to have taken the device from music—from Wagner in particular, to whom Thomas Mann confessed debt. Wagner called recurrent theme *"leitmotiv."* Rarely essential, this carrier of meaning helps other agents out, adding richness, depth, and immediacy to what we get from character and plot. The structural value of recurrent images is clear; for, winding in and out, they knit the whole together. Escaping the notice of a casual reader, they affect him beneath the level of notice. The alert reader, preferring to know what affects him, finds pleasure in its discovery.

Joyce experimented with motif in *Dubliners*, brought it to perfection in *A Portrait*, and triumphed with it in *Ulysses*. Joining parallel and isolated correspondence or epiphany, the running correspondence became favorite device. Joyce's value, partly moral and humane, owes much to such devices. Seeing reality plain, and master of words for it, he would have been great without motif and his other imagistic assistants, but his works would have been less rich, less formal, and less massive. It is likely, however, that though less rewarding to sensibility and intelligence without such assistance, his works might have been easier to cope with.

Many of the motifs that help make *A Portrait* dense and coherent are stated in the first two pages. This prelude, important literally for revealing Stephen's infancy and his delight in all five senses, introduces road, cow, water, woman, flower, and bird, the things to be elaborated. If we may abandon one metaphor for another, these are the threads that Joyce will weave to complicate and ensplendor the figure in his carpet. The ultimate design will hold the lesson of the master. But before following these threads through their labyrinthine design or, indeed, before proceeding with their identification, let us go back to the opening pages for another look; for these important pages, serving as the first context for weaver's thread or musician's motif or labyrinth's clue—choose your metaphors as you will and mix well before using—qualify the thematic elements while preparing them for reappearance in other contexts.

"Once upon a time and a very good time it was" is the tradi-

tional beginning of a fairy story.[23] Simon Dedalus is telling Stephen "that story" (lie?) about himself, a road, and a cow. The
end of a fairy story, according to Joyce, is this: "So they put on
the kettle and they made tea and they lived happily ever after."
Unlike traditional fairy stories, however, this story of boy and
cow on road, lacks this happy ending, whatever its beginning. The
teller of the story has a "hairy face" like a child's idea of God's,
and he looks at the child through a "glass" or monocle. A single
eye is synoptic, implying to one of Joyce's way of thinking the
gospels or three of them. Therefore Stephen hears a story of himself, a road, and a cow under paternal, godly, and gospel auspices.
Stephen seems an unlikely hero for so traditional a story, however; for he is the eldest son and it is always the third son who
wins in fairy stories. See Auden for this.

Mother plays the piano and Stephen responds to rhythm while
dancing to another's tune. Everywhere in these two crowded
pages are pressures of home, religion, and nation, the last represented by Dante's brushes. Subjected to these pressures, the child
alternates between desire and guilt. It is in this context that the
images of water, flower, bird, and woman begin their work; and, it
is from this context that they take something to be carried on.

Whatever the context, it enlarges and limits what is already
there, implied by image alone. Take the road, cow, and boy.
There he stands passively on a trodden way, maybe hedged. A
road implies direction, limited movement, past and future. A cow,
coming along it to accost the boy could imply everything agres-
sively maternal: church and country, for instance. (The cow is a
traditional image of Ireland.) These implications, confirmed by
reappearance in other settings, are no more than possibilities yet.
Later, Stephen loves to walk the roads around Stillorgan with tradi-
tion-loving Uncle Charles and to ride along them with the milkman. How nice to be a milkman, he thinks, until dismayed by the
cowhouse with its "foul green puddles." Since the Church
founded by Peter is a rock, it seems significant that the milkman's

23. For Joyce's idea of the beginning and end of a fairy story see *Letters* (400)
and *Finnegans Wake*. (69, 152, 320)

road is the "Rock Road." (310) Could this milkman suggest the priest, his cow the Church? Could Stephen's childish desire to follow one and milk the other suggest vocation? If so, these images embody and predict the future.

Still later, we find that Jesus was born not in a manger but in a "cowhouse." Stephen, becoming *"Bous"* or ox, as we have seen, goes to the Bull, emulates Daedalus the artificial-cow-maker, and, expounding an aesthetic theory, uses the cow to illustrate a point. (480) Near the end, Cranly, his critic, is reading *Diseases of the Ox.* (495) So enlarged to include the artist, the image of the cow, linking the books, recurs in *Ulysses:* in the milkwoman, for example, and in Mr. Deasy's campaign against foot and mouth disease. The motif achieves its climax and takes on further meaning of fertility in the Oxen of the Sun, the most bovine of chapters.

As for roads: sometimes straight, sometimes circular, they run everywhere through A *Portrait* to the last page, where "the white arms of roads," abandoning tradition, invite escape, like the bridge, which, to be sure, is a road in a way or, better, a way in a road. Most of the roads, however, are less encouraging: that dark country road where Davin sees the beckoning woman, and all those circular tracks. On the circular track in the park Mike Flynn trains Stephen to run in customary style. (306) Breaking his spectacles on the track at Clongowes, Stephen is all but blinded. (294) Not so the Jesuits, "walking round the cycletrack in the company of ladies." (415) The goatish creatures of Stephen's private hell—as if in Dante's—swish "in slow circles round and round the field." (394) Circular paths, implying custom and confinement are disagreeable throughout A *Portrait*—as they are in *Dubliners.* Transformed by other contexts in *Ulysses,* however, they become the race track, where the Gold Cup is won by Throwaway, and in *Finnegans Wake* the Vico Road or the cycles of history.

A more important image than road or cow, but not than the circle, is water, which also appears on the first page and also serves to link the books, one with another. Making water, Stephen wets the bed. From this infantile beginning the great image proceeds, becoming the sea at last and Anna Livia Plurabelle, the "river-run" of life and time in *Finnegans Wake*. Remember Gabriel's snow. Stephen's wet bed is warm at first, then cold, first agreeable, then disagreeable; for water, like road, has two aspects, good and bad. Were I not sworn not to use such words, I should call such images ambivalent. Their meaning at each occurrence is determined, of course, by their past and by their immediate setting. But by itself water traditionally carries the meanings of life and death; for it is our origin and our goal. We are a watery people, taking baths meanwhile and making what we can.

In the first half of *A Portrait* water is commonly disagreeable, agreeable in the second. The "square ditch," into which water-making Stephen plunges like a rat, is the cesspool for the college "square" or urinal.[24] The lavatory at the Wicklow Hotel says "suck" when you pull the stopper up to let the dirty water out. (250) The turf colored "bogwater" of the baths repels Stephen; for the color of Irish bogwater—even when lapping the lake isle of Innis-free—is yellow. (263, 420, 434) But the metaphysical fountain, dripping "pick, pack, pock, puck" into its "brimming bowl" seems the turning point. (285, 305) After this mysterious fountain in its context of cricket bats, offering more than we can easily guess, the image of water changes and expands. Conditioned by bad water, Stephen fears the cold "infra human" (427) sea; but it is wading there with the wading girl that brings renewal—as if by baptism at the wrong end. It is over water that Stephen flies to exile, and, before that, water flows under his bridge.

Flying, if not bridge-crossing, provides a natural transition to the bird, an image no less ambiguous. Encountered first as the eagle, a traditional symbol of authority, and reappearing as Heron, who not only threatens punishment but punishes, the bird becomes benign. As angel, Lucifer is a kind of bird, and Daedalus, promising creation and flight, is "hawklike"; for even birds of prey are friendly now. The wading girl is a seabird and a dove. (429,

24. Of the *graffiti* on the wall "Balbus," (287) evidently from a Latin primer, is the most interesting. A great engineer or builder, Balbus reappears through-out *Finnegans Wake*. (E.g. 4, 518, 552)

431-32) Birds flying over Molesworth Street, as Stephen leans on his augur's rod, seem symbols of departure or loneliness. (491-94) Finally Stephen takes off for Paris like a bird or Icarus himself. Temple, who seems a caricature of Stephen, is a kind of hen, (506) like Anna Livia Plurabelle. Remember the cooked goose of "The Dead" and all the wild geese of *Ulysses* and *Finnegans Wake* —not to mention the Phoenix.

But the bird is complicated by the bat, no bird, of course, but enough like one for ready association. Davin's beckoning woman on that dark, lonely road is a "batlike soul," the "type of her race," and Stephen wonders if E. C., his girl, is more like bird or bat. (444, 483, 488) Connected with the pandybat and the cricket bats of the first chapter, bats also seem connected with the theme of blinding: the famous spit, the broken spectacles, and the lowered blinds at the retreat. Moreover, the artist, less than the bird he wants to be, is a little batty. Davin's bat-woman lives a life of "darkness and secrecy and loneliness" that accords with the artist's prospect of "silence, exile, and cunning." (445, 518) Forgetting the problem of E. C., Stephen should have questioned his own condition. Morally blind, is he the bird he thinks he is? Stephen and E. C. are not alone; for bats, accumulating meaning and taking some along, reappear in *Ulysses* and, of course, *Finnegans Wake*.

Here and there in this catalogue of interwoven images I have hazarded an interpretation, no more than partial, to be sure; for these images are not signs with one fixed meaning. Tradition may have given the meaning of authority, Roman authority, to eagle, for example; but this meaning, enlarged by many connections, fails to limit or exhaust the meaning, which, though directed by tradition, remains indefinitely suggestive. In matters of this kind, limiting explanation is of less value than indication. It seems enough to point the images out and invite guesses, which, necessarily ingenious, must not be too ingenious.[25] Too much is not enough.

25. Shakespeare's "Bare ruined choirs, where late the sweet birds sang" made William Empson think of many things, among them "the cold and Narcissistic

Two images from those two crowded pages, the flower and the woman, await this pointing out. These important images, persisting throughout *Ulysses* as well as *A Portrait*, concentrate in Mrs. Bloom. In Molly all flowers are united.

Even the "green rose" that opens the sequence. This queer bloom, the object of Stephen's earliest desire, is not only unnatural—like art itself and the aestheticism of the nineties—but it suggests by color both unripeness and Ireland. However fascinated, Stephen is unable to articulate the name. There could be such a flower, he thinks at school, however unlikely its discovery: "You could not have a green rose. But perhaps somewhere in the world you could." (250-51) But the green rose has been complicated by now by the white rose and the red in an academic war of roses. Assigned the white rose, Stephen loses, but when he is able to choose, the red becomes his favorite. ("Canker," by the way, is a disease of roses.) We can never be sure whether this boy, detained by roses of another color, finds the green rose of an almost impossible Irish art or the green rose of aesthetic immaturity. The roses of his adolescence are white or red.

During piety, his devotions ascend toward that celestial cash register "like perfume streaming upwards from a heart of white rose." (402) But white, associated with cold and damp in his mind (as we know from the first chapter), never pleases Stephen. During his ecstasy at the Bull, his swooning soul beholds a red rose: "A world, a glimmer, or a flower? . . . breaking in full crimson and unfolding and fading to palest rose." (433) His second ecstasy, during the composition of mediocre verses, is attended by "overblown" red roses, indeed, by "a roseway" of these from where he lies upwards to a heaven "all strewn with scarlet flowers." (489) Green roses are never overblown.

Dante's rose, multifoliate but not overblown, unites rose and woman. Incapable as yet of apprehending this union, Stephen approaches it in *A Portrait* on hearing the servant singing "Rosie O'Grady" in her kitchen:

---

charm suggested by choir-boys." Following our suggestive text, we must try to stop this side Empson's bare, ruined choirboys.

> For I love sweet Rosie O'Grady
> And Rosie O'Grady loves me.

"There's real love," says Cranly. "Do you know what the words mean?" "I want to see Rosie first," says Stephen; (515-16) but, escaping him, she remains to be seen until the end of *Ulysses*. There Stephen approximates Dante's vision, but here, however roseate, Stephen's vision is pathetic from one point of view, comic from another. Overblown prose is his nearest equivalent for the green rose of his child's garden.

Women in *A Portrait* are associated with flowers more often than with bird or road, though these associations are common enough. There is the "guileless" flower girl offering Stephen blue flowers for which he cannot pay. (445, 487-88) There is Mercedes, his dream girl from *Monte Cristo*, who lives in a garden of roses by the side of a road. (308-09) Both girls suggest the Blessed Virgin; for her color is blue, one of her names is Mercedes, and she sits in the heart of Dante's multifoliate rose. Even Mary Green, the heroine of Blake's poem on William Bond (quoted by Stephen in his diary, 521) suggests the Virgin and the green rose too. Indeed, since most of the girls in *A Portrait* approximate or suggest the Virgin in one way or another, she seems as central in the book as in the mind of Stephen, prefect of her sodality and private adorer. Mary is woman to him and woman is Mary, remote, ideal, unattainable. Eileen of the cool, white hands, his first best girl (not to be confused with E. C., his second) is unattainable because Protestant; but even she is the "Tower of Ivory" from the Virgin's litany. (246, 278, 286) A shadow, Eileen is but first in a throng of girlish shadows, shadowing the Virgin forth.

These girls, at once less than girls and more, seem abstractions, allegorical personifications, or images. Woman, generally an "image" to Stephen, (445, 487) also appears in his thoughts as "the figure of woman" (444, 515) as it appears in liturgy. By this figure the foolish boy does not mean woman's figure but woman as figure or symbol.

Yet there are women with figures around, not only Davin's bat-woman but "Fresh Nelly" and the other whores. Stephen's trouble, or one of them, is seeing woman as Virgin or whore. E. C., who conforms to neither extreme, is rejected at last. The problem is to find someone who, at once Virgin and whore, pleasingly embodies the actual and the ideal. Mrs. Bloom does that. But until Stephen discovers her, he has to be satisfied with Rosie O'Grady, who, although ideal, existing only in song, intimates the proper compound. Rosie O'Grady is a rose—but a rose in an Irish kitchen, and what could be more commonplace than this? (515) Maybe this is "the little green place" where "the green rose botheth."

Less pleasing than the figure of woman, the kitchen nevertheless is one of the important figures of *A Portrait*. Not only a device for deflating Stephen and bringing him down to earth after his ecstasies and flights, the kitchen also represents family communion, as we have seen, and harmony. (403, 422-23, 434) A kitchen, not only a place for sitting around in, is a place for making things and putting them together. When Stephen compares his church to a "scullerymaid," (487) he implies more than he is aware of. What he misses is suggested by the scullerymaid singing "Rosie O'Grady" in her kitchen. Joyce himself found the real thing in a chambermaid in her chamber.

There are other motifs, of course, besides those assembled on the first two pages: dogs, heavy boots, light and dark. Lucifer, falling into outer darkness, is a bringer of light; and the director, dangling priesthood before Stephen, stands with back to light, as he suggestively loops the cord of the blind. (411) A sequence of dreams, constituting a kind of motif, is no less expressive: the first of dead Parnell, the second of goats in a private hell, and the third of little figures before great ones in a cave. (268, 394, 521) Dreams have always seemed symbolic. Joyce, who noted his dreams, uses these to present, with shocking immediacy, the political, religious, and domestic horrors of Stephen.[26]

Charged words and phrases, recurring, have the effect of more elaborate motifs. We have noticed the word "touch." Notice the

26. Joyce recorded and interpreted some of his dreams in a notebook (now at Cornell University) and others in his collection of epiphanies.

insistent repetition of "queer" in the first chapter and its reappearance in the last. But the most evident of these verbal motifs is "hither and thither," a phrase occurring in such a variety of contexts that I confess myself perplexed. (364, 394, 415, 420, 432) "Hither and thither" reappears in the "hitherandthithering waters" of *Finnegans Wake*. (216) It may be, of course, that, a favorite phrase, "hither and thither" recurs without special intention. Not even Flaubert, however, was more aware of his means than Joyce.

Expressive rhythm and montage or expressive juxtaposition, though not motifs, are closely related. We have noticed the overblown prose by which Joyce presents and mocks the ecstasies of his romantic double. In general, Joyce fits his rhythm and diction to the matter in hand. The bare, austere opening of the fourth chapter, for example, is in accord with the absurd austerities to follow. By montage Joyce brings motifs together to provoke interaction. Example: thinking of the square ditch (motif of water), Stephen thinks of mother (motif of woman): "How cold and slimy the water had been! A fellow had once seen a big rat jump into the scum. Mother was sitting at the fire with Dante. . . ." (249) This surprising juxtaposition, revealing dissimilarity and similarity at once and their dubious product (can mother be a sort of ditch?), makes one think. The pages on "smugging" (285 ff)[27] provide more elaborate examples of disturbing but radiant relationship. There, by proximity, "Lady Boyle" combines with Ivory-Towered Eileen (286) and the "square" with these unlikely associates.

By interaction these agents of harmony and radiance bring Stephen's aesthetic theory to mind. No sooner brought up, however, than questions prick their ears. Whatever the apparent clarity of Stephen's exposition, it has occasioned more misunderstanding and more debate than other parts of *A Portrait*. Here we question the sense of what he says, there Joyce's purpose. The question is not where the theory comes from but the sort of thing it is, what

27. The meaning of "smugging" is uncertain. The sin, like that of H. C. Earwicker, is indefinite.

it is doing, and why there. Are we to take it in relation to Joyce, to his works, to this work in particular, or to Stephen, his creature? Clearly, the application is not so clear as it seems.

Though not our problem, the origin cannot be avoided altogether. From documents printed by Herbert Gorman in his biography of Joyce we know that Stephen's aesthetic theory was Joyce's once. But there is no justification in the text of *A Portrait* for thinking the theory still his. We know Joyce's habit of taking what was handy from his life or experience and, transforming it, making it the matter of his art. Originally his, the theory is Stephen's now, serving to show his character forth and to advance the plot. Good on the whole, the theory nonetheless is of a kind that an arrogant boy, without aesthetic accomplishment, would display to keep his ego up. That this splendid theory precedes the mediocre verses supports, as we have seen, the prevailing irony. In the formal pattern, the theory provides one of the small elevations that interrupt the gradual decline of the last chapter. The theory, then, no longer Joyce's, takes its place in a structure as one of its working parts.

Concerning the theory itself: from a maze of definitions, illustrations, questions, interruptions, and digressions three main points emerge: 1) a distinction between the static and the kinetic; 2) a hierarchy of kinds (lyric, epic, and dramatic); 3) wholeness, harmony, and radiance as requirements of art and stages of its apprehension. This amounts to a theory of impersonality and autonomy. That an egoist maintains impersonality may seem ironic, but that he maintains autonomy is no more than we might expect. In this sense, the theory is another way of showing an egoist up.

For Stephen, art is all alone, as separate from morality as he himself from society. Kinetic art, whether moral or immoral, is bad because, connected with something, it arouses desire or loathing, inviting action rather than contemplation. His rejection of pornography is as easy to follow as his rejection of the didactic, which, for him, includes not only persuasion but morality and all significant matter. An end, he says, to "good and evil." (473) Stephen's theory, announced in 1902, is formalist. A theory of art for art's sake, it suitably follows Oscar Wilde's[28] and anticipates Clive Bell's. But to account for its character is not to explain the inconsistencies it gets Stephen into. As he stands before Maple's Hotel (now a parking lot) on Kildare Street, near the library, and thinks of the patricians there, he wonders: "How could he hit their conscience or how cast his shadow over the imaginations of their daughters . . . that they might breed a race less ignoble than their own?" (507-08) Not only moral but didactic, this desire seems out of harmony with his rejection of kinetic art. His desire "to forge in the smithy of my soul the uncreated conscience of my race" (525) is equally puzzling.

The word "conscience" is the difficulty. Father Arnall uses it throughout his sermons in the usual moral sense. In *Ulysses*, Stephen's "agenbite of inwit" means remorse of conscience in the usual moral sense. Can it be that Stephen, disdaining the sense of the marketplace, is using the word in another sense at the end of A *Portrait*—as Shakespeare did? "Conscience" can mean thought, consciousness, awareness, knowledge, self-realization. Maybe Stephen's static, contemplative art improves awareness. But even such improvement, plainly moral, is not altogether without didactic purpose.

Plainly moral and humane in purpose and substance, Joyce's work must be distinguished sharply from the theory of his inconsistent aesthete; but Joyce's purpose remains unclear at this point. We cannot be sure whether Stephen's inconsistency is another comic revelation, even subtler than the rest, or whether, nodding a moment and intruding his own moral concern, Joyce was inconsistent. Such possibilities aside, it remains apparent that, proclaiming static art, free from morality, Stephen's theory displays his aloof inhumanity again. His amoral proclamation becomes moral revelation.

Stephen's three requirements for art (wholeness, harmony, and

28. A connection between Stephen-Shem and Oscar Wilde is established by the "wilde erthe blothoms." (*Finnegans Wake*, 69) Like Wilde, Stephen is a perverse aesthete, accused by the rector (in *Stephen Hero*) of supporting the doctrine of art for art's sake.

radiance) are less formalist than his idea of stasis but formalist enough to harmonize with it. Wholeness, apprehended immediately by intuition, means that a work, separate from its surroundings, moral or human, is all by itself—alone and self-sufficient, like Stephen. Within this isolated thing is an intricate relationship or harmony of parts—of parts to whole and of this to these. Harmony, inviting critics, is apprehended by analysis. Wholeness and harmony together produce radiance or epiphany,[29] apprehended by intuition again and beyond critics. The important word is "relation," which recurs throughout his discourse. Truth and beauty depend upon "the most satisfying relations" of their materials. Wholeness and radiance also depend upon harmonious relationship—not, of course, with other things but of parts within the important, lonely thing. The "whatness" of the parts in relationship is left significantly vague, and so is their "result" or the whatness they radiate.[30]

In Joyce's works the parts in relationship are moral and human, and what they radiate, no less moral and human, expands our awareness or conscience.[31] Not so in unrelated Stephen's theory, where relationship and epiphany, lacking meaning, remain abstract and pure, like something by Mallarmé. Unrelated, the radiant relationship is autonomous. All right for autists, autonomy is unsuitable for artists, for literary artists at least; for more than shape, literature is shaped meaning. It may be that shape is meaning or meaning shape, but you cannot have one without the other or tell them apart in what deserves the name of literature.

The third important point of Stephen's aesthetic discourse is a theory of impersonality that he shares with T. S. Eliot (when without individual talent) and with Yeats with his mask on. According to Stephen, there are three kinds of art: lyric, epic, and dramatic, rising in this order from the personal to the impersonal

29. In *Stephen Hero*, Stephen identifies radiance with epiphany.
30. "Whatness" is the *"quidditas"* of St. Thomas Aquinas or the essence of a thing.
31. In *Letters* (62, 63) Joyce announces the purpose of *Dubliners* as the "spiritual liberation of my country." He hopes for the reawakening of "the Irish conscience," *Critical Writings*, 169.

and acquiring merit as they rise. His choice of terms is confusing; for commonly these terms apply to literary kinds. The lyric commonly means a short, personal song; the epic, a long narrative poem of wide scope; and the dramatic, a play. Not meaning this at all by his terms, Stephen uses them to distinguish three attitudes—three attitudes of writers toward their work. A lyric writer, incapable of distance, is one with his work, like Samuel Butler with Ernest. An epic writer, a kind of showman like Fielding, stands between his work and the audience, showing it to them. He is still around. But the dramatic writer, not around at all, has distanced himself to the point of disappearance. His work is there alone, speaking for itself. In Stephen's sense, therefore, a lyric poem could be dramatic or a bad play lyric, depending on the writer's attitude and position.

Though it is easy to see how this preference for dramatic, impersonal art agrees with Stephen's insistence upon autonomy, it is less easy to see why an egoist, one whose personality is the highest value, should praise an art without this value. Maybe, as we have suspected, this is another of Joyce's ironies or of Stephen's inconsistencies. But maybe—and this is more likely—the triumph of personality is the achievement of impersonality.

Stephen calls his theory "applied Aquinas," and so far as it concerns wholeness, harmony, and radiance it certainly comes from that philosopher, with allowance for free translation.[32] But if "applied" at all, Aquinas is applied to the point of being remade in another's image. "Liberally interpreted" seems a more suitable description. Indeed, less applied than denatured, the angelic doctor becomes the image of Stephen in his capacity of fallen angel, bringing light to self.

Not a proclamation of his own idea of art, the aesthetic discourse, I repeat, is Joyce's way of shedding more light on Stephen, another way of showing him up by letting him show off. A theory of art is a good device for that; for art, having two aspects, is autonomous, formal, and impersonal on the one hand and mor-

32. For the basis of Stephen's theory see St. Thomas, *Summa Theologica*, Part I, Question 39, Art. 8.

ally significant on the other. Taking sides, the theorist reveals part of art and himself entirely.

Many critics, taking Stephen's theory as Joyce's own, have applied it to his works to find if they are lyric, epic, or dramatic—as Stephen applies it to the bust of Sir Philip Crampton.[33] Some critics, working in the darkness of this assumption, have found A *Portrait* lyric, *Ulysses* epic, and *Finnegans Wake* dramatic. Some have found all Joyce's works dramatic, even the lyrics of *Chamber Music* and *Exiles*, that lyrical play. One critic finds all three kinds in A *Portrait*. Lyric at first, it becomes epic in the middle and dramatic at the end—though a diary, the epitome of lyric composition, remains a problem. Another critic finds the three kinds in *Ulysses*, with more justification from the text perhaps. Misled by an assumption and indifferent to texts, these critics are doing their best, like Samuel Beckett's parrot.

Let us accept their hypothesis for the moment, however, and apply it for fun to A *Portrait*. The text assures us that Stephen, diary-writer and bad lyric poet, is lyric in his attitude toward himself. Even when commending the dramatic, he is lyric, applying Aquinas to display Stephen. Not lyric in his attitude toward Stephen, Joyce usually seems distant, impersonal, dramatic. At these times he is the author of a dramatic book about a lyric hero. But often around as ironist, he seems epic sometimes, standing between audience and victim, indicating him to it. Pursuing our hypothesis, we may conclude that all of Joyce's works, even his lyrics, are dramatic in intention, harmonious and radiant, too. There is no harm in using Stephen's terms. "Harmony" and "radiance" in particular are critical conveniences that apply to any art. We are at liberty to apply them to Joyce as we are to apply any system that offers help.

However harmonious and radiant Joyce's works, Stephen's theory is inadequate nevertheless for estimating them—and too nar-

---

33. Sir Philip's bust, (480) which looks like a degenerate artichoke, is a Dublin joke and mystery. No one knows who he is or why the artichoke is suitable. Passing that bust on the way to the cemetery, Bloom wonders, "Who was he?" (*Ulysses*, 91)

row; for it lacks humanity, compassion, charity, and understanding—all that Joyce's works have. Maybe after meeting Mr. Bloom,
Stephen finds these too.

Exceeding his limitations after that, Stephen might find A *Portrait* a harmonious, radiant whole. But though we could agree, we
too are limited and questions remain. While satisfied that all the
parts enjoy satisfying relations with one another and that all are
functional, I do not pretend to understand them all or to follow
their workings. Why, for example, John Alphonsus Mulrennen,
who appears mysteriously in Stephen's diary? (524) Who is he
and what is he doing there?[34] We may understand or think we
understand Stephen's reference to Blake's "William Bond," but
why the song about "Bombados" (357)[35] and why the song that
Simon sings in Cork? (337) Unexhausted, the text seems inexhaustible.

Like any work of art—indeed, like life itself—A *Portrait* remains a riddle or an unanswerable question. Maybe that is why
Athy in the infirmary puts a riddle to Stephen, who cannot find
an answer. (266) Maybe that is why riddles figure in most of
Joyce's works.[36]

34. In *Stephen Hero*, a peasant uses Mulrennen's phrases.
35. There is an enigmatic reference to Bombados in *Letters*. (86)
36. E.g. *Ulysses*, 27, 130, 133; *Finnegans Wake*, 21-22, 170, 223, 231, 233,
311, 607.

Stephen Hero

A Note

A *Portrait* is a little world, compacted, globular, done. But that, like our world, this little world is the result of an evolutionary process, marked by trial and error, is proved by *Stephen Hero*, the surviving part of an early version, rescued from the fire. This fragment, which includes Stephen's years at the University, demands comparison with A *Portrait* or with the last chapter at least.

Joyce wrote *Stephen Hero* while finishing *Dubliners*. The wonder is that a man turning out the felicities of "Grace" or "The Dead" could turn the crudities of *Stephen Hero* out, the day before or the day after. Joyce himself called *Stephen Hero* "rubbish," (*Letters*, 362) but it is not quite that. Little more than document, however, a kind of footnote to A *Portrait* now, this discouraging fragment encourages scholars alone. There they sit, consulting it as paleographers a rune, palaeontologists a bone, or archaeologists a piece of pot. When, throwing the manuscript into the fire, Joyce called it "a young man's book," he was just and accurate in the main. If book at all, however, the rescued fragment is no portrait of a young man.

Nevertheless, the ordinary reader of A *Portrait* may find comparison not altogether without interest. Proving again how good A *Portrait* is, the disparity between book and fragment is a lesson in art. Without value in itself, *Stephen Hero* provides a clue to value, letting the glory of creation through. If art is significant form, here is insignificant formlessness. If art is shaped matter, here is matter awaiting shape—stuff for the forge. If *A Portrait* is a world, here is chaos before God got around to it. Any part could be left out—and should have been.

Commonly taken at his own estimate, Stephen, not victim here but hero, seems another person entirely. Nor is he the center of the same place. In *A Portrait* he is there alone, surrounded by shadows and things alluded to. Their subordination and his solitude seem the desired effects. Here he is lost in a crowd of facts and friends. Where he is seems more important than what. Indeed, there is no whatness here whatever.

But for those teased by shadows in *A Portrait*, *Stephen Hero* provides substance. E. C. emerges as Emma Clery. There is abundant news of Cranly, Lynch, MacCann, and Davin (Madden now). Bringing out details of many other things that were to be improved by the darkness of insinuation, bringing into foreground things better left back where they belong, *Stephen Hero* provides light.

Transforming this matter for *A Portrait*, Joyce left much out: the death of Stephen's sister, for example, the visits to Mullingar and the seminary where Wells (of the hacking chestnut) turns up again. A long passage on the Franciscans survives only in Stephen's visit to a Capuchin for confession and in a passing reference to Gherardino da Borgo San Donnino.[1] Stephen's brother Maurice all but disappears in the process; for nothing is left but essentials—whatever shapes Stephen, reveals him best, or improves his solitude and pride.

What is retained and developed is no less instructive. The final conversation with Cranly, loose, pointless, and rambling in *Stephen Hero*, becomes tight and significant. Scattered references to Stephen as an arrogant "egoist" or "inhuman theorist" expand

1. Gherardino or Gerardo (*Portrait*, 487) is a heretical follower of Joachim of Flora, who also interests Stephen hero.

into the great theme of humanity and charity.[2] The aesthetic theory, though substantially the same in both versions, becomes working part in the second.

Most impressive, however, is the change from trivial objective fact to object as symbol, trivial only in the sense of offering three ways or more. In *Stephen Hero*, Stephen, accompanied by Maurice, goes to the Bull, where, in *A Portrait*, he will see the wading girl. No girl is wading now. Indeed, nothing happens there nor is there apparent reason for including the scene. Yet in it is one insignificant detail that, transformed and developed, was to become splendidly significant: "As often as not he encountered dripping Christian Brothers" on the rocks of the Bull Wall. Changed utterly for *A Portrait*, this meaningless encounter with no directions, becomes the great encounter with Christian Brothers, marching westward two by two, in top hats, past Stephen, static, looking eastward, on the bridge.

2. It is true that in the recently discovered pages of *Stephen Hero* (included in the later editions as a kind of appendix) Mr. Heffernan of Mullingar, a typical provincial, commends humanity and charity to Stephen, who cynically rejects them.

Exiles

However simple its surface, *Exiles* is one of the more difficult of Joyce's works. Questions of theme, motive, and general meaning plague audience or readers, whatever their chairs, in pit or closet. As *Stephen Hero* is the poorest, so *Exiles* is the most painful, of Joyce's works. Critics have found it of little or no value and so have most producers. But Joyce, lost in admiration of his accomplishment, found merits that escaped less generous critics. His concern and disappointment attended the general neglect.[1]

Production denied him, Joyce insisted upon immediate publication, as if, for him, *Exiles* claimed a place in the sequence of his works between *A Portrait* and *Ulysses*. One may guess why; for here is another portrait of the exiled artist, this time as an all but middle-aged man. Thematic relations with *A Portrait* and *Ulysses* are close. Here too we find the conflict of pride with love, of inhumanity with humanity. Here, as in *A Portrait*, pride and inhumanity survive. Richard Rowan, the hero of *Exiles*, is kin not only to young Stephen, but to James Duffy of "A Painful Case" and to Gabriel of "The Dead"—but to a Gabriel who, lacking that last revelation, is unregenerate. Stephen is to be regenerated in *Ulysses*, but here, as in *A Portrait*, the proud, inhuman being who

1. *Letters*, 78, 86, 94, 97, 102, 105, 129, 142, 148, 150, 166, 289. Parenthetical numbers in the text indicate pages in *The Portable James Joyce*, Viking Press.

obsessed Joyce, remains a failure. Here is a kind of Stephen who, missing Bloom, remains loveless and alone.

The resemblance between young Stephen and middle-aged Richard is not surprising; for heroes related to the same image are related to each other. As if aware of Joyce's practice, Stephen says, we recall, that the artist uses his image. Joyce used it to create Stephen. In *Exiles* he used it again—or part of it—for Richard, who owes almost everything in character or circumstance to Joyce's idea of himself and to his experience. Like Joyce, Richard returns from exile in 1912. He still declines marriage with the intellectual and social inferior with whom he has eloped. Their son, like Joyce's own, calls father "babbo." Such resemblances, exciting biographers, are too numerous and obvious to list. That Joyce made use of part of his image is certain. The point, however, is not resemblance but difference. Whatever he owes to Joyce, Richard is not Joyce, but another person, more or less detached from his creator and observed from a little distance. Sending his creature "scouting on the globe," Joyce was impersonally personal again—or this, at least, seems his intention. That he failed to achieve the impersonality of his desire is one of the troubles with *Exiles*.[2] Not Joyce, maybe, Richard seems closer to Joyce and more involved with his feelings than Stephen ever was, even in *Stephen Hero*—closer than Shem. There is distance enough between Joyce and Richard to separate them, but it is only a little distance.

Not enough for irony. What best distinguishes Stephen from Richard is Joyce's attitude toward the one and the other. Though Stephen's kinsman and a sufferer from Stephen's complaint, Richard is taken seriously—as seriously as the Stephen of *Stephen Hero* or more so. Yet victim and hero are alike enough to make us wonder why Joyce bothered to change his image's name from Stephen to Richard. Was it an attempt to prove his image not himself, an attempt like that of Thomas Wolfe, who changed his image's name from Gant to Weber? Nothing seems likelier; but it

2. In his letter to Ibsen (*Letters*, 52) Joyce praises Ibsen's "lofty impersonal power," his "higher and holier enlightenment." Neither seems approximated by *Exiles*. See "Drama and Life," *Critical Writings*.

may be that, with *Ulysses* in mind, Joyce reserved an image named Stephen for eventual success. Richard is older than the Stephen of *Ulysses*, and if the encounter with Bloom in 1904 is to fulfill its promise, Stephen could not return to Dublin a moral failure or a psychological monster in 1912. Another name was indicated for Joyce's persistent image; for Richard is the exploration of another possibility, another aspect of the same thing.

The choice of Dedalus as Stephen's surname is easy to explain; but why Rowan for Richard? The dictionary—always of use for following a writer so attentive to words—provides a possible answer while raising other questions. A rowan is an ash tree, a tree of life. Stephen carries an "ashplant" as walking stick, and Shem significantly waves one. Does the name Rowan imply life or creative power? If so, is this implication ironic or literal? The former would be better and more consistent with Joyce's habit, but the context suggests the latter. That a rowan tree, as the dictionary informs us, produces "pomes" may be relevant or not. In *Pomes Penyeach*, however, Joyce took his image as solemnly as here.

Exiles seems a drama, and Stephen commends dramatic art, though his commendation at that time is not necessarily Joyce's at this. Commending the dramatic, Stephen does not mean a play, however, but an attitude of author to work. Novel or lyric poem, according to that boy, can be as dramatic as drama, and must be, if good. Yet Joyce, dramatic enough to please Stephen in *Chamber Music, Dubliners*, and *A Portrait*, longed for dramatic drama. He had adored Ibsen for years, and, though devoted to Dante, had read Shakespeare with approval. The pity is that Joyce's drama is less "dramatic" in Stephen's sense, than Joyce's stories, verses, and novels. Sufficiently impersonal to distinguish Richard from Joyce, *Exiles* is not objective enough to be a play. Inclining toward what Stephen would call "lyric" art, *Exiles* fails to play on a stage, remote from the author, where a play must play. Actors on a stage guarantee nothing. Small producers have attempted *Exiles* in little theaters without great success.[3] Maybe a

3. Ezra Pound reported *Exiles* "impossible" for the English stage; and Shaw, rejecting it for The Stage Society, found it "obscure." (*Letters*, 84, 133)

great director and great players could transform it, sensitive to its inordinate demands, and maybe a great audience could follow it; but in the productions so far (so far as I gather) neither players nor audience could follow what seems (though is not really) there. The reader, to whom this play is now committed, is equally at a loss. Joyce liked riddles and created many; but what he fooled with here seems less riddle than confusion.

That enigma can be successful on the stage is proved by *Hamlet* and *Waiting for Godot*; but enigma, as there, must be embodied—massively. Here, although Richard is central, he lacks body to carry and offer what Joyce burdens him with. The load is too great, its shape too uncertain, and its surface too slippery for Richard; and those around him are no help at all. We puzzle over Hamlet and Beckett's bums, but Richard, though puzzling, is not solid enough or sufficiently "there" to detain most of us. He bothers those around him on the stage, for they are somehow involved; but the man in the audience, lacking such involvement, gives up or, if something is expected of him, goes home to write an essay at once dogmatic and hypothetical. What matters is that the conflicts centered in Richard and caused by him remain unsettled for those on stage or off it alike. Whether the play is tragic or comic as Joyce insisted, (*Letters*, 78) no satisfaction is forthcoming. All is lost, unhappily scattered—though that, of course, could be Joyce's point.

T. S. Eliot has blamed the author of *Hamlet* for inability to find an "objective correlative" or a suitable embodiment for what, if anything, he had in mind. The charge, as critics have observed, could be applied more fittingly to the author of *Exiles*. But to those who like enigma or confusion, from whatever inadequacy it springs or whatever intention, Joyce's play has much to offer. Nothing comes quite clear, and one may puzzle endlessly.

Yet neatness of structure and a workmanlike tidiness seem to promise clarity of meaning. Exits and entrances, timed as if by stage-business machine, commonly leave two of the four contenders before us. When a third intrudes, he or another immediately goes off to the other room, conveniently awaiting him in both sets. The symmetry is almost that of *Cosi Fan Tutti*. But neatness is all; and what seems promised never comes from those two contending in the parlor and those two in the other room or, if separate, from one there, one elsewhere, both away anyway.

Neatness offering enigma instead of clarity is not necessarily displeasing nor does it lack eminent example. Consider "Who Goes With Fergus?" by W. B. Yeats. But in this great lyric, the contention of neatness with mystery creates something worth puzzling over. Of *Exiles* we ask as we ask of "Fergus": What is it all about? But we may add: What of it?

Not only neat, *Exiles* is familiar in kind. Familiarity also promises meaning without discomfort; for commonly what we are accustomed to yields more of the same thing. Like many of Shaw's plays, Joyce's play combines two traditional kinds: the well-made play, associated with Scribe or Sardou, and the play of domestic problems, associated with Ibsen.[4] The first of these is empty but neatly contrived. Exits and entrances click along and nothing unprepared for happens. The second, familiar fifty years ago, discloses unpleasant people with difficulties in a room with a door to open or to slam. Joyce found both kinds congenial. Liking symmetry, he liked the first; and having discovered domestic problems in *Dubliners*, especially in "The Dead," he came to like the second even more. The family with its tensions and its intruders, began to rival Dublin as his microcosm, offering all in little, all the world's concerns and all its history. Any family was pretty good for this, but a family in Dublin had everything.

Though familiar in kind, Joyce's well-made, domestic-problem play, disappoints our expectations. Apparently of Shaw's kind, *Exiles* is nothing of the kind. It resembles triangular *Candida*, to be sure—in reverse perhaps, with emphasis not here but there. Moreover, there is difference in shape since Joyce employs four characters instead of three. We may figure his extension of domestic geometry as a quadrangle complicated by internal triangles, as

4. Francis Fergusson, whose reading of *Exiles* differs entirely from mine, compares Ibsen in detail. (Introduction to *Exiles*, New Directions, 1945) "The *Portrait*," says Mr. Fergusson, "shows us the process of construction; *Exiles* gives us the completed masterpiece."

a three-sided quadrangle maybe or, better, a four-sided triangle. No geometrical extravagance seems too great for the inventor of "square wheels." But back to *Candida* and *Exiles*. Similar problems of choice, freedom, and loyalty vex the figures. In *Exiles*, however, the rational simplicity of Shaw is nowhere around to clear the matter up. We are left with the uneasy feeling that Joyce's play, however familiar in appearance, occupies an area beyond Shaw's limits and his lights.[5]

Before attempting this dark, indefinite area, let us survey the action or whatever they call what happens on a stage. The action of *Exiles*, if we confine ourselves to what seems to happen there, is deceptively simple. Approximating the condition of the commonest reader, let us read, mark, and digest what we can.

Assimilated, the dialogue proves much has happened before anything happens here. Rejected by his mother, as she by him, Richard, a writer, has left Dublin for exile in Rome, accompanied by Bertha, with whom his principles forbid marriage. Their union has been blessed with Archie, a bastard. Dublin, impressed meanwhile by something so far beyond good and evil and so far away, has responded with rumor and gossip. But Richard, having written something, becomes famous enough to be endured. That much for what precedes the action.

The first act, in Richard's Dublin parlor, consists of a series of interviews. At one point three of the four principal figures are present, but elsewhere exits remove the crowding third. Plainly unhappy, Richard, like some inquisitor or prosecuting attorney, questions all motives but his own, which, however uncertain, he applauds. Failing to clear things up for us or for his three companions, he succeeds in making others as unhappy as he. These subtle and intricate interviews, making all heads swim, more or less establish the relations between Richard and the others and the relations among these. Beatrice, useful for "intellectual conversation" and aesthetic concern, serves Richard as subject, reader, and inspiration. If love at all, their love is sublimated, whatever

5. Joyce dismissed Shaw as "didactic," a "born preacher." (*Letters*, 173) For domestic geometry see *Finnegans Wake*. (293-97)

Bertha suspects. Robert, the friend professing loyalty and commending prudence, is a smiling betrayer, bearing gifts. Like tempting Satan, he offers unworldly Richard the world or one of its parts, a chair in the faculty. Bertha, who is unable to read Richard's obscure celebrations of Beatrice, is simple, innocent, and honest. Doing her best, she tells Richard of Robert's plan for her seduction.

The quadrangular triangle, now fixed, is complicated by a line that Archie draws, in quest of horse and milkman. Initial letters bring hints of proportion to complicate Joyce's geometry. The two principal men bear names beginning with R, the ladies, with B. Is R to R as B to B, we ask, or is R to B as R to B? But such hints are deceptive, such questions vain; for there is nothing so plain as Euclid here.

The second act discloses Robert's love nest, once Richard's, too, and once the abode of Dublin's inadequate Muses. The seducer with his perfume pump and his Wagner awaits seductive Bertha. Richard is off with the vicechancellor, seeing about a job —or so prudent Robert, who has arranged this distraction, hopes. Not Bertha, however, but Richard comes through that door, with purpose far from clear. Is it to interrupt the scheduled seduction, to embarrass Robert, to dismay Beatrice, or to pain himself? Anyway, when Bertha enters to enjoy the flattery of notice, Richard proceeds to disguise passion by principle. Like Candida, Bertha is free to choose. Liberty must make no compromise with violence. But a natural woman prefers nature. Bertha is disappointed and annoyed when Richard departs, leaving choice to her and slamming Nora's door.

The third act, increasing Bertha's annoyance, confusion, and despair, increases Richard's incomprehensibility. It is morning and she is home again, probably intact; for Robert has spent the night in his office, praising Richard, and on the tiles, recovering. Archie has been out with his milkman, and Richard has been out with himself, as usual, on the strand. Attempting retaliation on his return, Bertha brings Beatrice up, and, failing there, tries curiosity and jealousy. But, disappointing her again, Richard prefers not to know what, if anything, has happened. Indeed, whatever her protestations, he will never know, he knows. This insufferable uncertainty means suffering for her and him alike, but he likes it; for suffering seems his pleasure. Calling her old lover back is vain. There is no lover there at all, and, lost between fraud and enigma, Bertha is alone.

Her quandary is exemplary. But although it ends this unpleasant play, claiming our attention for the moment, what detains us, relapsing into tranquillity, is not Bertha but her relations with Richard or, better, himself alone. Like Beatrice and Robert, Bertha seems there to show Richard forth. However pathetic, she remains a stooge, a word as nasty as this play and therefore suitable. Like Stephen in *A Portrait*, Richard is surrounded by shadows, who provoke him as he perplexes them. They spend their time trying to understand him, without success. He, with illusion of success, spends his time trying to understand their effect on him. And we, trying too, are likely to misunderstand these misunderstandings. To understand anything we must consider Richard's motives and his conflicts. This is hard because, as from Baudelaire's temple, only confused intimations emerge. What they correspond to is the question.

Conflicts are the stuff of drama, and Richard has them in abundance, externally, between self and circumstance, internally, between feeling and idea or between parts of self. There are moral, social, and psychological conflicts, all centering in him. So furnished, the play about Richard should be better than it seems. A trouble may be overabundance of conflicts, each good in itself, but each conflicting with the others. None emerges to claim our notice as each cancels others out. Moreover, a conflict of conflicts, though intricate, subtle, and worthy of admiration, may be too complicated for audience or reader to follow. Puzzled rather than moved, we are lost in the intricate diffusion. Beatrice, Bertha, and Robert are no better off. Even Richard, trying to know himself, seems disconcerted by the mess.

Many of Joyce's earlier works culminate in self-realization—not that that guarantees literary merit. Not lack of self-realization, then, but of any realization may be a trouble here. If, however, Joyce meant to embody confusion suitably or the state of being at a loss or the impossibility of knowing, *Exiles* is a triumph, or was, at least, for him. Maybe he was his only audience. To suggest that, however, is to find *Exiles* a dramatic failure, something imperfectly separated from its creator. Triumph of a sort maybe, but not a play.

Returning to those conflicts, let us single out a few, for listing all appears too much or, maybe, too little. The great conflict of pride with love or of ego with humanity underlies *Exiles* as it underlies A *Portrait* and *Ulysses*. There it is, determining the scenes. But almost unaware of what he illustrates and once confesses, Richard does not fully know his failure pride; nor does he see that Bertha offers love and humanity to his self-centered inhumanity. He does not see that even Robert, offering lust, is offering a nearer approximation of love. Yet Richard is fully aware of some less basic conflicts: that between exile and nation; or that, since he is an "artist," between art and journalism, represented by Robert; or that, since Robert is his competing opposite, between self and rival. Richard must be aware or all but aware of the conflict, evident to his companions and to us, between principle and feeling. Maintaining the moral principle of freedom and choice, he is victim of jealousy and of a possessiveness which, however natural, is at odds with principle—as his desire to follow Nietzsche beyond good and evil wars with common morality.[6] Richard is also more or less aware of the contention between the Beatrice-adoring and the Bertha-wanting sides of his nature, or, to reduce these to abstraction, between need of talk and need.

These conflicts, both outer and inner, but between Richard and circumstance for the most part, are simpler, however, than those deeper within him: that between exhibited coldness, for example, and latent heat. Of still deeper conflicts he is partly aware sometimes but mostly unaware. Sometimes the three people around him, though almost unaware, hit as if by chance upon

6. For Nietzsche see pp. 584, 585, and "A Painful Case." Joyce (*Letters*, 56) once signed himself "James Overman."

such conflicts. These are those that cause the difficulties.

Richard's deepest motives, though as nearly central as anything in this quarrel of motives, must be determined from what is hardly ever on the stage. Adequate signs, if there at all, are lost in a multitude of hints. Our position is not unlike that of Richard's three companions. We too are sure that something queer is going on within him or between him and them, but what that is remains uncertain.

The reason of this is certain enough, however. In a play the stage is where all is staged or adequately implied. In *Exiles* the stage itself, wooden and hollow-sounding, is where hints pass by, too fleetingly for capture. We begin to feel that whatever happens is happening somewhere else—inside Richard, we guess. Indeed, he seems to house the stage and the players on it. Since this private stage is out of sight and almost out of mind, their uncertainty about where they are or what is doing there is attended by anxiety. In the dark ourselves, we share their feelings—not without reason; for this interior stage, where they wander while we peer, is full of trapdoors to the cellar.

"We are approaching a difficult moment," as Robert says, fearing "a new trap." (552, 590) These traps and this private cellar, though not altogether unattractive to Freud, would have pleased Krafft-Ebing more. Analysts, however, crowd the actual boards, looking for cellar, and a crowd of confessors seems looking patiently for couches. "We all confess to one another here," says Robert (596)—and here all probe remorselessly for the truth, down there in darkness. None more pitiless than these analysts, whether of others or of self, and none more eager than these confessors have adorned the boards, whether actual or internal, in our time. Disguised and offered as a domestic-problem play of the 1890's, *Exiles* is a study in the psycho-pathology of the same period, a *Candida* in appearance, but a *Candida* gone morbid.

Unqualified, these analysts of Richard scatter their diagnoses, agreeing only that, as Brigid puts it, he is "a curious bird," always "off by himself," maybe "a little mad," and certainly hard to understand. (548, 603) "I am trying to understand," says Robert.

(591) "My God," says desperate Bertha to her husband, "tell me what you wish me to do." (589) Richard, on the other hand, complains that nobody understands him. (568) But scattering opinions, like pellets from a shotgun, sometimes find the mark. Richard is proud, self-centered, and loveless, according to some opinions and, to others, cruel. "Have you ever loved anyone?" asks Bertha, echoing Cranly's great question. "If you loved me or if you knew what love was you would not have left me. For your own sake you urged me to it." (611, 616) "All," she adds, "is to be for you." (566)

As for Richard's cruelty to others and to himself, Robert and Bertha are often in agreement. He finds Richard's "experiments" on them more than a little cruel, (573, 590) and she, his inquisitions pitiless. "I fear a new torture," says Robert, (590) anticipating other experiments, further inquisitions. Richard's cruelty to others seems obvious to these involved diagnosticians (whose findings we must check against his actions), but his cruelty to himself and his delight in suffering demand greater penetration— not too great, however for Robert and Bertha at their luckiest. Both find him a sufferer, inviting suffering. The motive, according to Robert, of Richard's lonely walk along the strand is "Suffering. Torturing yourself." (623) The motive behind Richard's curious conduct at the love nest, according to both victims, is a longing to be betrayed by them. The idea of it "excited him," (594) says Bertha, shrewdly. Even invited suffering is suffering, but he likes it.

Richard's "strange" conduct seems pretty well accounted for by these diagnoses, however amateur and partisan. But let us consider his own. "Struggling with himself" (according to a stage direction, 583), Richard offers an analysis of self that, although more enigmatic and more suggestive than their analyses of him, confirms them. Confessing "pride" and "guilt," Richard adds: "In the very core of my ignoble heart I longed to be betrayed by you and by her." There is, he finds, an "ignoble longing" deep within him and "a motive deeper still." (583-84)

However vague this diagnosis, it suggests psychological depths that his conduct seems to illustrate. His enigmatic hint becomes a clue to what has bothered Bertha, Robert, and ourselves. Our growing suspicion that Richard is victim of the defect of love that Krafft-Ebing called sadism and masochism and that Richard's morbid condition is an underlying theme, conflicting with moral surface and domestic guise, causing difficulties by conflict with other areas and by itself alone, is corroborated by Joyce's recently published Notes to *Exiles*.[7] Its "three cat and mouse acts," says Joyce, are "a rough and tumble between the Marquis de Sade and Freiherr v. Sacher Masoch. . . . Richard's Masochism needs no example." Like masochistic Bloom, Richard wants "to feel the thrill of adultery vicariously and to possess . . . Bertha through the organ of his friend." Although to us Richard's masochism seems complicated by sadism, its identical twin, for Joyce, not Richard but Robert is the sadist.

The intention is plain. What Joyce intended to do, however, is not necessarily the same as what he succeeded in doing. Intending one play, he may have written another. Our real evidence is the completed text, not these notes, which, however moving and instructive, are no more than work sheets for his guidance. So long as we take them for what they are, they may guide us, too, calling attention to much we might have missed and to much Joyce failed to do. Indeed, it is immediately apparent that the notes, not only clearer than the play, include more than it presents—and less.

As Joyce remains the true audience of *Exiles*, so he appears its true critic—though what he criticizes in these notes is not the thing before us but his idea of it. For him, the idea of *Exiles* includes his deepest obsessions and most personal concerns, displaying to his admiration that almost terrifying insight into self and those around him that others have found his mark. To us, judging by the text, *Exiles* seems his most painful case. However acute his notes, Joyce failed to embody his insights and obsessions in an object for an audience, something standing by itself without the aid of notes or comment, on a stage. Using the same

7. New York, Viking Press, 1951. References in *Ulysses* and *Finnegans Wake* prove Joyce familiar with Krafft-Ebing.

pathological materials, Joyce gave them dramatic shape and independence in "An Encounter" and in the Circe episode of *Ulysses*.

Richard's morbid psychology, clearing many difficulties up, fails to clear all, nor does it bring the confusion of motives and conflicts into order. No single element can do that for this. Other difficulties remain, calling for notice, the curious title, for example. Richard, to be sure, is literally an exile, home for a holiday, but who are the other exiles? In his notes Joyce says that since Ireland cannot hold a Richard and a Robert, one or the other must go away. This explanation seems inadequate since the title is plural and either-or is not. Richard accuses Bertha of separating him from Beatrice. Is each of the four chief characters an exile in the sense of being separated from something? Richard's deeper exile seems by pride and perversion from love. So exiled, he becomes exile's agent, making others as like himself, and raising as much Cain as he is able. Robert is exiled from Beatrice, Bertha, and Richard by Richard. Beatrice is exiled by Richard from himself, Bertha, and Robert. Bertha, standing for love, is the principal victim. That is my guess; but, as Richard proves, uncertainty is our portion. "I can never know," he says with equal pain and delight, "never in this world."

Not much of a world, *Exiles* lacks the roundness and harmony of Joyce's great creations. It also lacks his customary attitudes toward his creation and its observers, embodied attitudes that I. A. Richards calls feeling and tone. There is little here of Joyce's irony and little of the gaiety that was to return in *Ulysses* and *Finnegans Wake*. "I have always been a joyce crying in the wilderness," he said, (*Letters*, 337) but that joyous voice is silent now and only wilderness remains. Almost nothing relieves the heavy scene. When Robert asks Richard to "be gay," (558) he asks in vain; and vain his perfume pump, however absurd. Traces remain of irony, too, but too few. Selfish Richard accusing Beatrice of reluctance to give herself "freely and wholly" (536) is almost comic, and there is irony in Bertha's tragic call for her old "lover" back. Lover indeed.

The general heaviness and solemnity of *Exiles* may help us estimate Joyce's distance from his object and its nature. As we have
seen, he generally used his image and his wife's for his matter. But
insight, whether pitiless or pitiful, generally made this personal
matter impersonal. Irony, humor, and gaiety of manner are the
marks and agents of that distance from self he commonly
achieved. The feeling and tone of *Exiles*, possibly implying distance unachieved, may indicate lyric and personal involvement
with the matter, which, though handled remorselessly and with
the usual insight, remains too close to home. *Exiles* is too personal
for irony and humor. Untransmuted, the base matter never
emerges from alembic and pipkin into light outdoors as philosopher's stone.

There is in *Exiles*, however, a certain stone that figures among
objects of like importance: roses, water, and cows, for example,
and wind and light. Such images, serving to connect *Exiles* technically with *A Portrait*, are similar in purpose and no less elaborate. But here they work less happily with one another in what
they have for setting. What is good for novels need not be good
for plays, and what is good for a good novel need not be good for
a bad play. Noting such objects in his notes, Joyce calls them
"symbols" or "attendant images." The latter term seems happier;
for these images, far from essential, accompany the action, adding
meaning at times or condensing it. If meant to hold the play together, they fail, however. Moreover, some seem too perplexing
for the immediate apprehension the stage demands. Others, more
suitable, are obvious.

This stone is not one of these. Brought home by Bertha from
the beach, where Richard walks, the stone lies round and beautiful in the parlor. Robert picks it up and fondles it, comparing its
beauty and passivity to woman's. Robert swims "like a stone,"
and Bertha asks: "Do you think I am a stone?" Associated with
too many people, the stone corresponds to none. Richard, with
whom it is associated least, seems stonier than the others; but
Robert anticipates Shaun of *Finnegans Wake* and Shaun is a
stone. Bertha and the stone have nothing in common but round-

ness and beauty. Obviously important, this stone lacks definite import. (542, 555, 556, 614)

Not so the roses that Robert hands Bertha. Stage business of the corniest sort centers in these blooms, as red and traditional as those of Robert Burns. Plainly, the roses of Robert Hand signify his love and the quality of its object, who, with the aid of mixed simile, is also as "beautiful and distant" as moon and music. Fingering petals, Bertha tears some off, and interrogated by Richard, crumples a handful. Richard throws a rose at her feet. She picks it up. Seeing Robert's hand in roses, Richard finds them "overblown" (like the roses of Stephen's poetic vision) and their abundance a "mess." Are they too many or too common? Robert asks. They sadden him, says Richard. The roses of A *Portrait* and *Ulysses* are of a better sort and, with Dante's help, less commonplace. But here they help the action out as punctuation, the sentence. (540, 545, 551, 561, 563, 568, 569, 574)

Proceeding from A *Portrait* in their turn and anticipating *Ulysses*, cow and milkman are also in attendance. Like Stephen, Archie wants to horse around with milkman and see cows. That they are eleven in number is probably significant; for Archie is youth and eleven was to become Joyce's sign of renewal and hope in *Ulysses* and *Finnegans Wake*. Archie talks of "cow robbers" as Robert ponders assignation, and Richard calls Robert thief. We wonder if Bertha is a cow (as well as flower, moon, earth, and music) and Richard an imperfect milkman, to be replaced by another generation. (560, 561, 565, 575)

Images of light and wind confine themselves to love nest, save for the extinguished lamp in Richard's study. "I am in the dark here," says Robert from bedroom. "I must light the lamp," which, when lit, is pink. In the other room he turns the lamp up and down, putting it out entirely at last. But pink light shines from bedroom. "The wind is rising," he announces, anticipating *Finnegans Wake*. Probably Shelley's wind of desire, Robert's wind makes lamp flicker. (592, 595, 597, 601, 605)

Shakespeare and experience associate the wind and the rain. Those gusts at the love nest are accompanied by rain. Bertha, like

Gretta before her, has neither umbrella nor waterproof. Robert enters wet with rain, a summer rain, falling on earth. The second act ends with this symbolic shower, but Richard, dry in the downpour, contents himself with walking near water on the beach, like unregenerate Stephen or like Joyce himself; for what he liked almost more than anything, if not more, was walking beside the seaside.[8]

Most of such images must escape notice. But whatever they mean to an audience in the theater, their point for us, as careful readers, is this: giving the lie to some of Joyce's notes, they put Richard in his place, showing more than Joyce seemed aware of when he put them down. Writing is discovery; and in the process Joyce left his notes behind. The text before us—images and all —is all the proof we need.

Exiles resembles *A Portrait* not only in recurrent images that escape general notice but in parallels so ghostly that, invisible to any audience but Joyce himself, they seem meant for him alone. Brief references to the "fatted calf" and to "fierce indignation" (559, 613) seem hardly enough to establish Richard as the Prodigal Son and as Jonathan Swift; but Joyce's notes prove these parallels intended. We must agree that Swift, who became one of the principal parallels in *Finnegans Wake*, has much in common with Richard—in his degree. Both Dubliners, both writers, both psychologically odd, they both have two women to torture. Both torture them. But there are other parallels, about which notes are silent. Richard seems parallel to Jesus, Robert to Judas; Richard to Caesar, Robert to Brutus; and, like Stephen before him, Richard is like both Satan and God. To confuse the host, Richard seems Prospero, too.

Jesus, Judas, Caesar, and Brutus take their places in the theme of betrayal, one of the most evident in *Exiles*, and, if we may judge by its presence in *A Portrait* and *Ulysses*, one of Joyce's obsessions. Exiled artist is betrayed by friend. Robert professes himself Richard's "disciple" with a disciple's fidelity to his "mas-

---

8. Pp. 586, 591, 601-02. *Letters*, 244: "I could walk for ever along a strand."

ter." Seeing through his Judas, Richard-Jesus replies: "the disciple who will betray him." (558) That Richard-Jesus, like Bloom-Jesus, longs to be betrayed, joins this theme to that of masochism. (583, 601) The Caesar-Brutus parallel, less firmly established, is based on a single reference to the battle of Philippi, where Brutus died. (559) If Stephen thinks he is Napoleon, however, why should Richard deny himself the eminence of Caesar? Brutus and Judas occupy a single pew in Dante's hell.

Devils are also in attendance here. Robert, tempting his master with worldly glory, seems swapping the role of Judas for that of Satan. But Richard, called a "devil" by Bertha, Robert, and Brigid (565, 572, 604), seems better as devil than Robert and better as a Satan than as a Jesus. Stephen, of course, is both Jesus and Lucifer. Failing to bring light, Richard is no Lucifer, save in pride. Richard seems one of the lesser devils, assigned to torturing and delighting in it. Yet, like Stephen, he thinks himself God. "I am what I am," he announces, (616) putting it up to others to comprehend his august incomprehensibility.

No audience in the theater could follow such tenuous and conflicting parallels, still less, that of Prospero, which is even slighter and more dubious. Returning from the beach, Richard says, "The isle is full of voices." (612) How to take this reference to *The Tempest* is uncertain, however. Prospero may be intended; for he, too, is a man of letters, betrayed and exiled. Stephen raises *The Tempest* in *Ulysses* as a kind of Ferdinand; but although "manmonster" of a kind, Richard is no Caliban, and it is he, referring to Prospero's work, who says: "The isle is full of noises." Richard's "voices" are of those "who say they love me." (623) In this chorus, however, his own voice, louder than the rest, carries the air.

Such are the problems that vex readers of Joyce. However sure we are that a reference to *The Tempest* means something and the distortion of Caliban's words something more, we remain uncertain of what they mean or how they work. To change uncertainties to certainties is the delight of critics, but as readers we are sure of one thing only: that Joyce used nothing casually or in vain. Avoiding certainty where none is justified, we follow him as we can.

Allusions are still more doubtful. Is Beatrice, who suggests Dante by name and remoteness, a product of his "refrigerating apparatus," celebrated by Stephen? Do references by both Richard and Robert to Duns Scotus (581, 621) imply a shift from St. Thomas Aquinas, who presides over *A Portrait*, a change from the whatness of Thomas to the thisness of Duns? If so, why? *Exiles* seems happy with neither.

Yet, like the other works of Joyce, it rejoices in a number of characters and relationships that seem archetypal. Of these, the Fishwoman, calling "Fresh Dublin bay herrings," (620-21) is the most difficult, exceeding the milkman in mystery. The fish, an ancient image associated with Jesus and serving as the Eucharist in *Finnegans Wake*, is probably an archetype—if by archetype we mean an image or pattern, formed by racial experience, that emerges from the writer's unconscious, intentionally or unintentionally, to give his writing significance and depth. (Jung is the authority.) But why is this Fishwoman crying fish here? The other women—Brigid, Richard's mother, Beatrice, and Bertha—seem to compose the image of Woman, certainly one of Jung's archetypes and central among Joyce's. Poor old women, Brigid and Richard's mother seem almost allegorical representatives of the Poor Old Woman or Ireland herself. Both are critical of Richard's independence, both find him odd, and the mother has refused forgiveness. Protestant Beatrice seems a sterile ideal, like Eileen, the Protestant girl in *A Portrait* or even Mercedes, but Bertha, plainly of the better sort, is all but the real thing.

Based, according to the notes, on Nora Joyce, Bertha is another Gretta, unable this time to disconcert another Gabriel. Bertha and Gretta are studies for Mrs. Bloom, whose image is the earth. The relationship between proud Richard and earthy Bertha, anticipating the relationship between Stephen and Mrs. Bloom, is that between intellect and reality. Joyce tried many women out before hitting on Mrs. Bloom. Bertha, not altogether the image of his desire, is among these tries.

The two men must be counted, too, among Joyce's obsessive archetypes and so must their relationship. Joyce saw domestic reality as the contention of equal and opposite rivals for earthy woman. Their conflict forms the pattern of almost all his work from *Chamber Music* to *Finnegans Wake*, where it achieves finality in the contention of Shem and Shaun. Shem is the introvert, incomplete until balanced by earthy woman and worldly man. Shaun is the successful extrovert. Present in some of the stories of *Dubliners*, these rivals find better bodies in A *Portrait*, where Stephen is á Shem and prudent Cranly a Shaun. In *Ulysses* Stephen contends with Mulligan on one level while Bloom contends with Boylan on another, and on still another, Stephen with Bloom; for all is relative. Not absolute, the types emerge in relationship to others.

The rivalry of Richard and Robert, the first a Shem, the second a Shaun in their present relationship, finds a place in this developing pattern. Like Cranly, Robert supports conformity. Like Stephen, Richard is the lonely rebel. Richard is an artist, Robert a journalist. That their conflict ends in a kind of draw is part of the pattern; for Joyce's contenders are not only opposite but equal. Uniting in the end, Shem and Shaun become the complete man. But there is neither union in *Exiles* nor victory, whatever the abundance of conflict. Made of the stuff of drama, *Exiles* somehow escapes it. As we have suspected, the trouble may be that Joyce, lacking the distance and the divine impartiality he achieved in *Ulysses* and *Finnegans Wake*, embraced one of his contenders, loving him as himself.

Yet *Exiles*, like Bertha, is a good try. Trying to adapt old themes and methods to new form, to adapt a comic talent to heavy drama, Joyce was exploring. But exploration, however admirable, is not always triumphant. Exploring for Dr. Livingstone, the explorer may come upon Mr. Stanley. This parable, I am afraid, is not so plain as I meant it to be. Enough of parable, however. Enough of *Exiles*—or, as Robert says: "Enough. Enough." (584)

Ulysses

Ulysses is one of the great books of our time. Some—I among them—think it greatest of all, except *Finnegans Wake*, maybe. But, like almost every great book nowadays, *Ulysses* is too difficult for careless reading. Difficulties of method are complicated by density—by what Joyce himself called "enormous bulk and more than enormous complexity." (*Letters*, 146) One reading does not work, we readily agree, for works of Mann, Proust, Faulkner, or Conrad. After many readings of *Ulysses*, we should be ready to agree that many readings are insufficient. Returning to it again and again, we must pause at each sentence, every word, asking why and learning more and more, but never all. Even this reward, however, is worth the trouble. Increasing our awareness and formally triumphant, like all great books, *Ulysses*, differing from some, is good fun or, to borrow a phrase from Gibbon, "amusing and instructive."

Confusing the profound with the solemn and missing all the fun, a critic, who surprised me more than most, found the cheerful book tragic. A vision of reality, *Ulysses* is profound and serious, to be sure, but neither solemn nor tragic. Serious comedy is no paradox, nor is there room for quarrel here.[1] Comic in two senses

1. A similar union of playfulness, fanciful ingenuity, and seriousness is apparent in "The Wreck of the Deutschland" by Gerard Manley Hopkins. T. S. Eliot praised that "alliance of levity and seriousness by which the seriousness is intensified." Bloom's union with Stephen is "jocoserious," (661) and *Ulysses* is Joyce's "farced epistol to the hibruws." (*Finnegans Wake*, 228)

of the word, Dante's and ours, *Ulysses* has a happy ending, like *The Divine Comedy*, and, like something by Thurber, Joyce's "chaffering allincluding most farraginous chronicle" [2] is funny, however dark and terrible some of its materials.

Ulysses is the story of three Dubliners and their city during June 16, 1904. Nobody knows why Joyce chose this day, though there have been many speculations. Maybe it was the day of Joyce's own renewal by Nora or the date on a newspaper that lined the exile's trunk. However arrived at, June 16 is celebrated now as Bloomsday. Some celebrants send cards to others, and some have kidneys for breakfast. Stephen Dedalus, Mr. Bloom, and Mrs. Bloom, the three Dubliners, compose a trinity, the first member of which is least important, the last most important, and the central one, central. Likely at first to single Stephen out, we discover Bloom next, and finally, after many readings, Mrs. Bloom. Understanding her is the sign of understanding and its achievement. These three are individuals; yet, more than individuals, they represent man and two of his aspects. Stephen is intellect, Mrs. Bloom, flesh, and central Mr. Bloom, uniting the extremes, is almost everybody. Everybody and his incomplete extremes, taken together, compose mankind, which *Ulysses* celebrates. Celebrating it on Bloomsday or any other day, we celebrate art and man.

The relationship among these elemental figures and their individual characters determine action, structure, and theme. Deferring structure and theme awhile, let us consider action or what happens. The action of *Ulysses*, apparently inconsiderable for so long a book, is so simple and obvious that it escapes many readers; for simplicity in a formidable setting proves more difficult than difficulty sometimes. However complex the setting, and whatever our consequent expectations, the action of *Ulysses* is not only simple but archetypal. The journey or quest is one of the oldest and most familiar stories in the world.

---

2. P. 416. To chaff is to jest, and a chafferer is either a jester or a gossip. Since a farrago is a mixture, "farraginous" means formed of various materials. "Allincluding" is all-including.

Lying there in bed, inactive but not altogether inactive, Molly Bloom is the goal of Bloom's action and ultimately of Stephen's. The pattern of Bloom's action is that of almost all men's daily lives: leaving home in the morning, Bloom comes back at night. His day is a journey. All day, in street, pub, or brothel, he quests through Dublin for Molly, for she is home. There she is. His quest is more or less successful. Stephen's simultaneous quest, though its end is more or less implicit, is successful. Indeed, *Ulysses*, like the works of Horatio Alger in respect of this, is a success story. Having no home to leave, Stephen cannot leave it, yet seeking all that day, through street, pub, or brothel, he finds his home at last. His quest is that of youth for maturity and identity—for being rather than becoming. Not entirely aware of what he needs and wants, he finds both by meeting Mr. Bloom and, with his aid, apprehending Mrs. Bloom. Meeting human Mr. Bloom and suddenly understanding humanity, Stephen becomes a kind of Bloom, leaving pride for charity, and inhumanity for acceptance of mankind. It becomes increasingly apparent that in meeting Bloom and seeing what he sees in Molly, Stephen meets himself for the first time. Becoming mature, he becomes himself. Discovering the father, he becomes capable of fatherhood. That Stephen is Bloom, and Bloom Stephen at last is all we need to know; but how they establish this strange equation is our problem, as establishing it is Stephen's and the object of his quest.

Clearly, the theme of *Ulysses*, implied by the quest and determined by the characters, is moral. Like the Church he rejected, Joyce condemns pride, the greatest of sins, and commends charity, the greatest of virtues. Like any humanist, he favors humanity. Like an advertising man or, indeed, like D. H. Lawrence, he favors "togetherness," although his word for it is "communion" or "atonement," being at one with another. Having shown defects of love in "The Dead," *A Portrait*, and *Exiles*, he turned in *Ulysses* to love's triumph.

Plainly moral in theme, *Ulysses*, nevertheless, is not plainly moral. No wonder that some readers, diverted by occasional indecencies and confusing decorum with virtue, found the book immoral.[3] No wonder that others missed the theme entirely; for Joyce's "sinister dexterity" came between theme and them.

Yet these mistaken or frustrated readers were not altogether without justification for complaint, however unaware of its true reason. Even to us, it may seem a pity that a book celebrating mankind and its virtues, should separate itself from men by obscurity. But if, in the sense of separateness, *Ulysses* is less responsible than its theme, so is most good literature of our time; and if morality in this sense means conforming to the habits and expectations of foolish men, this kind of immorality may be a virtue—socially deplorable maybe, but nowadays a mark of art. Neither willful nor capricious, Joyce's method serves his vision. Like any great artist, he found the exact way to say what he saw. If the way he found shuts bad readers out, they must try to become better. Joyce's intricate celebration of communion is not incommunicable to good readers. That there seem few around is less his trouble than our own.

The structure of *Ulysses* may give some trouble although, determined, like theme, by the three characters, it falls naturally into three simple parts, the three great blocks of material with which Joyce built his book. By relationship with one another these parts indicate the relationship of the three characters. To bring them to mind—to the careful reader's mind, at least—the three parts begin with the letters S, M, P. The first part, devoted to Stephen, begins with S to suggest his devotion to himself. The second part, devoted to Bloom, begins with M to show his devotion to Molly. The third part, devoted to her, begins with P to show her devotion to Poldy or Leopold. That S, M, P are also traditional signs for parts of a syllogism may hint the logical progress of Joyce's structure.[4] Progressing through the first two parts, the quests of Stephen and Bloom, uniting, reach their climax in

3. In her diary Virginia Woolf calls *Ulysses* "illiterate, underbred . . . ultimately nauseating." That her complaint was social as well as moral is proved by her dismissal of Joyce as a "self-taught working man." D. H. Lawrence's objection was moral: *Ulysses* reveals "deliberate, journalistic dirty-mindedness." 4. Innocent of meaning, decorative in purpose, the enlargement of these initials in the American edition is a lucky accident, calling attention to what might have been missed.

the last part, where Molly, at once their goal and the great, em-
bedded conclusion to Joyce's syllogism, completes the incompleteness of premise and middle.

Molly Bloom is the great Woman who, terrible and adorable as
the sea, is our beginning and our end and all around us. She is
our object and, if we are poets, our subject and our Muse. Gretta
and Bertha are studies for Mrs. Bloom, but her brilliant success
is to their moderate success as the moral success of Stephen in
Ulysses is to his moral failure in *A Portrait* or to Richard's in
Exiles. Here as there, the Woman is only chief of many archetypes.[5] That of the rival, present in *A Portrait* and *Exiles*, emerges
splendidly here in Mulligan, Stephen's rival, and in Blazes Boylan, Bloom's. Not archetypal perhaps, the city is certainly microcosmic, showing all in little. As another celebrant of Joyce's city,[6]
Ulysses is a sequel to *Dubliners* as morally and technically a
sequel to *A Portrait* and *Exiles*.

Whether this sequel to these symbolist works is naturalistic or
symbolist is a question for critics, who, asking it, immediately take
sides. It is certain that, careful of external details, Joyce observed
his city as a naturalist would. He even wrote Aunt Josephine for
verification. (*Letters*, 135, 175) Yet, in *Ulysses*, as in the earlier
works, he used these particulars to suggest inner or general things
—in the manner of Baudelaire and Flaubert. Such usage is symbolist; for a symbol is a common thing, closely observed, suggesting other things. An observer of things, Joyce saw something else
within them and beyond, something they embodied and showed
forth. That much is plain, let critics quarrel as they will. And it is
plain that, however reliant upon details of Dublin, Joyce called
again upon parallel and motif to enlarge his particulars and hold
them together.

Of parallels Homer's *Odyssey* is principal, as Joyce's title,
helping the reader out, implies. To have called *A Portrait Daeda-*

---

5. Joyce calls Earwicker an "archetypt," (*Finnegans Wake*, 263) and *Ulysses*,
emphasizing Mrs. Bloom, "my mistresspiece." (*Letters*, 206)
6. To follow Joyce's epic of Dublin you need a map. The Ordnance Survey
Office, Phoenix Park, Dublin, publishes a *Plan of Dublin*, obtainable at four
shillings plus postage from Browne and Nolan, Nassau Street, Dublin.

lus—as, indeed, the French translator did—would have given suitable prominence to a parallel parallel. Not altogether reliant upon title as clue, however, Joyce told friends, who, as if horse's mouthpieces, published the news. Therefore, readers of French little magazines (T. S. Eliot, for example) had some idea of the Homeric parallel from the start. No reader of those, I had no idea of my luck when, having arrived in France on the S.S. *Homeric*, I bought a copy of *Ulysses* from Sylvia Beach on June 16, 1925, the day of the first Bloomsday celebration (so she told me later on) in her shop in the rue de l'Odéon. (For all I know, Joyce may have been sitting in the shop at the time.) I liked the book at once for its texture and massiveness, but title, date, and theme remained beyond me when, at that summer's end, I came home on the S.S. *Homeric*—and for long after. Today, what Joyce told Valery Larbaud and other friends is available to all in a convenient chart, published by Stuart Gilbert, one of those friends, in his study of *Ulysses*.

The structure of *Ulysses*, determined by character and theme, as we have noticed, is also determined by the co-operation of Homer. The three parts of *Ulysses*, embodying Joyce's three characters, imitate the three parts of *The Odyssey*. In the first of these Telemachus sets out to hunt his missing father; in the second, Ulysses travels, seeking home; in the third, son finds father, father finds son, home, and, after killing the suitors, wife. This action corresponds to what Joyce planned for his day in modern Dublin. Elaborating this fortunate correspondence, each of the eighteen chapters of *Ulysses* parodies an episode or a smaller element of *The Odyssey*, not entirely according to Homer's order, however, for other considerations, other parallels, interfered. Each of Joyce's major characters parodies one of Homer's. Stephen, hunting himself and fatherhood, is like Telemachus, hunting father. Buck Mulligan and Blazes Boylan seem a composite parody of Antinous, chief suitor and rival. As Gerty MacDowell, for example, suggests Nausicaa, so Molly, Penelope, and Bloom, Ulysses himself.

Suggesting Ulysses, Bloom is not that hero; for parallel is **not** identity. Joyce is not retelling Homer's myth, but using it for a story of his own. Joyce's people are individuals in modern Dublin. To give them another dimension and to make them general, Joyce called upon Homer for simile. *Ulysses* parodies *The Odyssey* only in the sense of using it to enlarge by resemblance and difference the actions and people of a Dublin day. Far from mock-heroic, *Ulysses* makes fun of neither Ulysses nor Bloom. However funny the analogy between Gerty and Nausicaa, a great princess, Joyce's parody is serious, intended to show man in our time forth. Homer, an assistant in this enterprise, deserves attention, but no more or less than he deserves. Not Ulysses but Bloom is the man before us, however improved by the comparison.

Persuaded that, like every man, he was Everyman, Joyce sought ways of presenting his image or parts of it—not to display himself but man. As Stephen, embodying part of Joyce's image, is every young man seeking maturity, so Bloom, embodying another part, is every mature man or what Stephen will become and what Joyce, writing of Bloom and Stephen, had become. That Stephen resembles Bloom and that both resemble Joyce are the likeliest things in the world. Not content, however, with the generality he found within himself, Joyce used familiar parallels to make the generality more apparent, Daedalus first, and now Ulysses. Placing this hero next to Bloom, Joyce suggests, without irony, that as it was in the beginning is now and then. Ancients both, Daedalus and Ulysses are mythical, and myth, lying deep in our unconscious and our past, is, as Erich Fromm puts it, "a message from ourselves to ourselves." Calling on myth and all that deep, though undiscoverable, meaning seems the triumph of generality.

"A good man," said Joyce of Ulysses to Frank Budgen. It is easy to see why, like many writers before him, Joyce found Ulysses congenial and suitable for his purpose. Outsider, stranger, and exile, family man and wanderer, "ever-scheming" trickster and man of valor, a man of sensibility, ever close to tears, Homer's "long-tried" hero is an all-round man, complex, full of surprises, and endlessly suggestive. For his qualities and the contradictions among them a multiplicity of adjectives is needed: moderate, rash, responsible, cunning, persistent, polite, boastful, tender, destructive, eloquent, and many more. But civilized on the whole and humane, he is the atypical hero, differing from great Achilles in most respects and in all from simple Ajax. In the first line of *The Odyssey* Homer calls Ulysses "polytropic," a word as ambiguous as this hero and maybe, therefore, the very word for him. "Polytropic" can mean man of many devices, turns, or tricks, or it can mean a man inviting many tropes or comparisons.[7] Joyce liked the many-sided humanity, the fortitude and prudence of this maverick. Here was a trickster to put beside his forger, here an image to enlarge Bloom's and serve as Stephen's model. " 'He's a cultured allroundman, Bloom is,' " says Lenehan, connecting Bloom with Ulysses; and, connecting Bloom with Daedalus, Lenehan adds, " 'There's a touch of the artist about old Bloom.' " (231-32) Joyce's Ulysses and his Daedalus are identical twins, yet opposites like Shaun and Shem. In a sense, Ulysses is Daedalus grown up; for Ulysses, like Joyce, knows himself.

As in *A Portrait*, Joyce used other parallels to support Daedalus, so in *Ulysses* he used other parallels to support Ulysses. Of these assistants, which work harmoniously together, the most important are Jesus, Elijah, Moses, Dante, Shakespeare, Hamlet, and Don Giovanni. That Jesus gets along with Ulysses is not so surprising as it seems; for allegorical fathers of the Church had found Ulysses a moral prototype of Jesus, who is, of course, a kind of Everyman. Moses is another exile seeking home and leading others there. Jesus and Moses are analogues for Bloom, and, since Stephen is a potential Bloom, for Stephen, too. Putting other parallels off awhile, let us look at Ulysses, Jesus, Moses, and Bloom again.

All but Ulysses are Jews, and if he is not Semitic, his voyage is, according to the theory of Victor Bérard, (*Letters*, 272, 401) which, delighting Joyce, made his parallels seem more nearly consistent and his image better. " 'Jewgreek,' " says Lynch, " 'is greek-jew.' " (493) Always seeking resemblances, Joyce found the Jew

7. See W. B. Stanford, *The Ulysses Theme*, 1954.

a fitting analogy not only for Ulysses but for himself—though not the only one—for himself as exile, seeking home. As Joyce's image, Bloom is fittingly Jewish.

Prized by mediaeval allegorists, a Christian Ulysses became one term of a simple equation, commonly moral. Joyce's Semitic Ulysses, however moral, is neither simple nor allegorical. Yet, though a romantic symbolist at heart, Joyce used mediaeval allegory to complicate parallel and image. (Both analogies, allegory and symbol differ in limitation. The allegorical image is definitely assigned.) Most of Joyce's chapters allegorically correspond to one of man's organs and his arts; for Joyce's subject is not only Everyman but all of man. There are even a few of the personifications that pleased mediaeval allegorists: the milkwoman as Ireland, for example, and Mrs. Bloom as the earth. Each chapter, as Stuart Gilbert's chart informs us, has its appropriate color, and each, though this is far from allegorical, its symbol: an object within the chapter to present its essence.

Further complications, all carriers of meaning, should give those familiar with *A Portrait* no further trouble. Here as there, Joyce called upon motif or recurrent image not only to link the parts together but to gather, carry, and deposit meanings—"a myriad metamorphoses of symbol." (407) In our survey of the episodes we shall encounter many such devices: tea, water, hat, potato, and soap, for example, the man in the macintosh and Plumtree's Potted Meat. Since all are symbolic, none has definite or fully demonstrable meaning; but nowadays we are used to this or should be. A world, like the world of politics or physics, *Ulysses* offers riddles with which we must try to get along, guessing and fumbling. Some parts of either world are clear at once. We can work some others out, but we are always baffled in the end.

The riddling motifs of *Ulysses* are complicated in turn by allusion, quotation, and single images or charged words—like those in *A Portrait* or, better, since *Ulysses* is a kind of poem, like those in "The Love Song of J. Alfred Prufrock." Reading, we must notice everything, forgetting nothing; for each thing in *Ulysses* is connected with other things.[8] Cross-references, demanding the alertness with which we approach poetry, help establish the harmonious relationship and the wholeness that young Stephen desires and Joyce achieved. Noticing each thing, we must notice, too, what each is next to. Of each proximity we must ask: what of it? For neighborhood in *Ulysses* improves the neighbors, who, working together, mean more than each alone. Master of the illuminating juxtaposition in *A Portrait*, Joyce is master of a more sardonic and a funnier variety here.

A last difficulty, and not the least, is the variety of methods Joyce used to present a variety of matters. Though none of his methods is altogether new, their combination and particular development may puzzle some accustomed to simpler ways—those of Frank O'Connor, for example, or of C. P. Snow. From each according to his needs. Joyce, too, found means appropriate to need and purpose, though having more to say, he needed more ways to say it. That he found them is our difficulty. His eighteen chapters, presenting eighteen problems, called for eighteen techniques and many points of view, each as suitable to the matter and its possibilities as glove to hand or—since techniques cannot be separated from their matters without injury—as flesh to bone. (*Letters*, 119, 128-29, 167) The stream of consciousness, question and answer, dramatic dialogue, and parodies of many styles are ways he found to set his matters forth. Agreeable to us, after some pardonable confusion at the start, they were the only possible ways for him. Joyce said (*Letters*, 146-47):

It is an epic of two races (Israelite-Irish) and at the same time the cycle of the human body as well as a little story of a day. . . . It is also a sort of encyclopaedia. My intention is to transpose the myth *sub specie temporis nostri*. Each adventure (that is, every hour, every organ, every art being interconnected and interrelated in the structural scheme of the whole) should not only condition but even create its own technique.

A great creation, we readily concede, a creation of the most intricate and ingenious sort, indeed, a world—as a waiter in the

8. Miles L. Hanley, *Word Index to Ulysses* is useful for following motifs and connections.

Dolphin Hotel in Dublin called the Dolphin Hotel. But is Joyce's great, intricate creation a private place, we may ask, and, if not, what are its public relations? "My brain reels," said Joyce (*Letters*, 168) "but that is nothing compared with the reeling of my readers' brains." If *Ulysses* communicates at all, to whom, how much, when, and what? The answers involve the questioner.

We may assume that *Ulysses* offers something of value to some-one. What part of this is received depends upon the capacity, experience, and taste of the receiver. Homeric simile: as a radio station of great power broadcasts in vain unless a receiver is there with the power on and all the tubes in order; as the power and quality of the receiver are the success of the broadcast; so with *Ulysses* and reader. Maybe the demands upon him are so great that few today are equal to them. Those who are get what they deserve of the plenty offered. Those getting most bring most, participate most, and stay widest awake; for Joyce is not for sleepy readers, relaxing after dinner. Addendum to Homeric simile: at-tempts at Joyce, like the book in hand, may tune receivers more precisely or improve their sensitivity.

So attuned, what can the wakeful reader with a past, both literary and practical, get from *Ulysses*, and why is it worth his while? He gets, as from all great books, amusement, instruction, delight in form, and greater awareness. Maybe, however, abstrac-tion is less of an answer than experience. I have read *Ulysses* again and again, bolt upright and wide awake; for, when relaxing, I read stories of espionage or P. G. Wodehouse. I have read what critics say about *Ulysses*, too. What I get from it is this, and this is why I find it worth my while:

Besides the attractiveness of surface—the wit, the verbal felic-ity, the rhythm and texture of the sentence, all of which delight me, I get from *Ulysses* the minor pleasures of exploration and puzzle-solving. Each time I enter the maze I find new corridors. Each time, I come closer to an apprehension of the great design and its working out, an apprehension of what Joyce called "lov-ingly moulded" form. (*Letters*, 126) Demanding a mixture of analogies, the form of *Ulysses* seems that of architecture, of sculp-ture, of music, and of all things beautiful and true. It is good to be aware of these; but the composer's embodied attitude toward his object and his tone are greater delights for me. At once aloof and compassionate, serious and gay, Joyce seems Mozart's rival. For me the significance of the form Joyce made and I all but apprehend is a humane and charitable understanding of mankind that makes me glad to be alive and part of it. Charity, for me, is the radiance of this great whole, this intricate harmony.

In the chapter-by-chapter account of *Ulysses* that follows, my treatment of each chapter is divided into two parts, the first a general approach to theme and method, the second a list, page by page, of less formidable matters. Both parts are necessarily brief and, therefore, incomplete, leaving much to the reader's enterprise. Marginal and parenthetical numbers refer to pages in the old Modern Library edition (1934). Those using the new Modern Library edition (1961) or the new Bodley Head edition (1960) may find the following table helpful.

	Modern Library (1934)	*Modern Library* (1961)	*Bodley Head* (1960)
Chapter II	p. 25	p. 24	p. 28
III	38	37	45
IV	54	54	65
V	70	71	85
VI	86	87	107
VII	115	116	147
VIII	149	151	190
IX	182	184	235
X	216	219	280
XI	252	256	328
XII	287	292	376
XIII	340	346	449
XIV	377	383	499
XV	422	429	561
XVI	596	612	704
XVII	650	666	776
XVIII	723	738	871

Part I

Telemachus

Overtly, nothing much happens in the first chapter of the first part. Stephen Dedalus, back from the exile attempted in *A Portrait*, is living in a tower on Dublin Bay at Sandycove between Kingstown and Dalkey, about eight or nine miles south of Dublin. With him are Buck Mulligan, a medical student, and Haines, a visiting Englishman. Plainly dissatisfied with his companions and his condition, Stephen resolves to leave the tower. The time is 8 A.M. Mulligan shaves, the three eat breakfast, a milkwoman delivers milk, and Mulligan swims in the "Fortyfoot," a cove in the rocks at the base of the tower. Well-adjusted Mulligan is gay; frustrated Stephen, gloomy, proud, envious. These externals, however trivial in appearance, embody many meanings.

Of these the Homeric parallel is most apparent. In the first book of *The Odyssey* (which every reader of *Ulysses* should read again) Telemachus, surrounded by his mother's suitors, feels neglected and dispossessed, though son and heir of Odysseus. Those intruders, eating his substance, rob him of his patrimony. Stirred from his childish ineffectuality by Athena, acting in disguise as messenger, he resolves to seek news of his missing father. In Joyce's parody, Stephen, representing sad, lonely Telemachus, is also preoccupied with mother, father, home, and self. Mulligan, the "usurper," (24) and Haines are the suitors. The patrimony of which they rob Stephen is at once the tower, for which he pays rent, and Ireland; but Athena remains problematical. Is she suggested by the milkwoman, "maybe a messenger" and "lowly form of an immortal"; or is she suggested by Mulligan, playing two parts? Malachi, his given name, is Hebrew for "messenger," and he is called "Mercurial." Mulligan calls Homer to mind not only by several references to Greece but by quotation. His "*oinopa ponton*" (the winedark sea) is Homer's favorite tag, but Mulligan's "*thalatta*" (sea) is Attic, not Homeric, Greek. The hunt for the father, commencing here, is suggested, as we shall see, in several ways.

This chapter also establishes the parallel of Hamlet, which works congenially in the Homeric context of father, mother, and son. Stephen will expound his theory of *Hamlet* in a later episode Looking forward to this, Mulligan says: "He proves by algebra that Hamlet's grandson is Shakespeare's grandfather and that he himself is the ghost of his own father." (19) Looking at the rocks around the tower, Haines thinks of Elsinore, but his theological interpretation of *Hamlet* is more significant: "The Father and the Son idea. The Son striving to be atoned with the Father." (20) Atonement, we recall, means becoming at one with. Finding his father, Stephen-Telemachus-Hamlet will become his father.

Establishing this central theme, the chapter also introduces several of the symbolic motifs and archetypes that are to bind the episodes together. Limp black hat, powerless stick, and the key, that Mulligan makes Stephen give up, will become important later on in connection with Bloom. But cow, water, and rival, proceeding from A *Portrait* and *Exiles*, are important here.

The milkwoman, replacing the milkmen who delighted Stephen and Archie, is Ireland. Calling her "Silk of the kine" and "poor old woman," traditional names for Ireland, Stephen sees her "serving her conqueror [Haines] and her gay betrayer [Mulligan]." (15) For this woman's favor Stephen must contend with these two suitors. Her milk introduces the great motif of cows that, reappearing in Mr. Deasy's letter on foot and mouth disease in the second chapter, reaches its climax in "Oxen of the Sun." A symbol of fertility, the cow is maternal and national, like the tower itself. Low and squat, with a vaulted room, entered through a passage, Stephen's tower seems more maternal than paternal— though the idea of tower is certainly paternal. Giving the tower up, as he scorns begging the milkwoman's favor, Stephen gives up parents, Ireland, and local or immediate success.

As for water: Mulligan, a lifesaver, swims in it, but Stephen, who almost never takes a bath, has little use for the vital element now, despite the wading girl of A *Portrait*. Green, bitter waters of the Bay remind him only of his dead mother, the great "sweet mother" of Mulligan's "Algy" Swinburne. (7) A drowned man, who may bob up that day, (23) implies renewal, after death by water—full fathom five of it. But the principal manifestation of water in this chapter is the confusion of tea and urine in Mother Grogan's pot. (14) (Compare the confusion of wine, water, and urine in Mulligan's "Ballad of Joking Jesus.") Along with plain water, tea and urine—one quested, both made—are to become increasingly important motifs.

Replacing Cranly as Stephen's rival, Mulligan also serves as St. John the Baptist, announcing his messianic successor. The connection with Cranly, who is John the Baptist in A *Portrait*, is made clear on p. 9. Mulligan's original is Oliver St. John Gogarty, whose middle name establishes another connection with the Baptist, but how did Joyce expect the reader to know that?

Most chapters of *Ulysses* have an organ and an art. That this one lacks an organ hints the incompleteness of intellectual Stephen. But that the art is theology seems suitable to the theme of father and son. Mulligan, whose blasphemy is functional, sings the "Ballad of Joking Jesus." His favorite exclamation is "God"; and, appearing in the first sentence as mock-priest, he burlesques the Mass. Like most of Joyce's opening sentences, this one implies more than it seems to say. Dressed in priestly robes, Mulligan holds a bowl of lather aloft, intoning "*Introibo ad altare Dei*," the beginning of the Mass. If it is the purpose of the Mass to create the Creator, to make His flesh and blood out of common wine and biscuit for the refreshment of communicants, then theological Mulligan is mocking the creation of a creator. If this book, in one sense, is about Stephen becoming a father or creator, Mulligan is irreverently announcing Stephen's transformation.[1] The Eucharist

---

1. Stately, plump, and gay, Mulligan, seeming an embodiment of Joyce's book, states its theme in Joyce's tone. Mulligan is a "gay deceiver"; Joyce is a gay trickster, in whose work opposites commonly unite.

becomes the central symbol of *Ulysses*. Razor and mirror, crossed on Mulligan's bowl and identified later on[2] as aspects of art, seem to prove this creator an artist and the book a story of his making. Does a fake priest imply a fake artist? Maybe so; for Joyce's artist is a forger.[3]

Theological Stephen thinks of heretical confusions of Father and Son, especially that of Arius, who warred against "the consubstantiality of the Son with the Father." (22) Whatever its theological fortunes, consubstantiality, in the literal sense of identical in substance, is a theme of this book: Stephen, the son, is or will be Bloom, the father. If Stephen is son or Son in this chapter, Haines, whose name means hate in French (as Klein points out), is the devil. An anti-Semite, Haines is God's enemy if, as Bloom maintains, God is a Jew. (336)

Haines' anti-Semitism and his nightmare of the "black panther" predict Bloom. Dressed in black, Leo Bloom moves with the step of a "pard" (215) or, since panther and leopard are identical, with the step of a Leo-pard. That devilish Haines had reason for his nightmare is proved by the mediaeval Bestiary, where panther is Christ.[4]

Mulligan calls Stephen "Japhet in search of a father." (19) Since Japhet is one of Noah's three sons, Stephen is one third of everybody, like Shem in *Finnegans Wake* and Hamm in Beckett's *Endgame*. Stephen's reference to urinating Mary Ann (14) seems to predict Marion or Mrs. Bloom on her pot. Malachi, not only Hebrew messenger but Irish king and saint, suitably combines the Irish and the Jews. Moreover, Malachi, the last and briefest prophet in the Old Testament, predicts the coming of Elijah; and

2. Stephen, a "knifeblade," refers to the "lancet of my art." The mirror, probably Shakespeare's, is a symbol of art and, as the servant's "cracked looking-glass," of Irish art. (6, 8) Mirror and razor include the externals and the inner penetration of art. A mirror, reflecting the artist's image, offers it to his analysis.
3. A. M. Klein finds this chapter a black mass. To be sure, Mulligan celebrates a black mass in the Circe episode, and there is good reason for thinking the whole book a kind of Mass, not necessarily black: "Was Parish worthe thette mess?" (*Finnegans Wake*, 199) asks Joyce, referring to *Ulysses*. His question, involving Esau and his mess of mottage, combines Dublin (province or parish) and the Paris of Henry IV. Mess or *messe* is Mass.
4. See T. H. White, *The Book of Beasts*, 1954, a typical Bestiary.

Elijah, as we shall see, is Bloom. Announcing Stephen as artist, Mulligan also announces Bloom.

The method—"Narrative (young)" according to Gilbert's chart —is conventional except for some intrusions of the stream of consciousness, its best examples the passages on Fergus (11) and heretics. (22) But on the first page the single word "Chrysosto-mos," Stephen's patristic reaction to Mulligan's gold teeth, is the stream at its source, from which Mrs. Bloom's river comes—and the "Missisliffi" of *Finnegans Wake*.

5 : "Kinch" is from kinchin, child, a good name for Telemachus-Stephen. "Toothless Kinch" (23) means that the infant has no bite. "Ouns" are wounds, Christ's wounds. "White corpuscles" are literally a medical man's view of sacramental blood; but ex-cess of white corpuscles is pathological. "Christine" is the Eucha-rist, but why feminine? Because a black mass (e.g. Mulligan's, 583-84) is celebrated on a woman's body? Joyce owned a copy of Huysmans' *Là-Bas*, the great book on black mass. Mulligan's priestlike robe is "yellow," his vest "primrose." Ecclesiastical white and gold are the colors of this chapter; but yellow is the color of decay in *A Portrait* as brown, the color of the next chapter, in *Dubliners*. The tower was built for coast defense during the Napoleonic wars.

6 : "Snotgreen" may owe something to Rimbaud's *"morves* [snots] *d'azur."* (Cf. "worms of snot," *Finnegans Wake*, 183.) Yeats and the other poets of the Celtic twilight, who liked "pearl-pale," might find snotgreen even more Irish.

7 : "Odor of wax" and "wetted ashes," like *"Liliata rutilan-tium,"* (12) a prayer for the dead, become motifs for dead mother. "Dogsbody" is opposite to "Godsbody." Note Mulligan's con-fusion of God and dog. (584) Stephen, a young dog, wants to be a god or creator. Remember dog-God in *A Portrait*. Compare "god in the manger" in *Finnegans Wake*. (188)

9 : "Hellenise": Mulligan wants to do for Ireland what *Ulysses* does for it. Bray Head cannot be seen from the top of the tower.

11 : The poem quoted by Stephen is "Who Goes with Fergus?"

by W. B. Yeats. The cloud (maternal) covers the sun (paternal). Mr. Bloom reacts similarly to the same cloud. (61) Both Stephen and Bloom are cheered by "warm running sunlight." (12, 61)

12 : "Mosey" or Moses connects Stephen with Moses-Bloom. A "kip" is a brothel. "No, mother. Let me be and let me live": Stephen's effort to escape mother and accept father is the process of growing up. Freud would approve.

13 : "Coronation day" refers not only to getting paid (in crowns) but to Edward VII, a son frustrated by a mother. Stephen means crown.

14 : "Dundrum": The "weird sisters" are Yeats' sisters, who established the Cuala Press at Dundrum to publish Yeats, serving in this chapter as father-image. Hence Stephen's mixed reaction.

17 : "Agenbite of inwit" is Middle English for remorse of conscience. "Here's a spot," from *Macbeth*, supports the idea of guilt.

19 : "Omphalos," navel or center, is certainly maternal. Cf. p. 9. As ghost of his father, Stephen is his essence.

21 : "Ashplant": ash is a tree of life. Stephen trails it now, but breaks the lamp with it in the Circe episode. Stephen took up his stick when he saw the wading girl.

22 : Haines' "history is to blame" looks forward to the next chapter, which deals with the pressure of history.

23 : "Five fathoms" suggests Ferdinand and his father in *The Tempest*. Cf. Milton's drowned Lycidas. (26) The "Photo girl" in Westmeath (Mullingar) is Milly, Bloom's daughter. (See 65-66)

24 : Note several references to Nietzsche, a favorite with Joyce's characters (e.g. "A Painful Case" and *Exiles*). "The Ship" was a pub.

CHAPTER II

Nestor

It is now 10 A.M. of a Thursday morning. At school in Dalkey, Stephen attempts lessons in history, literature, and algebra. In an

interview with Mr. Deasy, the headmaster, Stephen, having received payment and advice, agrees to submit Mr. Deasy's letter
on cows to a newspaper. Then Stephen leaves the school for good,
as he has left the tower.

Homer's Telemachus, in the parallel episode, goes to wise, horse-
loving Nestor for news of father. Sitting among his sons, Nestor
gives Telemachus a history of the Trojan war, a discourse on
treacherous women, such as Clytemnestra, and sends him along to
Menelaus, husband of Helen. Nestor sacrifices a young cow to a
goddess. In *Ulysses* Mr. Deasy, with his pictures of race horses, his
traditional wisdom, and his concern for cows, is not altogether
unlike Nestor. Mr. Deasy's remarks about faithless women (Helen,
MacMurrough's wife, and Kitty O'Shea) parody Nestor's. As Nestor is surrounded with sons, so Mr. Deasy with pupils. Like Telemachus, Stephen defers on the whole to an elder's wisdom.

The art of this chapter is history, the "nightmare" from which
Stephen is "trying to awake." (35) To him the past is intolerable,
its shape arbitrary, its materials fictive and uncertain, "fabled,"
as Blake says, "by the daughters of memory" (25) or the Muses.
Confined to time and space, history is impermanent and unreliable: "I hear the ruin of all space, shattered glass and toppling
masonry, and time one livid final flame." (25) No more than "an
actuality of the possible," as Aristotle says, history limits "infinite
possibilities." As unsubstantial as it is impermanent and limiting,
history is woven of wind by wind. (26) "As it was in the beginning, is now," says Stephen; (30) for history, as tiresome as unreliable, is more of the same thing. Pyrrhus stands for the general
past; but in weak-eyed Sargent, a mother's darling, Stephen meets
his own past, as he meets it again in the algebraic equations that
once detained him. All the past, whether personal or general—all
that the rejected tower includes—is to be rejected by this freedom-
seeker. It is ironic that, shaped and conditioned by his past and
all the past, repeating the ancient quest of Telemachus, Stephen
wants to escape not only what never escapes him but what he
cannot escape.

Envious and egocentric, Stephen applies the lesson on Pyrrhus to himself. A "pier" to the spooning pupils, Pyrrhus, uniting in Stephen's mind with himself, becomes "a disappointed bridge." Plainly the disappointment is that of the exile (and maybe the love) Stephen has attempted. "*Another victory like that and we are done for,*" said Pyrrhus. Another hollow victory like his exile and Stephen is done for. Asked for a "ghoststory," the bitter jester responds not only with drowned Lycidas but with a riddle, which, as his "shout of nervous laughter" hints, also applies to his own condition. Too clever by far, foxy Stephen is trying to bury his "grandmother" under a "hollybush," a tree of life, promising renewal.[1] "Grandmother" seems to include all the oppressive past: country, Church, and Stephen's own mother, recalled by the motif of "rosewood and wetted ashes." Like *Hamlet* and, indeed, like history itself, the riddle is a ghost story. Trying in vain to bury the past, Stephen finds it returning to haunt him. (27-29) In the infirmary at Clongowes, Stephen is asked a riddle he cannot solve. That he asks the riddle now and knows the answer seem hopeful signs. Applying his riddle to himself, he is beginning the contemptuous self-examination that may help to save him from his pride.

Knowing himself a "learner" is another hopeful sign. No teacher, he certainly has much to learn about himself and all mankind if ever he is to become mature and creative. "To learn," says wise old Deasy, "one must be humble." (36)

Like his advice, Mr. Deasy's crusade against foot and mouth disease is good; for if the cow is a common symbol of fertility, Mr. Deasy, campaigning against a disease of cows, upholds fertility.[2] "I will help him in his fight," thinks Stephen, becoming "the bullockbefriending bard." (36) Though Mr. Deasy's anti-Semitism is far from admirable, it is more easily pardoned than that of Haines; for Mr. Deasy's anti-Semitism, unlike that of Haines, is "unhating," (31) harmless on the whole and absurd— like the "toothless terrors" (36) at his gate.

1. Eleven can mean renewal or the penultimate. Stephen's riddle reappears, pp. 543-45. Probably the fox killed his grandmother, says Stephen.
2. Reading *Diseases of the Ox* in *A Portrait*, Cranly is not supporting fertility but criticizing Stephen, the "*bous*" or ox. *Bous* Stephen, supporting Mr. Deasy, is supporting his own artistic fertility. Cf. the "debagging" of the ox. (9)

In a sense, Mr. Deasy's references to Jews, like those of Haines, constitute news of Bloom, the hunted father. But there is further news of father a little farther on. "A shout in the street," (35) Stephen's god is as commonplace and secular as Bloom in his capacity of God the Father. Mr. Deasy's name, pronounced daisy, suggests Bloom as bloom or Henry Flower. Indeed, fatherly Mr. Deasy seems a father-image on the way to a better one. That Lycidas-Stephen, "sunk though he be beneath the watery floor," will be brought back up "through the dear might of Him that walked the waves" is an evident prophecy of Jesus-Bloom.

Imagery of light and dark, ending in a "checkerwork" of these extremes, abounds in this chapter. Jews sinned against the light, says Mr. Deasy, pointing to the darkness in their eyes. (34-35) Beginning with the "mind's darkness," (27) proceeding to the "tranquil brightness" of art and soul, then back to the "darkness shining in brightness" of Semitic algebra, (29, 49) Stephen ultimately finds brightness shining in darkness when dark-eyed Mr. Bloom (in the penultimate chapter) shows him the light in Molly's window.

Stephen's mind moves from contemplation of the "form of forms," (27) the thing in itself or the idea of things or the shaping principle for other philosophers, to its manifestations in the coins and hollow shells of Mr. Deasy's collection—Caesar's tribute or things as things. Husks of the real thing, shells are history, of course, as well as a fitting introduction to the next chapter, where Stephen walking beach, crushes them. By those shells Nestor-Deasy sends Stephen to Menelaus and the protean seaside.

The method of this chapter is "Catechism (personal)," according to Joyce, reported by Stuart Gilbert. But question and answer, suitable to school room and interview, interrupt the stream of consciousness, which proceeds by free association, one thing suggesting the next. Our point of view, centered in this process, is necessarily Stephen's.

25 : Vico Road in Dalkey suggests the historical philosopher Giambattista Vico to A. M. Klein, who finds the structural pattern

of the chapter consistently Viconian. Vico is the philosopher behind the structure of *Finnegans Wake.*

28 : Fox: Parnell or Mr. Fox (482) is associated with Stephen (*Portrait*) and with ivy, if not holly (*Dubliners*).

29 : "He proves by algebra . . ." Compare p. 19. Algebraic symbols move in a "morrice" or Moorish dance. Compare Stephen's equations in *A Portrait.* The equations of algebra, applied to literature, may mean correspondence or parallel. "Secrets, silent, stony sit in the dark palaces . . ." Compare Stephen's dream of tyrannical parents in his diary in *A Portrait.* For darkness in brightness see John 1:5.

32 : King Edward: Compare 13, 213, and Edward King, the hero of "Lycidas." Edward VII recurs throughout *Ulysses.* "Croppies lie down," is an Ulster song about the crop-haired Irish of the South. A "soft day" in Ireland is a rainy day.

33 : Horses and riders establish the motif of the race, which centers in the Gold Cup. Cyclical history is a kind of race.

34 : "The harlot's cry" is by Blake.

36 : The City Arms Hotel, near the cattle market, was once Bloom's residence.

CHAPTER III

Proteus

The action of this comparatively difficult chapter, the last part of the "Telemachia," is mostly interior and fluid, hence suitably presented by the interior monologue or stream of consciousness. Alone at last, lonely Stephen talks to himself, his only audience. Never has solipsism achieved more triumphant display. The time is 11 A.M., the place Sandymount strand in Dublin and the Pigeon House breakwater. Apparently in no time at all, Stephen has come nine miles by train or tram from Dalkey to walk the mudflats here. Not for swimming in (with Mulligan) or for wading in (with a girl), the waters of life and death are for walking beside at a safe distance and for thinking about. Stephen sees cocklepickers and a dog; and he sits down at last to write a poem on a bit of paper appropriately torn from Mr. Deasy's fertility-commending letter. The interior action, composed of thought, imagination, memory, and immediate sensation, is the record of a fine mind idling. Not logical, its process is that of free association, an inner flow that mimics the outer flow of tides and the shifting of the sands. The bitter, searching, and healthy self-analysis that Stephen began at Mr. Deasy's school continues, revealing himself to himself and to us, his privileged sharers. We find ourselves peeping into the mind of a philosopher-poet, a rich, learned, and allusive mind, always a little beyond us. Since Stephen is master of words and rhythms, some of the most poetic prose of the book is concentrated in his monologue.

However slight, the Homeric parallel is significant. The story of Proteus, on which Joyce concentrates, is a small part of the long interview with Menelaus, who tells Telemachus how on the voyage home he extracted news of Ulysses from slippery Proteus, an Egyptian god of the sea. Despite the constant inconstancy of protean Proteus and all his agility, Menelaus gets him down and fixes him. Stephen-Telemachus, assuming the role of Menelaus, encounters an artist's or philosopher's Proteus and the Proteus within himself. Less considerable than that of Menelaus, Stephen's victory over his Proteus yields nevertheless some news about himself as father and a hint or two of Bloom.

Proteus stands—if he stands at all—for instability, change, and flux, external, internal, and, what is worse, verbal—as if to illustrate the Greek conviction that all things flow. All things are streaming here, conscious or not. By his nature Proteus suggests Stephen's nature and his idea of nature. The pursuit of Proteus suggests Stephen's attempt to fix flux by form, which philosophy imposes and art composes.

Less formidable than they seem, the first two pages (continuing the Dalkey meditation on the "form of forms" and outer husks) establish the philosophical position. Manifested reality consists of the inevitable but temporary forms of the visible and the audible. The shape of the visible, meeting the eye, is space or *"nebeneinander"* (things next to each other). The shape of the audible, meeting the ear, is time or the *"nacheinander"* (one thing after another). Mr. Deasy's shells, encountered on beach by ear in time, are seen in space. Stephen's thoughts about time, space, and eternity, about accident (color) and body, about subject and object are based upon Jacob Boehme and Aristotle.[1]

The world of time and space lacks form, "you see. I hear." It is now, however, that "rhythm begins" or the poet's effort to compose flux by art, "creation from nothing." Thoughts of midwives, wombs, navel cords, Adam and Eve, father and mother support the idea of creation, artistic as well as biological. The creator's number in the umbilical telephone exchange ("Edenville. Aleph, alpha: nought, nought one") suitably combines the Jews, the Greeks, and creation from nothing. Arius, reappearing with consubstantiality (now complicated by "jew"), brings up Father and Son, who, of the same substance, are partners in the great creation; for the Son is the Word or the Father's creative tool. "In the beginning was the Word," according to St. John, and, according to Stephen, "As it was in the beginning, is now."

It is fitting that the art of this chapter on the Word should be words or philology, their study. Unlike the unchanging Word, however, words are as shifting as the protean reality they must compose. (Yet, in a world of "changing things," as Yeats observes, "Words alone are certain good.") Philology is a study of change. The poet's problem is more formidable than God's; for God, the unmoved mover, is static, like art itself, while the poet is as kinetic and fluid as the flux he tries to make static with fluid tools. Monkwords, roguewords, the lingo of gypsies, and a multitude of terms for the same thing illustrate the variety of words—as inconstant

1. "Signatures of all things" (38) is from Boehme, a follower of Thoth. Aristotle is the bald millionaire, Dante's *"maestro di color . . . ."* or master of those that know. (*Inferno*, IV, 131) "Diaphane" means transparency. The conflict of ear and eye, beginning here, continues in *Finnegans Wake*, where Shem is ear, Shaun eye.

as moon, woman, and Shakespeare's "seachange." [2] The very sands
are "language tide and wind have silted here." (45)

Yet Stephen manages three creative acts, one with words, two
without. He makes water, (50) deposits a piece of snotgreen snot
on a rock, (51) and writes a poem. (48) That these acts seem parallel and of equal importance serves irony and humor more than
indecorum. But self-critical Stephen is also aware—or partly
aware—of his creative incapacity. The account of his Epiphanies
"on green oval leaves, deeply deep" (41) is bitter; and, though he
cannot know this, his "very like a whale," a reference to the cloud
of Polonius, connects him (as we have seen) with the little cloud
of Little Chandler, whose creative desires were also greater than
his accomplishment. Certainly the verses that Stephen writes (to
be found in the Aeolus episode, 131) seem an inadequate climax
to his philosophy—as the verses he writes in *A Portrait* seem less
than his brilliant theory. Yet, like the God of the Vulgate Genesis,
Stephen looks, during a post-creative "sabbath," at his work and
finds it good: *"Et vidit Deus. Et erant valde bona."* (50) A god
maybe, Stephen is a little god.

As for news of father: one piece of it is greater than the rest.
Stephen remembers a dream he has had of a smiling Oriental
who offers him a "creamfruit" melon: "You will see who." (47-48)
Plainly of Bloom and his offer of "melonsmellonous" (719)
Molly, this dream is prophetical—like Haines' parallel dream of
the black panther. The "threemaster" Stephen sees sailing along
the breakwater towards home[3] predicts not only Bloom but the
trinity of which he is a member. (51) References to Moses and
Jesus are further news of Bloom.

But of protean things, disguised, "clutched at, gone, not here,"

2. That Proteus is Egyptian calls gypsies to mind. (48) "White thy fambles"
is a poem in rogues' lingo, to be found in Richard Head, *The Canting Academy*, 1673. "Fambles" are hands, "gan" is mouth, "quarrons" is body. "She
trudges, schlepps, trains . . . ." illustrates the variety of languages.
3. Sails are never brailed on crosstrees; but when Budgen pointed this out, Joyce
kept "crosstrees" for the connection with "crosstree." (195) Cross and tree
suggest both Jesus and Adam. The ship is the *Rosevean*. (246, 609)

(44) most concern Stephen more immediately. He sees himself in exiled "wild geese" (44) and in "pretenders" (46) or tricksters. Unable to seize his own identity, he is Jesus, Lucifer, Hamlet, Shakespeare, Swift, and a bald-headed priest by turns.[4] But what proves him as protean as external nature and words is the dog, (47) which seems hare, buck, bear, calf, wolf, and pard by turns. "Ah, poor dogsbody," says dogsbody Stephen, who, not yet godsbody, fears "poor dogsbody's body" as he fears himself.

Not even certain of his sex, Stephen anticipates the sexual ambivalence of Bloom.[5] But that Stephen is basically sound is shown by his adoration of Woman, the archetypal figure that Berkeley, Bishop of Cloyne, will bring from the ideal world through Mallarmé's "veil of the temple" into the world of manifested things: "Touch me . . . I am lonely here . . . . touch me." (49) Getting into touch, Stephen's problem in A *Portrait*, (515) is his problem still.

That the techniques of the first three chapters are repeated with differences in the last three shows progress from youth to maturity, from the personal to the impersonal, from ego to humanity.[6]

38 : "*Los Demiurgos*": a demiurge is a creator.

39 : Mananaan is the Irish god of the sea, comparable to Proteus. "Orient and immortal" is from a work by Thomas Traherne; but since it was not published until 1908, the reference is anachronistic. Adam Kadmon is the symbolic complete man of the Kabala.

40 : "*All'erta*" and Ferrando: from Verdi, whose name means green, the color of this chapter. "Napper Tandy" (45) is from

4. "I thirst" (51) connects Stephen with Jesus; "Allbright he falls" (51) connects Stephen with Lucifer; "A hater of his kind . . . Houyhnhnm" (40) connects Stephen with Swift; "Cockle hat" (51) connects Stephen with Hamlet. "Delta of Cassiopeia" (49) connects Stephen with Shakespeare: Cassiopeia, having the shape of W, is William. W on its side is Greek sigma or Stephen, and the delta of this constellation stands for Dedalus. For proof see p. 207.
5. Note Esther Osvalt's shoe and Oscar Wilde. (50) Compare Bloom in the Circe episode. (528) A union of male and female is needed for creation.
6. Chapter I: "Narrative (young)." Chapter XVI: "Narrative (old)." Chapter II: "Catechism (personal)." Chapter XVII: "Catechism (impersonal)." Chapter III: "Monologue (male)." Chapter XVIII: "Monologue (female)."

"The Wearing of the Green." Marsh's Library, in St. Patrick's close, is where Stephen reads Joachim de Flora in *Stephen Hero*. "Abbas" means father, and Flora means bloom. As a horse, Swift takes his place in the motif of the horse race. Cf. 558.

41 : "Descende, calve . . . .": Come down, bald priest, lest you be deballed. "Cousin Stephen . . . ." parodies Dryden's remark to Swift: "Cousin Swift, you will never be a poet." Compare the mirror with that in *A Portrait*—not the mirror of art but of ego, here and there. "Mahamanvantara," a great manifestation.

42 : By free association the Pigeon House (Cf. "An Encounter") suggests *"le pigeon"* or the Holy Ghost, Mulligan's bird in "Joking Jesus," and wild geese. "Fleshpots of Egypt" anticipate Moses and Plumtree's Potted Meat. (73)

44 : "Green eyes": cf. "An Encounter." Note the recurrence of "shattered glass and toppling masonry" (25) or the ruin of time and space.

46 : "The two maries" and "bulrushes" suggest Jesus and Moses. Malachi with the collar of gold is the Irish king. Compare the blubber-eating Irish with those in *Finnegans Wake*. (13) Mulligan is now an "enemy."

47 : Like the fox, the dog digs for his buried grandmother. Not only Stephen, this dog is buck and pard.

48 : "Behold the handmaid of the moon [Lord]," from the Angelus, suggests the Virgin. "My tablets" from *Hamlet*: " 'Tis meet that I put it down," fixing Proteus by a pin.

50 : "Pan's hour, the faunal noon" suggests Mallarmé's *"L'Après-midi d'un faune."* "Cock lake" is both a tidal pool off Sandymount and the bladder. Note "hising up their petticoats" from p. 15. "Five fathoms" and "Sunk though he be . . . ." recall the drowned men of *The Tempest* and "Lycidas."

Note: Most of the other names and words in this chapter may be found in the dictionary or the encyclopedia. It is worth-while looking everything in Joyce up.

Part II

CHAPTER IV

Calypso

This sunny and pleasing chapter, where after many predictions Mr. Bloom at last appears, has the "tranquil brightness" of Stephen's desire. While Stephen breaks his fast in the tower, Bloom breaks his at 7 Eccles Street, ten miles away. Beginning at 8 A.M., the chapter ends at 8.45 by St. George's clock. It is the 16th of the month. (66) Bloom talks to the cat, gives it milk, and goes around the corner to Dlugacz's on Dorset Street for a kidney. Back home, he brings Molly her breakfast in bed. They talk of metempsychosis, literature, and her concert tour with Blazes Boylan. Down in the kitchen again, Bloom saves his burning kidney, eats it, reads a letter from Milly, his daughter, and goes to the jakes in the back yard. From there, having read a story by Philip Beaufoy in *Titbits*, he leaves for a bath at a public bath on the way to Paddy Dignam's funeral. Bloom is suitably in black. Paddy dead! says Alf that afternoon. " 'He is no more dead than you are.' " " 'Maybe so,' says Joe. 'They took the liberty of burying him this morning anyhow.' " (295)

Beginning the second part of *The Odyssey* in the middle of things, Homer reveals his hero, longing for home on the island of Calypso, where that amatory goddess has detained him for more than seven years. Forced at last to let him go by the intervention of Athena and orders from Zeus, Calypso sends Ulysses along on a raft.

In Joyce's parody, which is not immediately clear, Calypso seems represented by the picture of the Greek nymph from *Photo Bits* on the wall over Mrs. Bloom's bed[1] and by the "laughing

---

1. Plainly identified with Calypso on p. 532, the nymph descends from her "grotto."

witch" of Philip Beaufoy's story. Since Mr. Bloom is at home, how
does his nymph keep him away from it? Bloom is away in the
sense of having had no carnal intercourse with Molly for almost
eleven years, since the death of Rudy. What keeps Bloom from
home is Molly herself on the one hand, and on the other, his
amatory fantasies, centering in the nymph, Molly's substitute.
The jakes, a good place for fantasies, serves as Calypso's grotto.
The pictured nymph is "not unlike" Molly. (65) Moreover, Calypso is the daughter of Atlas, and Mrs. Bloom comes from Gibraltar, across the strait from Atlas, equally near the center of the
world. Although Bloom prefers Molly to her fantastic substitutes,
he can come no nearer to "her ample bedwarmed flesh. Yes, yes."
(61)

That the art of the chapter is economics or the science of home
reveals his longing. Mourning Paddy Dignam, Bloom is Ulysses
mourning his lost companions. "That we all lived on the earth
thousands of years ago," Bloom's explanation of metempsychosis,
adds hints of "transmigration," "reincarnation," and renewal of
fertility to Joyce's revival of Homer. (64-65) The parody is inexact,
however; for Calypso gives Ulysses a bath before he leaves. De-
pendent on an imaginary nymph, Bloom has to take his own.

However inadequate as husband and father, bourgeois Mr.
Bloom is as well adjusted as most men are—as mature as "other
heroes of that kidney"; for there are no absolutes in this. Whatever
his frustrations and his consequent fantasies, Bloom, looking out
as well as in, has grown more nearly up than Stephen. Interested
in swinging hips, Bloom is also interested in science, commerce,
and literature, of which he knows little—as if half educated by a
progressive school. What distinguishes him best from Stephen,
with whom he has much in common,[2] is an interest in the body
and its organs. The chapters on Stephen lack organs. This, on
Bloom, begins with the "inner organs of beasts"; for the complete
man is no less organic than intellectual. "Most of all," Bloom

2. Bloom and Stephen not only respond to the same cloud but often share
thoughts: Compare Bloom's "full gluey woman's lips" (67) with Stephen's
"glue 'em well." (48) Compare Bloom's taste in women (59) with Stephen's
(41)

likes kidneys, "which gave to his palate a fine tang of faintly scented urine." (55) The kidney is vital, but Stephen, walking his lonely beach, finds "urinous offal" dead. (51) Words all but conceal the action of his kidneys on that beach.

Mrs. Bloom is organic entirely. There she lies in bed over her "orangekeyed chamberpot," [3] planning infidelities. Plainly the boss at home, she keeps a "mocking eye" on Poldy. But her immediate interests are *"Là ci darem"* from *Don Giovanni* [4] and "Love's Old Sweet Song." As selections for that tour with Boylan, the latest of her suitors, these songs are suitable. No less suitable, her literary interests include sadistic *Ruby: the Pride of the Ring* and the works of Paul de Kock. "Nice name he has," says Molly.

The theme of this organic chapter is fertility and infertility. There is a drought. Bloom's back yard, a kind of wasteland, is waiting for manure and rain. Going out there to the jakes, fertilizing Bloom provides what he can of both. His visions of the Orient may be an Oriental's dream of home; but, filled as they are with cattle and fruit, these visions of his Ithaca are also dreams of a fertility which, disenchanted, he knows impossible. "Agendath Netaim," [5] however, continues to haunt him all that day with promise of abundance. That Milly is in Mullingar confirms this theme; for this town, at the center of Ireland, is a great cattle market, and every girl of Mullingar is "beef to the heels like a Mullingar heifer." Here, as elsewhere, the photo business concerns reproduction. Milly's father, who once worked in Dublin's cattle market, dreams of a tramline from there to the docks to help cows on their way. Plainly Bloom and Stephen, Mr. Deasy's "bullockbefriending bard," are in agreement. It is hardly surprising, then, that kidney-favoring, cattle-centered Bloom should admire Philip Beaufoy and, later, confuse him with Mrs. Purefoy,

3. P. 63. "Scald the teapot," she says to Bloom. (62) Cf. the confusion of tea and water pots in the first chapter.
4. *"Là ci darem"* introduces the rather slight parallel of Don Giovanni. *"Voglio e non vorrei,"* misquoted from *"Là ci darem,"* should be *"Vorrei, e non vorrei"* (I'd like to go but then, again, I wouldn't).
5. Agendath Netaim (Hebrew) should be Agudath Netaim, a company of planters. Moses Dlugacz has shown Bloom the Promised Land, as Moses Bloom will show it to Stephen.

abundant mother; for Beaufoy, a creator, is as fertile as cows in his degree, though in his kind, manure.

The motifs of cow and urine persist from earlier chapters. Key, tea, and hat are equally familiar. Like Stephen, Bloom lacks key, and, like Mulligan, makes tea;[6] but in the hats there is a difference. Bloom's bowler, unlike Stephen's limp black Latin Quarter hat, is what the French call *melon*, the very fruit that Bloom has offered Stephen in a dream. Yet Bloom's hat is imperfect; for the inscription on its band reads "Plasto's high grade ha," (56) lacking a "t." That Bloom quests tea in vain that day is not irrelevant. The potato that he carries in his back pocket is a new motif that comes to climax in the Circe episode. A potato, not only Irish, is root and seed.

The method, "Narrative (mature)," seemingly conventional, invites comparison with "Narrative (young)" in the first chapter and "Narrative (old)" in the sixteenth. Neither young nor old, Bloom is more or less mature.

55 : "They call him stupid": "Him," seeming to confuse the sexes, in the Random House edition, is only a misprint for "them." Note the expressive variation in the cat's cries. Are we to associate Bloom, the black panther, with his female black cat, who wants to curl up on Molly's bed? Stephen is a dog. Homer's Ulysses is recognized by his dog in Ithaca.

56 : "Mn," Molly's first word, is negative, but her last is "yes." The jingling of the "loose brass quoits" becomes a motif, associated with Boylan. The "white slip of paper" in Bloom's hat is Henry Flower's card.

57 : Note fragments from the Lord's prayer on this page and p. 60. *Turko the Terrible*: cf. p. 11.

59 : The "sting of disregard," giving Bloom pleasure, hints his masochism. Cf. the mice who "seem to like it," p. 55.

62 : "Seaside girls," who include Calypso, Nausicaa, and the Sirens, become a motif.

6. Making tea, Bloom seems to parody Mulligan, making his god. Bloom's tea, however, must be *thea* (the botanical name of tea) or goddess.

64 : "Metempsychosis" becomes a motif, associated with Molly; and her "O, rocks!" unites at last with Gibraltar, Howth, and yes.

66 : "Swirls" in the last line is a misprint for "Swurls," Boylan's pronunciation.

67 : "Will happen, yes. Prevent. Useless" reveals concern, acceptance, and equanimity. Note lines from "Sing a Song of Sixpence," pp. 67-68. Cf. p. 74.

68 : The stinging bee becomes a motif, prominent in the Oxen of the Sun.

69 : Bloom's creative work will be co-operative, "By Mr and Mrs L. M. Bloom." Bloom taking notes on Molly is like Stephen collecting trivial matters for his epiphanies.

CHAPTER V

The Lotus Eaters

Though it is 10 o'clock of a bright morning, the air is heavy with sleep. Mr. Bloom, strolling idly along Westland Row, pauses at post office, church, drugstore, and bathhouse. At the post office he gets a letter from Martha, whom some might call a "pen pal." At All Hallows he ponders the Eucharist. At the chemist's he buys a cake of soap with which he retires to a tub. Bloom is alone; yet, like a story of Dubliners, this episode, displaying the city, is crowded with Dubliners.[1]

The Homeric analogue is as simple as the action. On a shore the companions of Ulysses, eat the local vegetable. At once a flower and a drug destroying all enterprise, the lotus makes them forget their homes. But Ulysses, mindful of his quest, rouses his

1. There are encounters with or references to these characters of Dubliners: M'Coy, Bantam Lyons, Hoppy Holohan, Martin Cunningham, Bob Doran, Tom Kernan.

men from lethargy and drives them back aboard the black ships. Bloom, at once drugged and alert, seems to include both Ulysses and his men. Maybe, however, M'Coy, Lyons, and the other dopes of Dublin also serve as members of the crew. Post office, church, and bath provide the flower of idleness.

Nothing could be more suitable than "Narcissism," the method here;[2] for Greek Narcissus admired his image in the water before falling in and becoming a flower. Like Stephen on the beach, Bloom in his capacity of Henry Flower, is detained by self.[3] In M'Coy, his caricature, Bloom meets himself as he meets his private parts in bath water. Narcissus and his pool imply regression and the death wish or retreat from responsibility in the external world. As a "womb of warmth," (85) Bloom's tub is the very image of regression.

Botany and chemistry, the arts of this chapter, support the lotus with a variety of flowers and drugs. Mr. Bloom, who knows "the language of flowers," (77) imagines the Far East a kind of hothouse. (70) Anything that promises peace—gelding, for example, or pre-atomic physics—finds congenial place in Bloom's sleepy revery. Galileo offers the law of falling bodies (32 feet per second, per second); and Archimedes, also concerned with heaviness, attempts his principle. (71) "The weight of the body in the water is equal to the weight of the," says Bloom's incompetent Archimedes, sitting in his tub—and there is no "Eureka" when he emerges, dripping. Among the drugs supplied by botany and chemistry are tea, tobacco, Guinness' porter, perfume, and all the things in jars in Sweny's shop. But the Eucharist, that "lulls all pain," (80) is the most potent drug and, according to Joyce, the "symbol" of this chapter. A symbol is an embodiment and radiator

2. By "Narcissism" Joyce evidently meant a more than usually self-centered variety of the stream of consciousness. Note, however, the interview with M'Coy, (73-75) in which Bloom's mind moves on at least three levels. Compare the agricultural fair in *Madame Bovary*. Morally, Narcissism can mean pride; psychologically, infantilism or megalomania; mythically, death and rebirth. Narcissus is a drowned man who bobs up.
3. Stephen's "faunal noon" on the beach, (50) sleepy, watery, flowery, parallels Bloom's lotus-eating. Note Stephen's "foampool, flower unfurling." (50)

of meaning. Joyce's Eucharist, embodying all, is an offering to communicants.

In All Hallows, Bloom sees communion as an agent of communion or togetherness, something to make communicants "feel all like one family party. . . . Not so lonely." Are the wafers "in water?" he wonders; but he is sure that they are "*Corpus*. Body. Corpse." *Corpus* is a fitting word; for Latin "stupefies" communicants. (79) That Bloom thinks the Eucharist a "pious fraud" (80) as well as dope is ironic since it becomes increasingly clear that he himself is the Eucharist or *corpus*. "How's the body?" asks M'Coy. (72) When Bloom in tub says, "This is my body" (*Hoc est enim corpus meum*), his tub becomes a chalice or ciborium and he, Jesus Himself or the wine and bread of the Eucharist. (85) Chemistry becomes transubstantiation and botany suggests the twelve-petaled rose or the Jesus who, with twelve disciples around Him, is commemorated in the rose windows of churches. A "mosque" in appearance, the bathhouse in Lincoln Place—as nearly church as Bloom is Christ—is suitable for Bloom's chalice and his body.

Bloom in tub is anticipated by three pots, each containing flesh. Like Stephen, (42) Bloom recalls the "fleshpots of Egypt." (85) In his newspaper (another kind of dope), he reads an advertisement for Plumtree's Potted Meat, without which home is incomplete. (73) This product, which, reappearing in many contexts, acquires meanings from each (corpse in coffin, for example, and embryo in womb—"Puzzle find the meat," 169), appears first in the immediate context of his wife and the general context of the Eucharist. Not only a valise with "double action lever lock," (75) Molly is a kind of meat pot; and Boylan, come to think of it, is potted meat, completing home. But the main reference is to Bloom himself, the flesh and blood in the chalice or ciborium. This meaning is confirmed by the "cod in the pot." (85) The metaphorical cod is a racing cyclist; but the fish is a traditional icon of Christ (less a matter of iconography, however, than of ichtheology), and the pot, immediately preceding Bloom's tub, is plainly another chalice. That Joyce loved pots and potted gods is proved by the "goddinpotty" of *Finnegans Wake*. (59) Pot as potty also suggests the flesh-supporting pot, lacking which no chamber is complete.[4]

The Eucharist is central, but "flower," the last word of the chapter, is the last word, including all the meanings. A metaphor for the genitals (the organ of the chapter),[5] flower refers not only to Bloom's Eucharistic body but also to the lotus and to Martha's Henry. "Now could you make out a thing like that?" asks Mr. Bloom. (78)

Several motifs begin or significantly continue in this chapter. The lemon soap, meaning little here (aside from suggestions of fruit, perfume, and bath), will reappear. Mr. Bloom, looking at "family tea" in the window of the Belfast and Oriental Tea Company, looks also into his "high grade ha," connecting the images of hat, tea, and maybe pot.[6] He resolves to get tea from Tom Kernan; but this quest will be disappointed. The Gold Cup race, resuming a motif that began with Mr. Deasy, suggests the chalice again. Mr. Bloom's unintentional tip on Throwaway, the winner, (84) will be disregarded. Indeed, all Bloom's offerings to Dublin are disregarded except, of course, his offering to Stephen, whose communion is his triumph.

Biblical references help the meaning out. Bloom's confusion of Abraham with Isaac is a significant confusion of father and son. Bloom's revery on Martha and Mary, sisters of Lazarus, is even more significant. (76) Trying hard, the original Martha gets nowhere with Jesus, who prefers listening Mary, Bloom's Marion. If Bloom is Jesus in this parallel, Stephen must be Lazarus, to be raised from the dead.

Intent on such analogies, we must not forget that Bloom in tub or church, Martha's letter, and that lady at the Grosvenor are very funny.

---

4. Remember Mother Grogan's tea and water pot (14) and Mulligan's shaving bowl. Plumtree, of course, suggests the fruit-bearing tree of Adam's fall as well as the tree of redemption with Eucharistic fruit.

5. "Languid" genitals in this context may imply impotence, not only Bloom's but Dublin's. Cf. the heart in the next chapter.

6. P. 70. Bloom calls his hat a pot. (79) Belfast is the goal of Molly's tour with Boylan. (74) Bloom dreams of a fertile Orient.

70 : "Hat" is a misprint for "ha." Other misprints: Martha's "that other word" (76) should read "world." Cf. pp. 113, 275. "Smart," (80) not Joyce's word, was added by the printer. This text is corrupt. Note literary references (70): "Flowers of idleness" (Byron); "Botanic garden" (Erasmus Darwin); "Sensitive plants" (Shelley). Is literature a kind of dope?

73 : Notice *"Esprit de corps."*

74 : "Love's Old Sweet Song": cf. p. 63. "Queen was in her bedroom": cf. p. 68. Note the "drowning case" at Sandycove, a reappearing "body."

75 : Brunswick Street is now called Pearse Street. The "hazard" is a cab stand next to the Westland Row station. Mosenthal wrote *Deborah*, not *Rachel*. Bloom is also confused about Nathan. Compare Bloom's theory about *Hamlet* with Stephen's.

76 : *"Voglio e non"*: cf. p. 63. Martha's flower is yellow like Mulligan's vest and Lynch's Dublin. Several phrases in Martha's letter become motifs. She and her letter are varieties of dope. Lords Iveagh and Ardilaun, who figure in *Finnegans Wake*, were directors of Guinness' brewery. All Hallows is actually St. Andrew's church.

79 : Bloom is right in connecting wafers with "mazzoth."

80 : "I. H. S." is Greek JES or Jesus. "I. N. R. I." is Latin for Jesus of Nazareth, King of the Jews. Bloom finds wine more "aristocratic" for communion than Guinness' porter or ginger ale. But Joyce uses tea, coffee, cocoa as symbols of Bloom's communion. "Hokypoky" is a suitable corruption of *Hoc est enim.*

81 : Consider Bloom's account of confession: "And I schschschschschsch. And did you chachachachacha? And why did you?"

82 : "P. P." is parish priest. "Brother Buzz": cf. pp. 485, 488. The "low tide of holy water" is remarkable.

83 : Bloom likes the idea of being bathed by a woman. Not so Stephen. (44) A waterlover, Bloom takes baths frequently; Stephen, a hydrophobe, almost never. Compare Bloom's "Water to water" with "foul flowerwater." (63)

85 : The cycle race, parallel to the Gold Cup race and to Vico's

history, recurs. Is Hornblower a kind of Gabriel announcing Bloom in womb? The weather is "heavenly."

In this holy chapter Bloom has proceeded from synagogue (70) to church (78) and mosque (85).

CHAPTER VI

Hades

This visit to Hades also brings stories of *Dubliners* to mind. Like them, it is an epiphany, showing Dublin forth and up. Not only Dublin but Bloom's Dublin, however, this chapter differs from those stories in being centered in an outsider's experience. The connection of lotus-eating and Hades is logical. We pass by an easy transition from *corpus* to corpse and from Plumtree's Potted Meat to Paddy Dignam in his coffin. "A corpse is meat gone bad," thinks Mr. Bloom.[1]

Soap uncomfortably in pocket, he attends Paddy's funeral. With him in the carriage are Cunningham, Power, and Simon Dedalus, Stephen's father. Tom Kernan, from whom Mr. Bloom seeks tea, is in another carriage. All the characters of "Grace" are there, except M'Coy, there by proxy, however; for Bloom has agreed to represent him. (74) The conversation in Bloom's carriage, like that of "Ivy Day" (recalled by the presence of Hynes), reveals the citizens of Dublin, witty, sentimental, malicious, kindly, and faithful to an empty rite. The sky, says witty Dedalus, observing a drop or two of rain, is "as uncertain as a child's bottom." (89) From Sandymount to Glasnevin cemetery, the cortege crosses Dublin from end to end, passing Stephen on his way to the beach (for it is 11 A.M.) and Blazes Boylan on his way to Molly. At the mortuary chapel, full of "bad gas," toad-bellied Father Coffey, conducts a hasty service. Bloom's thoughts, concerned with the burial of the dead, are suitably charnal, indeed gruesome. At the grave, there is a mysterious stranger in a macintosh. At the gate,

1. P. 113. Cf. "Plumtree's potted under the obituaries, cold meat department"; (152) and "Dignam's potted meat." (169)

Bloom imprudently speaks to Mr. Menton, an eminent solicitor, about his hat.

The Homeric parallel is this: Ulysses visits Hades, the abode of the dead, for news of home and of journey home. Tiresias prophesies.[2] Ulysses interviews the ghost of his mother, sees the dead men of his crew and some of the more illustrious dead, Achilles, Agamemnon, Ajax, and many more. Soft words to Ajax are in vain; for, still nursing a grudge about the armor of Achilles, Ajax snubs Ulysses. All those shades are eager for blood.

It is fitting, therefore, that the heart is the organ celebrated in Joyce's parody. The cemetery is the heart of Dublin, and all its people, like those of "The Dead," are bloodless shades. "The Irishman's house is his coffin," (108) thinks Mr. Bloom, alone alive. Mr. Menton, nursing a grudge about bowling, is Bloom's Ajax. That the caretaker with his two keys (the symbol of the chapter) resembles St. Peter more than Tiresias is also fitting; for Peter founded the Church, and the art of this chapter is religion as distinguished from theology. Concerned with ritual and empty forms, like the religion exposed in "Grace," the religion of Father Coffey's Dublin, like that of Father Purdon's, is devoted to burial, commerce, and other signs of death. Devoted to the Sacred Heart, Dublin wears this heart on its sleeve. (112)

Kernan, M'Coy, and Bloom are "in the same boat," (75, 104) as Bloom observes. All three are outsiders, all disregarded or snubbed. Cunningham interrupts Bloom's story of Reuben J. Dodd, the drowning son, as he interrupts M'Coy in "Grace." M'Coy, who has a job in the morgue, is seeing about the reappearance of the drowned man at Sandycove. Kernan, still indifferent to ritual in spite of Cunningham's efforts in "Grace," has the missing tea. It is natural for Bloom, M'Coy's representative, to pair off with Kernan at the grave.

---

2. That Tiresias, the dog, the burial of the dead, death by water, Bloom's back yard waiting for rain, and the method of allusion and quotation bring Eliot's *Waste Land* to mind is more than coincidental. The early chapters of *Ulysses* were appearing in magazines in 1918, several years before Eliot wrote his poem, which, as Joyce implies in *Finnegans Wake*, seems an unacknowledged parody of *Ulysses*.

"Eager and unoffending," like Stephen's Jews, (35) Mr. Bloom nonetheless invites what he gets from Mr. Menton, whose dented hat, taking its place beside Mr. Bloom's imperfect hat, invites speculation. In the previous episode Bloom's hat was a pot. (79) Here in the context of burial and piety it seems no less important. Yet, though Bloom's hat is as conspicuous as Kernan's in "Grace," Bloom's remains mysterious, and so does Mr. Menton's—though both may have inspired the hats of Samuel Beckett, who, whatever his understanding, never tells.

But the man in the brown macintosh is a greater mystery. "Now who is he I'd like to know?" (108) says Bloom.[3] Macintosh is number thirteen at the grave, "Death's number." His waterproof, as brown as decaying Dublin, keeps rain off. Hynes puts "M'Intosh" down among the mourners, though by now he has "become invisible." (110) Suggesting Jesus (number thirteen at the Last Supper) and death, macintosh seems to include life, death, and, because Bloom is analogous to Christ, Bloom. "If we were all suddenly somebody else," (109) thinks Bloom, who should be used to that possibility by now. Becoming a motif, the man in the macintosh reappears throughout *Ulysses*, hinting this and that.[4] The "selfinvolved enigma" still teasing Bloom at his journey's end, and teasing readers more, is "Who was M'Intosh?" (714) Who indeed?

"Incubism," Joyce's name for the technique, means brooding over, as "Narcissism," his name for that of the previous chapter, means concerned with self. Both techniques are varieties of the interior monologue.

86 : Martin Cunningham opens the chapter because as a "good practical Catholic," (216) he embodies formal religion—as he does in "Grace."

3. Passing Sir Philip Crampton's bust, Bloom asks: "Who was he?" (91) Cf. Stephen's remarks about Crampton in *A Portrait*. Bloom also passes Elvery's Elephant House, (92) a shop specializing in macintoshes. Maybe Gabriel got his goloshes there. Since "Mac" means "son of," macintosh includes father and son.
4. See Miles Hanley's *Word Index to Ulysses* under macintosh and M'Intosh.

87 : Stephen, "lithe" and black, suggests Bloom as panther.

88 : Stephen as son suggests Rudy, Bloom's dead son, who would have been eleven now. Eleven is the number of revival. (Cf. 593) Milly is Molly "watered down."

89 : Bloom thinks of his dead father as Ulysses of his dead mother. For Ben Dollard's "Croppy Boy" see pp. 278-79.

92 : Bloom corrects his "*Voglio e non vorrei*," suggested here by Boylan.

93 : Reuben J. Dodd and his son take their place in the themes of father and son, drowning and emerging. In 1954 Reuben J. Dodd, the son, sued the Joyce estate for libel. Dedalus' "One and eightpence too much," suddenly discovered, was too much for Mr. Dodd.

94 : Nelson's pillar: "Eight plums for a penny," prepares for the next chapter. (143) Paddy died of heart failure.

96 : Bloom's bee sting and Dixon, the medical student who treated it, reappear in Oxen of the Sun. The funeral cortege meets a drove of cattle (life).

98 : The Childs murder case (fratricide), recurs pp. 137, 403, 405. Though as full of garbage as the Liffey, the canal leads to Mullingar or "to heaven by water." (97) Yet the bargeman salutes Dignam with a "brown" hat.

102 : Bloom's ignorant view of ritual (the priest takes "a stick with a knob at the end of it" out of a bucket) is no less amusing than his view of the Mass at All Hallows. "Tiresome kind of job." (103)

106 : Bloom's ghosts are tantalized by the "smell of grilled beef-steaks" as those of Ulysses by blood. For "Keyes' ad" see the next chapter.

107 : "Holy fields" are Elysian Fields. The seaside girls "swurl" like maggots now.

111 : Hynes, though still devoted to Parnell, doubts his reappearance. Bloom thinks of the death of Ivy Day. (109)

112 : The rat in tomb is like the rat in Guinness' vat (150) and the rat in Stephen's square ditch. (*Portrait*, 249)

114 : Menton is one of Molly's lovers, (716) all of whom seem bad hats.

If you think these notes exhaust the text, you are deceived. Some things that I know remain unmentioned for lack of space. There are things I do not know, that others know maybe, and there are more that nobody knows. The world is almost all before you to make of what you can.

CHAPTER VII

Aeolus

Mr. Bloom is a canvasser for advertisements. At once an outsider and a bourgeois, he follows the central trade of bourgeois society. Minding his business, he enters the newspaper office at noon. He leaves, and bullockbefriending Stephen enters with Mr. Deasy's letter to the press. Like talkative idlers in the committee room, the Dubliners in the editorial office have little on mind, less to do. Hanging around, they talk incessantly until invited for a drink by Stephen at Mooney's pub across O'Connell Street. Going out, they meet Bloom coming back. "K. M. R. I. A.," says Myles Crawford, editor, to uninvited Bloom.

Near the "Heart of the Hibernian Metropolis" or Nelson's Pillar, the "Daily Organ" is not Dublin's heart, which remains the cemetery. This newspaper is lung. Yet heart and lung have much in common—circulation, for example. Attending to this, the machines downstairs thump away in heartless imitation of heart. But upstairs lungs, like mortuary chapel, emit bad air. It is not surprising that rhetoric, the art of Dublin, is the art of this windy chapter, over which Aeolus, god of the winds, presides.

Homer's Aeolus helps Ulysses homeward by tying up winds in windbags. But, almost home, Ulysses nods. His foolish crew, untying those windbags, loose the winds. The ship is driven back to Aeolus, who, understandably annoyed, refuses to hear the excuses of Ulysses. "Tell him go to hell," says Crawford. (135)

Myles Crawford, the "Harp Eolian," is Ireland's Aeolus. "Begone," he says to Bloom. "The world is before you." "Back in no time," says Ulysses Bloom. (128) We have seen what Crawford says when Bloom comes back. Thinking of home, (122) he does not get there, nor does he join his Telemachus. Metaphorical winds and windbags abound. The action, imitating Homer and lung, is in and out, back and forth. People go out, come in, collide. The structure, too, is a series of ins and outs, exits and entrances, as Dublin's lungs inhale, exhale. Newsboys rush past like the winds, providing a kind of tail for Bloom's kite—and Bloom is "gone with the wind." Meanwhile the windbags of Dublin, talking of wind while raising it, proceed along the scale of oratory from the "high falutin" stuff of Dan Dawson, an "inflated windbag," faithfully reported in the paper, to the eloquence of Seymour Bushe and John F. Taylor. Of windy journalism, Ignatius Gallaher, whom we met in "A Little Cloud," is the great example.

As plainly an outsider here as at the cemetery, Bloom is ignored, snubbed, or condescendingly tolerated by the gang. But his quest for keys supports him through these trials. Crawford jingles keys in his back pocket as the caretaker at the cemetery "puzzles" his in his hand. Without a key in pocket or hand, Bloom seeks crossed keys in a circle for the House of Keyes. A circle is the perfection of enclosure. St. Peter's crossed keys are to heaven and earth. The crossed keys of the parliament on the Isle of Man (known as the House of Keys) imply "home rule," as Bloom points out. (The "homerule sun rising up in the northwest," 57, is in the right quarter for Bloom's.) Those keys for Keyes, implying all this, are home for Bloom. As he fails to place Keyes' advertisement, he fails, like Ulysses, to reach his home, an Isle of Man, however ruled. That Keyes is "tea, wine and spirit merchant" (119) enlarges the implications. "Family tea," (70) already associated with hat, joins the missing key to Bloom's house. Wine implies communion, spirit, and everything in heaven and earth or what Molly means to Bloom.

Stephen is an outsider, too. Yet Crawford treats him with deference, for his father's sake maybe, and solicits him for the "press-gang." Write something with "a bite in it" for a Dublin audience, Crawford tells toothless Kinch. (134) "Put us all into it . . . Father Son and Holy Ghost and Jakes M'Carthy"—though when Joyce did this in *Dubliners*, Dublin was dismayed. Crawford and his pressure put Stephen in mind of Father Dolan ("Lazy idle little schemer," 133; cf. *Portrait*, 294) and all the Church's tyranny. Weighing journalism in the bàlance with literature, represented by Dante and even by those mediocre verses composed near the Pigeon House on a corner of Mr. Deasy's letter,[1] Stephen quietly reaches a decision. His exile from all that Dublin wants and stands for is voluntary. As the newspaper is another cemetery for Bloom, so for Stephen it is history, the nightmare from which he is trying to awake—the nightmare, he says hopelessly to himself, "from which you will never awake." (135)

The parallel of Moses, as prominent here as that of Aeolus, seems to include Stephen, Bloom, and the work of art. Occurring first in Bloom's thoughts of "Pessach" or Passover, Moses recurs in the speeches of Bushe and Taylor, and in Stephen's parable of Nelson's Pillar.[2] As the leader who will point the Promised Land out without getting there himself, Moses suggests Bloom pointing the way for Stephen—the way to Molly. As the young outsider, resisting priestly demands of conformity, Moses suggests Stephen, who, observing the "pillar" by day, will lead the Irish out of cultural bondage maybe and write tables of the law "in the language of the outlaw." As Michelangelo's "stony effigy," Moses suggests the work of art, both "frozen music" and "sym-

1. Stephen's poem: pp. 130-31. Cf. p. 48. The passages from Dante (136-37) are *Inferno*, V, 92, 94, 96, 89; *Paradiso*, XXXI, 142. Illustrating rhyme, they also indicate progress from hell to the rose of heaven (Mrs. Bloom?).
2. Pp. 121, 138, 140, 141, 143-48. Cf. 372, 682. Bloom's "into the house of bondage," (121) an apparent confusion, is a significant reference to his home.

bol." Like Bloom, the work of art is "soultransfiguring." Stephen's "Child, man, effigy," recalling his lyric, epic, and dramatic, all but confirms this possibility.

Stephen's parable, though remaining indefinite, suggests much. We can be sure that "Pisgah" means Moses seeing the Promised Land. We know that "parable" is the favorite method of Jesus. Similitude, analogy, parallel, or correspondence, the parable is Joyce's favorite method, too. But however adequate to its purpose, parable is not mathematical equation. What, we must ask, without being sure of an answer, does Stephen's enigmatic parable correspond to? Or, better, what hints does it provide? "I have a vision," says Stephen, introducing his parable, "Dubliners." Plainly his parable, like a sketch for *Dubliners*, is an epiphany, showing something forth. It is our only evidence that he is the artist he thinks he is.

Florence MacCabe is a midwife. (38) Plumtree's plums and their seeds imply fertility, but spitting seeds out onto barren ground implies infertility. The pillar, its ascent, and the "one-handled adulterer" seem sexual. The two vestals look up at Nelson, symbol of British empire, and down at Dublin's churches, symbols of Roman empire. "I am the servant of two masters," Stephen has told Haines, "an English and an Italian." (22) Professor MacHugh has scorned the Roman and British empires, preferring Pyrrhus, imagination, and the "lost cause" of Greece. (129-32) If the Promised Land seen from this artificial Pisgah means nothing but subjection, what promise does it hold? What sort of Moses is Florence MacCabe and what birth will she assist at? Stephen is bitter, his tone ironic; and his sudden shout of laughter implies personal involvement.[3]

"You remind me of Antisthenes," says MacHugh. "None could tell if he were bitterer against others or against himself." (147) Antisthenes, the Cynic, defending Homer's Ulysses against the

---

3. "On now. Dare it. Let there be life." (143) Stephen may mean that, however desolating, his parable is living art or what Crawford calls "God Almighty's truth." (148) Were it known, it might tickle us as Nelson's hand the old ones. If Joyce's artist is a trickster or forger, is a onehandled adulterer a kind of artist? MacCabe as midwife may imply Bloom, Stephen's midwife.

charge of immorality, praised him for being able to adapt his rhetoric to the occasion. Stephen has adapted his parable to his despair.

Polytropic Joyce adapts his method too. "Enthymemic" here, the method is as suitable to journalism as to the plights of Stephen and Bloom; for an enthymeme is a syllogism with part suppressed. The figures of speech that crowd this chapter illustrate rhetoric.[4] The headlines, mocking journalese, show its development from the eighteenth century, when the *Freeman's Journal* was founded, to modern times.

115 : Headlines and noisy trams, moving in and out, were afterthoughts, Joyce says in an unpublished letter to Valery Larbaud.

119 : The design for keys in a Kilkenny paper sends Bloom to the National Library.

121 : The cat, dog, and stick are from the Passover ritual.

122 : Note soap and Molly's perfume. "The ghost walks" (*Hamlet*) and "Agonizing Christ" introduce Bloom.

124 : "Reaping the whirlwind" is at once an enthymeme and a reference to Aeolus.

126 : Lenehan ("Two Gallants") favors Sceptre for the Gold Cup, not Bloom's Throwaway.

130 : The "cloacal obsession" of the Romans and English was Joyce's own, according to H. G. Wells.

132 : "Kyrie Eleison," from the Mass, means "Lord, have mercy." "They went forth to battle" is from Arnold by way of Yeats.

133 : Balfe's *Rose of Castille*, the answer to Lenehan's riddle, suggests Mrs. Bloom to O'Madden Burke ("A Mother") and Lenehan, as, later, it does to Bloom. (481) A rose from Gibraltar, she is a common carrier, like a railway.

139 : "That hermetic crowd" (A. E. and Mme Blavatsky) prepares for the references to theosophy in Scylla and Charybdis and Oxen of the Sun.

4. Stuart Gilbert (*James Joyce's Ulysses*) provides a list of figures of speech. W. B. Stanford (*The Ulysses Theme*) discusses Antisthenes. Enthymeme may suggest the incompleteness, hastiness, and inadequacy of journalism.

142 : "Dublin. I have much, much to learn." Stephen has, indeed, and that he learns it seems proved in Ithaca and Penelope.
143 : MacHugh's "wise virgins" connect this parable with Christ's.
147 : "Penelope Rich" is Sir Philip Sidney's Stella. As Vergilian sophomore, Stephen seems second-rate as yet. Someday he may become Homeric senior, like Bloom.

MacHugh's repeated "I see" is an ironic echo of Matthew 13:10-17, on interpreting parables.

CHAPTER VIII

Lestrygonians

Now one o'clock, it is time for lunch. On his way to look up that advertisement at the library, Bloom has food in mind or, rather, on it. However dominant, his hunger seems lightly satisfied. He eats a sandwich of "feety" Gorgonzola at Davy Byrne's pub and drinks a glass of Burgundy. But on the way he has adventures. Outside Graham Lemon's candy shop on O'Connell Street, a pious young man hands Bloom a throwaway, which he throws into the Liffey along with cake for gulls. In Westmoreland Street he meets Mrs. Breen and passes the office of the *Irish Times*. He sees sandwich men, wandering loonies, a squad of constables, and, in Grafton Street, a window of rich silks. He looks into the Burton with disgust before crossing Duke Street to Davy Byrne's. After lunch he helps a blind young man across Dawson Street and into Molesworth Street. A notion about the statues of goddesses diverts Bloom from the library in Kildare Street and into the museum next door. About to enter the home of a stony Venus, Bloom sees and avoids Blazes Boylan, still on his way to the home of a bouncing Venus. Plainly we are all at sea in Dublin's streets. Not such externals, however, but internals and what externals suggest are the more important matter and Bloom's lunch-hour fodder. A ruminant, Bloom chews the cud of memory and desire, swallows, regurgitates, and chews again.

Homer's Ulysses was not indifferent to food. Indeed, as Henry Fielding says: "Ulysses seems to have had the best stomach of all the heroes in that great eating poem of the Odyssey." But in this adventure, the Lestrygonians do all the eating. Hurling rocks, they pounce from their heights upon the ships of Ulysses and eat his sailors up. Only prudence enables him to escape those cannibals. In Joyce's parody the gulls, swooping "from their heights, pouncing on prey," (151) suggest the habits of Lestrygonians as do table manners at the Burton. "Eat or be eaten. Kill! Kill!" ruminates Bloom, digesting the limerick of the Rev. Mr. MacTrigger and his cannibals. (168-70)[1] The gate to the museum is the mouth of the harbor, the way of escape. "Safe!" says Bloom, reassured by soap, escaping Boylan, who confirming the union of hunger and sex, is the last of Bloom's Lestrygonians.

The entire chapter confirms the union of hunger and sex, desire and disgust, mind and body. All of Bloom's chapters are organic, but this one, celebrating the digestive tract, is the triumph of organism. His thoughts owe substance, shape, and sequence to the digestive process. Even his metaphors are foody. "Poached eyes on ghost" is notable, but consider the greater ambiguity of "all go to pot." (162-63) Bits of it here and there, the Rev. Mr. MacTrigger's limerick is partly digested. Sentences, responding to stomach and bowel, lose shape, go soft and mushy: "Wine soaked and softened rolled pith of bread mustard a moment mawkish cheese." (172) "Touched his sense moistened remembered." (173) Hungry and erotic, all five senses conspiring with memory, Bloom pauses before the petticoats and stockings of Brown Thomas: "A warm human plumpness settled down on his brain." (166) The word for this is psychosomatic.

"Peristaltic," Joyce's name for the method (which, as always, suits the matter), applies to structure and movement, too. The shaping principle is recurrence with change. For example: Bloom's verses on the gull reappear with variations. (150, 164) "Happier

---

1. MacTrigger is potted meat, and so is Dr. tinned Salmon. (162) The references to Plumtree in this chapter, (152, 169) connecting food and death, connect this chapter with Hades.

then," his refrain, is both constant and various. (153, 154, 165)
Prophetic thoughts of Parnell and Lizzie Twigg all but coincide
with actualities. (161 and 162; 158 and 163) Parallax recurs, but
recurrent thoughts of Molly, then and now, provide most matter
for digestion. "How's the main drainage?" asks Nosey Flynn, his
dewdrop impending and withdrawing. (176) But the general
movement, like that of food, is from mouth to bottom. On his
way to inspect the fundaments of goddesses, Bloom passes a display of plumbing. The processions he meets in the street seem
parodies of the great internal process: not only H E L Y 'S and
the squad of constables[2] but the singular processions of Mr. Farrell,
neurotically walking outside the lampposts, and of crazy Mr.
Breen. Dublin's streets become its bowels, which "having fully
digested the contents," (177) pass on the passers-by. "The
stream of life," says Mr. Bloom, crossing the Liffey. All passes, all
changes, yet all goes on the same, he ruminates in College Green.
(162) Whether of bowel or consciousness or of both together,
the stream is life. Life is a stream, beginning and ending in a pot.

Molly is in the middle of Bloom's stream, breasting it—not
Molly alone, of course, but Boylan with her—as with her once a
happier Bloom. Shabby Mrs. Breen and creative Mrs. Purefoy-
Beaufoy are what Molly might have been. Bloom is always meet-
ing substitutes and shadows. The blind stripling with a cane, who
looks "like a fellow going to be a priest," not only recalls the
Y. M. C. A. young man with his throwaway but foreshadows
Stephen.[3] Helping the blind boy on his way, Bloom gets small
thanks as, getting still smaller thanks, he will help Stephen. But
Bloom will open Stephen's eyes. The stripling, doing more for
Bloom than he for him, brings teasing Penrose back to mind.
(153, 179) If Stephen is a penman who will celebrate the rose
someday, "priesty-looking," weak-eyed Penrose is also Stephen's

2. Constables are the "symbol" of this chapter as caretaker and editor are the
symbols of the two preceding chapters. All have keys. The squad of constables
is not unlike Stephen's squad of Christian Brothers in A *Portrait*.
3. Recalls him, too. Remember priestly Stephen on the beach, who, closing
his weak eyes, feels his way with a stick. (38) "Way for the parson." (424)

surrogate. As Penrose has been, Stephen will be, Molly's lover. (716, 739)

Bloom's bowels are bowels of compassion. His kindliness and humanity include poor Mrs. Breen, poor Mrs. Purefoy, and that poor blind boy. "In the craft," according to Nosey Flynn, Masonic Bloom stands for "Light, life and love, by God." [4] "Is that a fact?" says Davy Byrne. "Decent quiet man he is. . . . He's a safe man, I'd say." ("Safe!" echoes Mr. Bloom.) Mr. Menton's view of Bloom is not the only one. That it is far from that may account for "parallax" (152, 164) and Bloom's concern with optics. Parallax is the apparent displacement of an object by a change in point of view. Mr. Menton's is one, Davy Byrne's another, Bloom's own, changing with time of day and circumstance, another still, and there are many more. Puzzle: where or what is Bloom at all or any one of us for that matter? What, after all, is identity?

But Elijah "Is coming! Is coming!! Is coming!!!" (149) Already associated with one throwaway, (84) Bloom is now associated with another, announcing the coming of Dr. John Alexander Dowie from Zion, Illinois, where the world is flat. "Bloo . . . Me? No. Blood of the Lamb," says Bloom, reading that throwaway and about to throw it away. Yet, anticipating Christ, Elijah confirms Bloom in his capacity of savior. There will be further news of Ben Bloom Elijah.[5]

150 : Both Bloom and Stephen seem the ghost in *Hamlet*. Cf. 122, 186.

151 : "Kino's 11/- Trousers." Cf. 479. K is the eleventh letter,

4. P. 175. Bloom passes the Freemasons' Hall. (180) Molly also thinks Bloom a Mason, (733) and there is corroboration in the Circe episode. Freemasonry, conspicuous in this chapter, may imply architecture, the art. In Bloom's litany, (488) "Charitable Mason, pray for us" suggests this chapter. "Pineapple rock, lemon platt, butter Scotch" and King Edward, a Mason, (149) may refer to the Scotch rite, the stones, and the levels of masonry, as Leonard Albert has pointed out. Architecture or recurrence with variation and coincidence may indicate the structure of this chapter.

5. E.g. p. 339. Malachi 4: 6, predicting the coming of Elijah to turn the hearts of fathers to children and of children to fathers, is the last verse of the Old Testament.

implying renewal. In *Finnegans Wake* the Liffey is the stream of life and the female principle.

152 : Molly's "base barreltone," like Joyce's wit, "all works out." Bloom's explication seems a key to Joyce's method.

153 : Bloom's inability to recall Penrose's name would interest Freud.

155 : Compare Breen's nightmare of the ace of spades with Haines' of the black panther.

156 : "U. P.," which gets a "rise" out of Mr. Breen, suggests urination and erection as well as the course of this book.

157 : Martha answered Bloom's ad in the *Irish Times*.

158 : "Word" in the first line should be "world," Martha's error. (76)

160 : Bloom as "mackerel" suggests Christ. The "meeting of the waters" is from Moore's verses on Avoca. The two waters, meeting under a poet's finger, may be Stephen and Bloom. "Ought to be places for women," says humane Mr. Bloom. Dixon and bee reappear. Thoughts of politics prepare for the meeting with Parnell's brother.

163 : Bloom, like Stephen, takes a dim view of vegetarian theosophists.

165 : Bob Doran from "The Boarding House" is trying to forget.

166 : That Molly's birthday is September 8 (the birthday of the Virgin Mary) will become important. The Burton (actually The Bailey) is now one of Dublin's best restaurants. All chromium and red leather, Davy Byrne's no longer caters to Nosey Flynn and his kind but to another kind entirely.

168 : Note the references to Hades: "blood" and "famished ghosts." Hunger, disgust, food, death, and sex seem confused.

169 : Nosey Flynn, at Davy Byrne's in "Counterparts," is still there.

173 : "Stuck on the pane two flies buzzed." Bloom and Molly? Boylan and Molly? Compare Bloom's memory of Howth with Molly's. (767-68) Giving chewed seedcake to Bloom, Molly becomes mother and Bloom child, receiving pablum—as Jesus from Mary.

174 : The goddesses, no longer in the museum, have been replaced by Irish crosses.

175 : Slipping off "when the fun gets too hot," Bloom is like Ulysses, slipping cable.

176 : Bantam Lyons and the Gold Cup. Cf. p. 84.

177 : The lines from *Don Giovanni* combine food, statue, and death.

180 : The excursionists on the *General Slocum* were roasted or drowned on June 15. Bloom thinks of "karma" and "met him pikehoses." Handel's *Messiah* recalls Dowie's Elijah.

181 : Soap and statue seem reminders of Molly or substitutes. When Bloom gets home he becomes "adorer of the adulterous rump," not so "safe" as that of a stony goddess but more "melons-mellonous." (518, 719)

CHAPTER IX

Scylla and Charybdis

In the director's office of the National Library Stephen discusses Shakespeare with George Russell (A. E.) and three librarians: Lyster, Best, and Magee, better known as John Eglinton. Jesting Mulligan intrudes. Having observed Venus (in the museum next door) and having found Keyes' design for keys in the Kilkenny paper, Bloom passes between Mulligan and Stephen, now standing at the door.

It is two o'clock. The organ is the brain. No less suitably, the art is literature and "dialectic," the method, is what scholastic philosophers use. Displaced by these circumstances from the central place he otherwise deserves, Bloom seems less Ulysses now than ghost.

Homer's Ulysses, forced to pass between Charybdis, a whirlpool, and Scylla, a monster on a rock, steers nearer the latter. Scylla, sticking her necks out, picks one man up in each of her six mouths; but during her supper prudent Ulysses gets away with what she has left. Her hideous voice, says Homer, is that of "a young dog." Parodying his great original, Joyce's displaced Ulysses passes between Mulligan and monstrous Stephen, whose incessant yapping, as he sticks his neck out, is that of a young dog—and Bloom steers nearer him, no doubt. Calling for aid upon Aristotle, Aquinas, and Loyola, dogmatic Stephen is the rock of dogma, like the "bulldog of Aquin" himself.[1] The debate between Stephen on one hand and A. E. and Eglinton on the other—they for Plato or Blavatsky, he for solider Aristotle—has established Joyce's rock and whirlpool. Mulligan, a substitute for his theosophical and Platonic friends, serves at the door as the whirlpool of "formless spiritual essences." (183)

This framework, both simple and absurd, is covered with closely woven stuff of all but impenetrable thickness and forbidding appearance. As we discovered in the Proteus episode, Stephen's mind is both complex and richly stored. Alone again, an egoist among enemies, he is showing off. However natural, the display is childish. His obtrusive learning may be shallow, yet we are put to it to keep up with him. Hundreds of allusions to books and systems that we may not know cloud the issue—if, we may well ask, any. To explain everything in or on his mind seems impossible, but some pains, uncovering essentials, may disengage a few from all those flickering allusions.

Bloom is ghostly and Stephen an authority on ghosts, the ghost of Hamlet in particular. "He proves by algebra," Mulligan has said, "that Hamlet's grandson is Shakespeare's grandfather and that he himself is the ghost of his own father." (19) The boys at Mr. Deasy's school have clamored for a "ghoststory." (26) Here, then, is the algebraic or scholastic demonstration of that ghost and, at last, this story. A shadow is the substance of Stephen's argument.[2]

Stephen himself calls Hamlet a "ghoststory." Not only ghost by

1. P. 205. Cf. p. 621: "san Tommaso Mastino" (mastiff). Aquinas is a dog because he was a Dominican or, according to a mediaeval pun, Domini canis, dog of God. Not yet a god or creator, Stephen, still a dog, aspires to the position of dog of God.
2. His main points are made pp. 185-87, 192-94, 204-05, 208-10.

death, a ghost may be ghost by absence or exile. Exiled from Stratford (Stephen's Dublin), Shakespeare, a ghost by absence, played the part of the ghost in *Hamlet*. Not Shakespeare himself as Eglinton holds, the Prince is Shakespeare's son, Hamnet, a ghost by death. No longer a son when he wrote *Hamlet* (as Joyce was no longer a son when he wrote *A Portrait* and *Ulysses*), Shakespeare was a father. But father and son are consubstantial. Father is son, son father, and both are ghosts or shadows of the same substance. We have, therefore, a kind of trinity of father, son, and ghost, unholy ghost maybe. This secular trinity is god and god, identical with artist, is the creator. As a god, Shakespeare created a "world" in which he found "as actual what was in his world within as possible." As an artist, God wrote "the folio of this world and wrote it badly." The godlike artist, composed of father, son, and ghost, is "all in all," the "father of his own grandfather" and of everyone else. "Himself his own father," adds Mulligan.

As the ghost in *Hamlet*, Shakespeare wore the "castoff mail of a court buck" as Stephen wears Buck Mulligan's castoff shoes. Exiled son and ghost by absence, Stephen thinks himself the ghost in *Hamlet*. But this ghost is a father, the condition to which Stephen inadequately aspires and now, without reason, assumes. Bloom, another ghost by absence,[3] is a father—though Stephen is unaware of him as yet. Meeting in their ghost, Stephen the son, and Bloom, the father, will compose a consubstantial creative trinity or the artist Stephen wants to be and thinks he is.

The central mystery, he says, is that of fatherhood or creativity. Therefore the madonna or the guilty queen in *Hamlet* is little more than peripheral. Stephen has much to learn. Standing beneath Mrs. Bloom's window with Bloom that night, Stephen will learn at last the importance of the madonna he once esteemed and now neglects. *Ulysses* is proof that Joyce, fully aware of her centrality, was her adorer. Nothing reveals Stephen's immaturity more plainly or more plainly distinguishes Stephen from Joyce than their estimates of woman. Ten or twelve hours away from Mrs. Bloom, Stephen is unready for her.

3. E.g. "The ghost walks" p. 122, and Bloom's quotation from *Hamlet*, p. 150.

But as guilty queen, Stephen's woman takes her place in a kind of holy family of father, mother, son, and rival—in a family situation like that of *Exiles* or, indeed, like that of *Ulysses*. The faithless wife, the betrayed father, the dispossessed son, and the rival seem Joyce's, as well as Stephen's, obsession. "The theme of the false or the usurping or the adulterous brother" (209) and the figure of the brother-rival (Shakespeare's Richard), without which Joyce's home is incomplete, include Cranly, Mulligan, Boylan, Robert, and Shaun.

The domestic situation of Hamlet and Shakespeare takes its place beside that of Ulysses, as another parallel to domestic Bloom's. Stephen's Ann Hathaway, "loosing her nightly waters on the jordan," (204) anticipates Mrs. Bloom. Shakespeare, Hamnet, Ann Hathaway, and Richard are to the ghost of Hamlet, the Prince, Gertrude, and usurping Claudius as Bloom, Stephen, Molly, and Boylan-Mulligan are to Ulysses, Telemachus, Penelope, and the suitors. What you have shown us, complains Eglinton, is a "French triangle," (211) another of the four-angled figures of Joyce's domestic Euclid. But, like Venus-observing Bloom, Joyce's Euclid is "Greeker than the Greeks." (198)

Not only useful for establishing parallels, Stephen's tiresome argument is also a device for showing Stephen up again. That many of his observations apply less to Stephen than to Joyce or any artist is part of the irony; for, whatever Stephen says, he is no Joyce. Talking about art is no substitute for art. That Stephen, who once maintained the dramatic impersonality of art, makes a personal or lyric poet of dramatic Shakespeare is further evidence of Joyce's irony. For lyrical Stephen, Shakespeare displaces his plays and Stephen displaces Shakespeare. Even A. E. and Eglinton, as if new critics, are able to detect Stephen's fallacy. The artist may use his own image but not as Stephen supposes. Not autobiography, Shakespeare's plays are distanced and dramatic. About families maybe, his plays are not about his own.

Mulligan's entrance is Stephen's necessary and overdue deflation. Pretentiousness is defeated by gaiety. More of a creator than Stephen, Mulligan writes a play. (214) However indecorous,

Mulligan's remarks about masturbation are functional; for Stephen's self-centered discourse is more like masturbation than criticism. Hints of perversion, occurring throughout the chapter, are no less functional. Applying less to Shakespeare than to Stephen, they also suggest his infertility.

But there is hope for the boy. As Bloom walks out with the step of a pard, Stephen, connecting Bloom with his dream, recalls the "creamfruit melon" and thinks of augury. The twining smokes of *Cymbeline* augur union with Bloom. "Kind air" (215) over Kildare Street, recalling the "mollis aer" or "mulier" of *Cymbeline*,[4] augurs "wide earth an altar" or Mrs. Bloom.

182 : The Quaker is Lyster, a "Christfox" or George Fox. (191) Goethe's *Wilhelm Meister,* a novel of adolescence, contains a discourse on *Hamlet.* "Ed egli . . ." (Dante, *Inferno,* XXI) applies to Stephen here: "Of his arse he made a trumpet."

183 : Stephen associates Cranly with Mulligan. "The shadow of the glen," a play by Synge. Dunlop, Judge, K. H. are theosophists. H. P. B. is Mme Blavatsky.

184 : "Dagger definitions": Scholastic Kinch is still a knife blade, requiring "whetstones," (208) or friend-rivals: Stephen's brother, Cranly, Mulligan, Lynch. (493) "Bound thee forth. . . ." by Douglas Hyde.

185 : MacKenna is a neo-Platonist. Mallarmé's Hamlet (Pléiade edition, p. 1558), like Stephen and Stephen's Shakespeare, is reading the book of himself.

186 : Stratford is to London as Dublin to Paris.

187 : Russell, a better critic than Stephen, is against "prying into the family life" of a poet. The lines on Mananaan MacLir, suggested by Lear and A. E., are from A. E.'s *Deirdre.* "I, I and I. I." are four of Stephen's changing personalities. But his "form of forms" or soul is constant. "I" is this egoist's favorite word.

---

4. *Cymbeline,* V, v, 446-48. "Let a Roman and a British ensign wave" (line 480), following the quoted lines, introduces Father Conmee and the Lord Lieutenant of the next chapter. Reread the final scene of *Cymbeline* to see what Joyce made of it.

Money ("A. E. I. O. U.") is one of the themes in this, as in the Nestor episode.

189 : "Between the acres. . . ." is from *As You Like It*. Most of Shakespeare's works are referred to in this chapter. *Isis Unveiled* is by Mme Blavatsky, in whose theosophical whirlpool A. E. is "engulfed."

190 : Stephen, an outsider, is not asked to contribute to A. E.'s anthology, nor is he invited to George Moore's party. Stephen, sexually ambiguous, is Cordelia, the rejected daughter of Lear-Lir (A. E.). However, Stephen submits Mr. Deasy's letter to A. E.'s *Homestead*.

191 : Thoth or Hermes Trismegistus, dog-headed god of analogies. Cf. *Portrait*, p. 493. "Christfox," quarry of a "hue and cry," may also refer to Stephen, burying his grandmother, or to Parnell. (557-58)

192 : "*E quando vede. . . .*" is from Dante, *Inferno*, VI. "That mole is the last to go": Stephen is referring to *Hamlet*, I, v, 162. Hamlet's "mole" is the ghost, speaking from underground.

193 : "His own image [to an egoist] . . . is the standard of all experience."

194 : "The tusk of the boar has wounded him" (*Venus and Adonis*). Homer's Ulysses is scarred by the tusk of a boar.

195 : "He who Himself begot . . . ," a parody of the Credo. Note "crosstree" from p. 51.

197 : Stephen's perplexing telegram quotes Meredith's *Richard Feverel*, a novel about father, son, and the failure of both. Cf. p. 418. Mulligan parodies Synge, whom Stephen has met in Paris.

198 : Bloom's "Galilean eyes" combine Jesus with Galileo, who also observed Venus. Ann is Penelope. Cf. p. 199.

199 : "Love that dare not speak its name" is from Oscar Wilde. Cf. p. 50. The many references to perversion may also imply that a union of male and female elements in one person is required for literary creation.

201 : The dramatic form is imposed by Stephen's mind. "Woa!" suggests Wagner's Rheinmaidens. Epicene Best, who echoes Stephen, seems his second best bed.

202 : "*Mingo*," Latin for "I piss," is Stephen's ironic estimate of what he is doing. Shakespeare as Jew suggests ghostly Bloom.

203 : "The new Viennese school," studying Oedipal incest, is a reference to Freud. Cf. "the doctor," p. 202. "*Pogue mahone*," Gaelic for "kiss my arse."

207 : "Delta in Cassiopeia": cf. p. 49. "*Bous*": cf. *Portrait*, p. 428.

208 : "Pillar of cloud." There are several other references to Moses, e.g. "fleshpots of Egypt." Stephen bitterly admits that he is Icarus, not Daedalus. "Lapwing" means leap and fall. "*Pater, ait*": "Father, he cries." As falling Icarus calls to his father, so Jesus, another forsaken son, calls to His in His extremity.

213 : "I hardly hear the purlieu cry," a parody of Yeats, Lady Gregory's flatterer. Mulligan's "jew jesuit" predicts the union of Bloom and Stephen.

214 : Augury: cf. *Portrait*, p. 492. "Creamfruit": cf. p. 47. Bloom is both "wandering jew" and "ancient mariner."

CHAPTER X

The Wandering Rocks

There are no wandering rocks in Homer's *Odyssey*, except by allusion. Warned by Circe against these distant hazards to navigation, that only Argonauts can get around or through, Ulysses decides to go the other way, past monster and whirlpool. It is not surprising, then, that these petrified yet restless ghosts by absence are not an episode of *Ulysses*—not an episode, that is, in the usual sense. Joyce called this chapter an "*entr'acte*," a "pause in the action," which, though occupying the middle of the book, has "absolutely no relation to what precedes or follows." (*Letters*, 149) There is plenty of movement, to be sure, and the relationship among elements is constantly shifting, but the plot, petrified and motionless, does not advance.

Mixing his myths, Joyce named the method "labyrinthine."[1]
So far as we can guess his purpose from his text, he planned a
vision of Dublin for the center of his book. At once the labyrinth
that Daedalus designed for his ambiguous bull and the moving
obstacles that scared Ulysses off, Joyce's city, more than scenery
or setting, is microcosmic, our world in little. Physical relativity
and discontinuity seem embodied in his symbolic city, and all our
social disorder. The organizing principles are ineffectual. The
human elements, like parts of fractured atoms, collide, part, go
separate ways, or sink, inert. However human, these elements
lack human contact. Related by time and place, they lack vital
relationship. Moving or inert, they lack meaning or value. "Sure,
the blooming thing is all over," as Master Dignam says—or so it
seems from the vision before us.

Nineteen brief scenes display Joyce's wandering Dubliners.
Each scene is connected with others—but arbitrarily and by
temporal coincidence alone—as if time on hands at the same time
were all these citizens have in common, as, indeed, it may be.
Processions of all sorts seem to connect the separate scenes without
really connecting them. Farrell still walks outside his lampposts,
colliding with the blind stripling. H E L Y ' S and Breen go their
customary ways. Elijah, Bloom's throwaway, moves up and down
the Liffey with the tides, with the other garbage. But the principal
processions are those of Father Conmee and the viceregal cavalcade. These alone have purpose and both are leaving town. Representing Church and State (the "Roman and the British ensign"
of *Cymbeline*), Conmee and the Earl of Dudley are Dublin's
governors yet they have almost no relationship with one another
or with the Dubliners they pass. A crossing of their paths would
imply integration. But a glance at the map shows no such cross.
Conmee, leaving the Gardiner Street church, goes northeast, then
northwest toward the Artane orphanage. The Lord Lieutenant,
leaving Phoenix Park, goes southeastward toward the Mirus
bazaar. They miss each other by a mile and by almost half an

1. Homer's Ulysses, to be sure, pretends that he is from Crete, "where the race
of Minos dwell."

hour. Conmee occupies the first section and the Lord Lieutenant the last. Hats are raised or left alone, but Stephen and Bloom, lost in the crowd, see neither of their departing governors.

Nor do Stephen and Bloom meet each other. But, pausing before displays of books, each is concerned with literature, Bloom with pseudo-Aristotle, (232) Stephen's area, and Stephen with pseudo-Moses, (239) that of Bloom. With money in his pocket, Stephen gives his sister Dilly nothing, preferring the enjoyment of his private misery. (240) But charitable Bloom has given five shillings to the Dignam fund. "There is much kindness in the jew," says Nolan. (242-43) Stephen is solicited in vain by Artifoni, another outsider. But Bloom is· noticed by an insider. "He's a cultured allroundman," says Lenehan. "There's a touch of the artist about old Bloom." (231-32) Could they meet, Bloom would have charity, humanity, and art to offer Stephen.

"A mighty maze," says Alexander Pope of macrocosm, "but not without a plan." Like any maze, Joyce's Dublin is amazing; but, aside from planned confusion, is there a plan at all? Blind alleys abound, promising corridors lead nowhere, appearances deceive, and clues are generally false. Bloom, the dentist, for example, is unrelated to Leopold. Kernan sees the "windscreen" of a motorcar; yet the cars of 1904 had no such thing. Deceptive complexity, without apparent center, may be Dublin's epitome and that of our world, but is it also the epitome of Dublin's labyrinthine epic, Joyce's world? Is his underlying plan a parody of *Ulysses?* Claiming "absolutely" no connection between this chapter and the rest of the book, Joyce, in his capacity of trickster, may be tricking us at last. Certainly this central chapter has characters in common with the other chapters. But the great question is whether these nineteen parts, connected by cross-reference, correspond somehow to the eighteen chapters of *Ulysses.* Nineteen is not eighteen, to be sure, but maybe Joyce threw one part in for good measure— as a summary of the others, as a musical coda, or as the epitome of this epitome. If eighteen of these parts parody eighteen chapters, the extra part may be the first, the last, or one in the middle.

Hypothesis in mind, book in hand, let us look at it again. Part
1 of this chapter (216) seems remotely parallel to Chapter I of
Ulysses. Conmee is a theologian and the art of the first chapter
is theology. In Part 2 (221) Corny Kelleher's "daybook," his
"coffinlid," and his readiness to "pass the time of day" could
imply history, the art of Chapter II. That the setting of Part 4
(223) is a kitchen could imply economics, the art of Chapter IV,
and Bloom's kitchen. In Part 5 (224) Boylan, unfaithful to Molly,
flirts with a fruit girl as Bloom in Chapter V flirts with Martha,
a flower girl. Bloom orders lotion for Molly. Boylan buys her
fruit, a "small jar" (of Plumtree no doubt), and acquires a "red
carnation." These resemblances are almost convincing, but others
depend on slighter connections. Part 8 (226) and Chapter VIII
share the art of architecture, but Part 8 suggests food only by a
sneeze, Lambert's "Chow!" Part 9 (228) is connected with
Chapter IX, the library scene, only by the fact that Rochford is
a "booky." Part 18 (246) suggests Chapter XVIII, Mrs. Bloom's
monologue, by Master Dignam's porksteaks (flesh) and by his
favorite word, "blooming": "The blooming stud was too small
for the buttonhole." Mrs. Bloom's monologue is the "blooming
end to it," if we take Master Dignam's "it" to mean *Ulysses*. But
this is absurd. These correspondences are trivial or grotesque.
Bear in mind, however, that *Ulysses* is a funny book.

The correspondences among other parts and other chapters are
even more dubious. Ingenuity, invited and challenged, may come
up with possible connections for Parts 3, 14, and 17. But, try as we
may, these connections are unconvincing.[2] Some parts, such as
13, (238) suggest several chapters with equal persuasiveness, and
some suggest nothing at all—to me, now.

But we are in a labyrinth. Meant to try, to follow clues down
this corridor and that, and ultimately to fail—meant to guess and
go astray—we share an experience with Minotaur-hunters in a maze
without a Minotaur. Our immediate sensation of wandering

2. Part 3 (222) with its sailor, "urchins," and Muse could correspond to the
Proteus episode. But ingenious as I am, I can make little or nothing of Parts 14,
(240) 15, (242) and 17, (246). Maybe you can make more. Parts 6, 11, 12,
and 16 seem almost too easy.

through a maze seems one of Joyce's ends and an explanation of these teasing but unsatisfactory correspondences. His labyrinth is Dublin and this book. Ours is this book and the world, which, exploring hopefully—successfully now and then, we never understand.

A labyrinth is a puzzle composed of little puzzles. Many detain us in our wanderings here. The man in the brown macintosh, dodging the cavalcade, eats dry bread. (251) The one-legged sailor, who suggests the onehandled adulterer, seems both Stephen and Bloom, getting a handout from Molly's window. (222) Miss Dunne, Boylan's secretary, suggests, without being, Bloom's Martha. (226) Posters of Marie Kendall and Eugene Stratton mysteriously preside over Dublin. Conmee and the Lord Lieutenant are plainly parallel, yet one is within a possible system of eighteen parts and the other out of it. The Poddle, a disappointed river, hangs out "in fealty" to the Lord Lieutenant "a tongue of liquid sewage." (249) The Poddle sticks its tongue out at the reader, too.

216 : Father Conmee (see *Portrait*) has no money for alms because, a Jesuit, vowed to poverty, he has been given only enough money for this trip. Father Vaughan is Father Purdon of "Grace." The placid, benign style reveals benign, placid Father Conmee. There is no better example of expressive rhythm and diction.

221 : "Sin," a Hebrew letter from the 119th Psalm, becomes a pun by juxtaposition. The young sinner is Lynch. Cf. p. 409.

225 : Artifoni, music teacher, advises Stephen in idiomatic Italian to give up literature, take up singing, and stay in Dublin. Compare the solicitation of Myles Crawford.

232 : Bloom is familiar with Masoch. Phrases from *The Sweets of Sin* become motifs.

234 : J. A. Jackson seems James A. Joyce, son of John Joyce. But why is that cyclist cycling here—and in the grounds of Trinity College? Ingenuity is invited.

237 : Kernan has sold tea and drunk gin. Emmet's hanging and "missed that by a hair" predict the Cyclops.

244 : The D. B. C. (Dublin Bakery Company) tearoom may correspond to the coffee stall of Eumaeus.

245 : Mulligan and Haines estimate Stephen's condition and his future. As Yeats' "Wandering Aengus" Stephen is both wandering rock and unsatisfied seeker.

246 : Stephen's schooner (51) is now identified as the *Rosevean*, from Bridgwater, with bricks. Cf. p. 609.

251 : The salute of Artifoni's sturdy trousers prepares us for the music and farting of the next chapter.

CHAPTER XI

The Sirens

That done, the action begins anew. On his way to meet Martin Cunningham at Barney Kiernan's pub, Bloom interrupts his charitable mission (like Father Conmee's in the interests of Dignam's orphans) by a stop at the Ormond Hotel for another lunch or early dinner. He is joined by Richie Goulding, Stephen's uncle. True to inner organs, Bloom orders liver. In the adjoining bar, the barmaids flirt with Dubliners. Lenehan is there, of course, jesting as usual, to meet Boylan, who, boiling with impatience, is soon off to keep his appointment with Molly. It is 4 P.M. now and all is lost. Simon Dedalus sings a tenor aria from *Martha*, and Ben Dollard, the "base barreltone," sings "The Croppy Boy." Of such is the music of Dublin. The blind stripling comes back for his forgotten tuning fork. Meanwhile, Bloom eats, answers Martha's letter, and broods about Blazes and Molly.

This chapter of eating, ear, and song distantly parallels Homer's account of the singing, man-eating Sirens, whom Ulysses and crew escape, the one by rope, the other by wax. Like Homer's Sirens, Joyce's barmaids lure men on—in vain; for here, aside from a feeble attempt, no Sirens sing unless Dedalus and Dollard are

Sirens, and that is unlikely. The barmaids are "seaside girls" of a sort, but the real Sirens seem Martha and Molly, especially the latter, for whom Miss Douce, another "rose of Castille," is the resident substitute. Avoiding authentic Molly, keeping Martha at bay, and slipping by Miss Douce, prudent Bloom gets safely away. As metaphors of food suitably crowd the Lestrygonian episode, so metaphors of sea, shore, and music, this one. There are shells and mermaids here, and pun after pun includes music.

Music (the art) and ear (the organ) determine matter, texture, and structure. The method is fugal,[1] says Joyce, and the structure that of a fugue, a musical form that is doubly suitable; for Dublin is on a *Bach* and the word fugue means "flight." In a fugue the subject or basic melody is announced by one "voice" or part. Entering one by one, other voices state a counter-subject or imitate and modulate the subject. The relationship among these parts—neither harmonious nor inharmonious—is contrapuntal. To follow Joyce's verbal imitation requires considerable knowledge of music; but even without such knowledge I hazard a guess that Joyce employs five voices. The subject, which, reduced to fundamentals, seems to involve flight and pursuit, is stated in the "bronze by gold" of the barmaids. "Bloowho" or "Greaseabloom" is the second voice, stating the counter-subject. "Jingle jaunty" is the third voice and "Tap. Tap," the fourth. "Rrr," modulating into "Pprrpffrrppffff," completes the fugue. "Done," says Mr. Bloom as if conductor; but my conclusion is tentative. All other elements imitate these voices in other keys, agreeing or disagreeing.

Music and literature are different arts entirely. Yet words and notes, having rhythm, sound, and feeling in common when put together, are not unrelated. As music, according to Bloom, is "a kind of attempt to talk," (283) so talk or, at least, the talking here, is a kind of attempt at music. Joyce's parody of one art by the other—grotesque, comic, and hopeless on the whole, whatever its

1. Compare "Patself on the Bach" and "his manjester's voice" (*Finnegans Wake*, 73). Using a Bach fugue as form for the sentimental voices of Dedalus and Dollard is no more of a discord than using the form of Homer for the matter of Dublin.

resemblance to the attempts of Mallarmé—goes as far as words without music can. However polyphonic, the fascinating result is plainly literature, literature which, nonetheless, suggests music not only by the structure of the whole but by that of the parts and by their texture. Even the syntax, abandoning all laws of discourse, imitates the structure, rhythm, and sound of music; and all the musical resources of language, called into play, conspire. The puzzling fragments that precede the fugue may be taken as a thematic index, an overture, a prelude, or a tuning-up. "Begin!" says the conductor. Yet, however well rehearsed or tuned his Dublin orchestra, true pitch abides in a forgotten tuning fork.

While Simon Dedalus sings Lionel's song to Martha, his lost one, Bloom becomes "Siopold" (271) and Stephen's two fathers are one. Even in absence, Stephen and Molly are important elements of the fugue. As Miss Douce, with satiny bosom, jumping rose, and smackable thigh, takes Molly's place, so the Croppy Boy and the blind stripling take Stephen's. The Croppy Boy, who has not prayed for his mother's rest, is also a rebel, betrayed by false priest or father. The blind stripling, already associated with Penrose and Stephen, feels his way toward the tuning fork, of which he is the careless custodian. Promising attunement, his tapping adds Stephen's voice to the fugue of Molly, Bloom, and Boylan.

Bloom's wind instrument, the fifth voice, recapitulating the second, carries the fundamental tone, out of harmony maybe with Robert Emmet's noble voice, but related by counterpoint. This strange relationship, which would seem irreverent to an Irish patriot, seemed indelicate to Virginia Woolf: "First there's a dog that p's," she complained to Lytton Strachey, "then there's a man that forths." "Forths" indeed. But the counterpoint of Emmet and Bloom, joining the above with the below, approximates the reality to which we must try to adjust ourselves. Neither altogether irreverent nor altogether indecorous, the disagreeable agreement of words and music suggests what we are stuck with. Moreover, since Emmet was hanged, drawn and quartered, he provides fitting introduction to the Cyclops episode, a vision for patriots.

252 : The fragments composing this prelude reappear in the body of the chapter, fusing, as Joyce says, (*Letters*, 128-29) only "after a prolonged existence together," first in his mind, now in ours. Bloom's stream is largely composed of allusions to his experiences in the earlier chapters, as the careful reader, jotting cross-references in margin, will notice.

254 : Example of musical rather than logical development (line 4): "Miss Kennedy sauntered sadly from bright light, twining a loose hair behind an ear. Sauntering sadly, gold no more, she twisted twined a hair. Sadly she twined in sauntering gold hair behind a curving ear."

257 : "Idolores" is from *Floradora*.

259 : "The bright stars fade" is from "Goodbye, Sweetheart." Bloom is a "black wary hecat" now.

264 : Bloom was once in the old clothes business, and, as Dedalus says, Mrs. Marion "has left off clothes of all descriptions." Cf. pp. 158, 266.

265 : Molly is established as a Siren, by "met him pike hoses" no doubt. Cf. "We are their harps." (267)

271 : Compare this fusion of music and sex with that of food, sight, and sex in the Lestrygonian episode.

277 : The minuet from *Don Giovanni* implies seduction, off-stage.

279 : The Croppy Boy (alluded to 89-90) reappears p. 578.

282 : Bloom's soap is sticky again. "Glad I avoided," says Ulysses-Bloom.

284 : The "last sardine of summer" on "bier of bread" in belljar is an image of loneliness, which, however, connects Bloom with rose, bread, and fish or the Savior. For Bloom's "wonderworker" see p. 706. "The Last Rose of Summer" (by Moore) is from *Martha*.

285 : Macintosh puzzles Bloom again. "A frowsy whore," adroitly avoided, is the last Siren and an imitation of Douce and Molly.

CHAPTER XII

The Cyclops

The scene is Barney Kiernan's bar in Little Britain Street, near courthouse, market, St. Michan's Church, and the Ormond. It is five o'clock. The citizen, a violent nationalist, is here with Garryowen, a formidable dog with "the hydrophobia dropping from his jaws." Joe Hynes, back from a meeting of the cattle traders at the City Arms Hotel, stands the citizen drinks. Bob Doran, still on his bender, droops in a corner. The usual Dubliners are hanging around as usual: Lenehan, of course, together with Alf Bergan, Nolan, Lambert, and O'Molloy. Mr. Breen passes and Mr. Bloom enters. Out of place again, he awaits Martin Cunningham, with whom he is to undertake an errand of mercy. Bloom makes two mistakes. He joins the conversation and fails to stand the company a drink, though thought a winner in the Gold Cup race. The threat of violence culminates in violence itself. Blind with rage, the citizen hurls a biscuit tin at Bloom, fleeing in Cunningham's jaunting car. In a book so visionary and all but static, depending for epiphany upon conversation and inconspicuous movement rather than conspicuous action, the citizen's violence is shocking. Little wonder that the observatory of Dunsink registered "eleven shocks, all of the fifth grade of Mercalli's scale." (337)

But here at last active Homer demanded action of his static parodist, who is faithful in his fashion to the familiar tale. As one-eyed as the gigantic Cyclops, the citizen is blinded in his cave among his sheep by the fire-sharpened stake of Ulysses-Bloom. "You don't grasp my point," (301) says he, waving his cigar. Champion of all Ireland at "putting the sixteen pound shot," (311) but off his form by reason of drink, sun, and rage, the citizen does his best with that biscuit tin. (Muscle is the organ of this chapter.) As prudent Ulysses becomes imprudent at last, taunting his oppressor and victim, so Bloom, "the prudent member," forgetting all prudence, becomes aggressive. Bitten by a sheep, the citizen is amazed.[1] Joyce transfers the anonymity of Homer's "Noman" to the citizen and the narrator.[2]

This nameless narrator, a typical Dubliner and in a sense the most important person in the episode, is one of Joyce's achievements. "Cute as a shithouse rat," (335) the nameless one is also "all wind and piss like a tanyard cat" (322)—if we may apply his own phrases to one whose sardonic malice is as suitable to the occasion as Joyce's scrupulous fidelity in "Ivy Day," and, somehow, not unlike it. But the report of this observer is not all we have to go by; for half the story comes to us in the form of interruptions by journalists, and writers of epics, sagas, or chronicle histories, whose accounts of what happens at Barney Kiernan's are among Joyce's most hilarious parodies. "Gigantism," his word for the method, means Cyclopian inflation. Defeating itself, gigantism tends to tedium; but if we skip lightly through the Rabelaisian catalogues[3] of people and things that fill these parodies, we miss such beauties as the "Herr Hurhausdirektorpräsident" (302) and "S. Marion Calpensis." (333) Not only funny, these grotesques are useful; for each provides a point of view to supplement that of the narrator.

The cheerful acceptance of horrors by journalist, historian, and spectator may be discouraging and dreadful; but an unconquerable gaiety, like that of Yeats' artist, transfigures all that dread. Not by the satirist's indignation, still less by the reformer's zeal, but by this gaiety (a gaiety recaptured by Samuel Beckett) Joyce reveals something terrible and terribly funny. However implicit his attitude, there can be little doubt about it. It is the quarrel of

1. What riled the sheep-keeping Cyclops, Bloom reflects, (642) "was a bite from a sheep."
2. Compare Samuel Beckett's "Unnamable," another narrator. The artist, according to Stephen, is impersonal, hence nameless. Like Beckett's Unnamable One, Joyce's "Nameless One" (461) may suggest the artist. Cf. "Nobodyatall," the outsider, provoking "Wholyphamous," *Finnegans Wake*, p. 73.
3. Compare the Rabelaisian catalogues in *Finnegans Wake*, e.g. pp. 71, 104.

matter with tone that, creating the epiphany, assures our response.

The horrors so cheerfully reported by these narrators are not merely local or peculiar to a time, nor are they the consequence of nationalism alone. The citizen, around whom violence concentrates, may be a "Fenian," an Irish patriot of 1904, but his intolerance, megalomania, and brutality are those of our world, too. Joyce's vision, ranging in space and time, includes stormtroopers, secret police, witch-burners, inquisitors, lynchers, segregationists, and bigots of every sort. The anti-Semitism of the nameless narrator and the citizen is one manifestation of a general defect. Joyce had the trouble with one-eyed man in mind.

But two-eyed Joyce observes man's virtue, too. Nowhere else in *Ulysses* is its moral theme more explicit or more evident. The conflict in Barney Kiernan's is the conflict of hate with love, of inhumanity with humanity, and of compassion with indifference or malice. In his capacity of Elijah, Jesus, and God, Bloom embodies and defends all that is opposite his surroundings. "Are you talking about the new Jerusalem?" asks the citizen. "I'm talking about injustice," says Bloom. "Force, hatred, history, all that . . . it's the very opposite of that that is really life." "Love," says he, "I mean the opposite of hatred." (327) As one of the outrageous catalogues reminds us, "God loves everybody." (327) "Your God was a jew," Bloom reminds the citizen. "Christ was a jew like me." "I'll crucify him," says the citizen, throwing a biscuit tin that becomes a "silver casket" (336) as it clatters down the street. This misused ciborium is empty of wafers, however. There is no communion here.

"Jesus," the narrator fittingly exclaims, as dog chases god along the street. In his "chariot" old "sheepsface" (or Lamb of God) becomes Elijah, a type of Christ. Ulysses-Bloom neglected for the moment, Elijah-Bloom ascends to "the glory of the brightness at an angle of forty-five degrees over Donohoe's in Little Green Street like a shot off a shovel." Nothing in *Ulysses*, and little elsewhere, is more masterly than the final paragraph of what Joyce called this "lovingly moulded" chapter. (*Letters*, 126) It "takes the biscuit," as Lenehan would say. And as for Bloom: "Gob, he'd have a soft hand under a hen." (310)

287-88 : "D. M. P.," Dublin Metropolitan Police. A "t. t." is a teetotaler. The conversation with Hynes is one of the best in the chapter. Legal jargon is the first example of gigantism.

289 : The "shining palace" with "crystal roof" is Dublin's meat and vegetable market.

291 : The citizen becomes a stone-age barbarian in this parody of a prose saga. Note the catalogue of Irish heroes.

292 : "Cod's eye" implies Jesus. The "old woman of Prince's street" is the *Freeman's Journal*, of which the citizen disapproves. That Bloom works for it is significant in this illiberal context.

294 : Notice the description of a penny in the epic manner. The citizen, like all of Joyce's patriots, knows a few tags of elementary Gaelic.

295 : As a "bloody freemason" Bloom stands for brotherhood.

296 : Pseudo-Sanscrit "talafana . . . wataklasat" improve this report of a spiritualistic séance.

298 : Rumbold's letter, like the accounts of pugilism (313) and lynching, (322) is fitting material for this chapter.

299 : Bloom's "natural phenomenon" is a vain attempt at reason and science.

307 : "Wife's admirers," a slip of the tongue. Cf. the list of suitors, p. 716.

314 : Calpe is Gibraltar. Cf. Calpensis, p. 333.

315 : Bloom alone has sympathy for the Breens. Cf. pp. 157, 293. "Neither fish nor flesh" could imply Jesus.

327 : Notice the references to Gerty MacDowell (of the following chapter) and the man in the brown macintosh. What dead lady does he love?

329 : As a "dark horse" Bloom becomes Throwaway, the winner. Boylan backed Sceptre. (320)

330 : For Crofton see "Ivy Day."

331 : Virag, Bloom's original name, means flower in Hungarian. "That's the new Messiah for Ireland," says the citizen.

332 : As "Ahasuerus" Bloom is the Wandering Jew. Note "blind your eye." Cf. "beam" in the eye. (320)

333 : Saint Owen Caniculus is Garryowen. Saint Anonymous is the patron of this chapter.

334 : *"Epiphania Domini"* is Bloom's epiphany. *"Adiutorium nostrum"* is from Vespers. *"Deus, cuius verbo"* is the *Benedictio ad omnia*, a formula for blessing.

339 : "When, lo. . . ." is a parody of Biblical English. For the ascent of Elijah, thought to foreshadow the Ascension of Christ, see II Kings, 2:11.

CHAPTER XIII

Nausicaa

Having visited poor Mrs. Dignam at Sandymount, Bloom re-treats to the beach, the place of Stephen's protean walk that morning. Bloom sits on the rocks (no longer there) at the foot of Leahy's Terrace, near the Star of the Sea, Dignam's parish church. There, at a temperance retreat, the Benediction of the Blessed Sacrament is in progress. On the beach Gerty MacDowell of Sandymount and her two "girl friends" are airing the Caffrey children and throwing (or, in Gerty's case, kicking) a ball around. Gerty looks at Mr. Bloom and he at her. Their reactions to each other are the principal substance of this chapter. She becomes an exhibitionist, he a voyeur. The Bailey light at Howth, a bat, the fireworks at the Mirus bazaar, and a cuckoo clock, striking nine, announce the coming of dark. Gerty goes sadly home, taking Bloom's image with her, and Bloom, exhausted by the view and his response, dozes a little before setting out for the maternity hospital, where poor Mrs. Purefoy is in labor.

In the Homeric original, Ulysses, having drifted on a plank, crawls from the sea at Phaeacia and, exhausted, falls asleep in the bushes. Nausicaa, the king's daughter, arrives at the beach with her maids to do the washing. As the girls play ball, their screams wake Ulysses up. He terrifies the maids, but Nausicaa, undismayed by nakedness and dirt, cleans him up, clothes him, and takes him home to father. Joyce's parody, which stops short of this point, includes a game of ball, to be sure, but what comes out in the wash is more important. As Nausicaa exposes her washing on her beach, so Gerty hers on hers. The difference is that Gerty has her washing on. A baby carriage replaces Nausicaa's cart. Bloom muses on "seaside girls" (365) and on sailors away from home, "hanging on to a plank" maybe. (372)

Of the two parts of Joyce's chapter, the first is centered in Gerty's mind, the second in Bloom's. These parts are so private that they incurred the displeasure of the censor long ago; but, less illiberal nowadays or more insensitive, we can eye them at a suitable distance as Bloom eyes Gerty, Gerty Bloom. For Bloom's part Joyce chose interior monologue of the most interior sort. For Gerty's part he wickedly chose the style of a cheap Victorian "novelette"—what he called "a namby-pamby jammy marmalady drawersy . . . style with effects of incense, mariolatry, masturbation, stewed cockles. . . ."[1] The ultimate indecency of the chapter is not Bloom's action but this style, which, embodying and presenting Gerty, is Gerty—as the style Joyce chose for Father Conmee is Father Conmee. Though style tells all, some particulars of Gerty's "ladylike" thought and nature invite notice. Her continual blush is as "delicate as the faintest rosebloom"; (342) for "from everything in the least indelicate her finebred nature instinctively recoiled." (358) As the Caffrey twins play with spade and bucket in the sand, she digs away herself, never calling a spade a spade, however—though once a bucket a bucket. Transformed by Gerty from the Nameless One's old "sloppy eyes,"[2] Bloom becomes the dark romantic stranger, a man of sorrows, a "dreamhusband." Not only a man of distinction but a

1. *Letters*, 135. Joyce's aunt in Dublin sent him a bundle of "novelettes" to serve as models. Plainly the presiding Muse is the "bawd of parodies." (*Finnegans Wake*, 296)
2. Far from "sloppy," Bloom's eyes seem "wonderful" to Gerty. A variety of views, here and in other chapters, gives Bloom multidimensional solidity.

man of discernment, who eyes her "as a snake eyes its prey," Bloom becomes her real ideal. "Art thou real, my ideal?" the poet asks, (357) and Gerty answers yes, yes, yes. The transition from Gerty's Bloom in part one to Bloom's Bloom in part two is shocking in more ways than one. Joyce's name for his technique, inseparable from his matter, is "tumescence and detumescence."

"Virgin," said Joyce, is the "symbol" of the chapter. What virgin did he have in mind—Gerty or the Blessed Virgin, whose litany occupies those at church, or Molly herself, whose surrogate Gerty seems to be? All at once, of course, and all together, or "womanly woman," the chief subject of Bloom's meditation. Gerty's half of the chapter alternates between Virgin in church and Gerty on the shore. However impious, their juxtaposition or "montage" is as significant as that of Gerty and Nausicaa, impious too in its degree. Gerty, Molly, and the Blessed Virgin are connected by the rose and by incense or perfume. Both Gerty and Molly are "rosebloom," and so is Dante's Virgin. "What kind of perfume does your wife . . . ?" asks Martha. Molly uses "opoponax," Bloom recalls. (368) However rosy, Gerty's scent, wafted in Bloom's direction by cotton wadding, is "sweet and cheap." It may be that all the girls are one, but they are one with differences.

As organs of this chapter nose and eye seem fitting. Nose is lured by scent of one kind or the other and eye by a variety of exhibitions. "She saw that he saw." (360) Unlike the rest of *Ulysses*, allusive on the whole, this chapter is pictorial and descriptive, though no more smelly than most. Exceeding transparent stockings and even drawers, fireworks, the ultimate picture, include most of Gerty's vision, much of Bloom's:

And then a rocket sprang and bang shot blind and O! then the Roman candle burst and it was like a sigh of O! and everyone cried O! O! in raptures and it gushed out of it a stream of rain gold hair threads and they shed and ah! they were all greeny dewy stars falling with golden, O so lovely! O so soft, sweet, soft! [3]

3. P. 360. "My fireworks," says Bloom. "Up like a rocket, down like a stick." (364) Cf. "phallopyrotechnic," p. 473.

But there is another identified flying object here. The bat, flitting from its belfry, is a "ba," (371) recalling Bloom's "ha." We have met the bat in A *Portrait*, (444-45) where, embodying "darkness and secrecy and loneliness," it serves as image of Irish womanhood and artist. It will preside over the benighted washerwomen of *Finnegans Wake*. (215) The bat at Sandymount seems to include both Gerty and Bloom. In A *Portrait*, bat is almost never without bird. Here the bird is the cuckoo, announcing the hour and Bloom's condition.[4]

As Stephen writes verses on the vampire, a sort of bat, on this beach, so Bloom, using a stick, writes a message in the shifting sand: "I AM A" (375)—a literary creation no less satisfactory than Stephen's, and no more. Whether Bloom's "A" stands for Alpha (or God) or whether, an indefinite article, it precedes an unwritten word such as cuckold or Jew we shall never know. "What is the meaning of that other world?" (375) asks Bloom's Martha, confusing world with word, like Joyce himself. All we know for sure is that Gerty's Bloom, "a man of inflexible honour to his fingertips," (359) offends fertility here as he defends it in the following chapter. Gerty, no doubt, will continue to gaze "out of the window dreamily by the hour at the rain falling on the rusty bucket, thinking." (348)

340 : It is notable that "Mary, star of the sea," a beacon to "stormtossed" man, figures in the opening paragraph.

341 : The Martello tower is not Stephen's at Sandycove but another at Sandymount. These towers dot the coast.

342 : Gerty's rosebud mouth is "Greekly perfect."

343 : For the boy with the bicycle see p. 327, and for his brother, W. E. Wylie, and the cycle race see p. 234.

4. Bloom's cuckoo is Gerty's canary. (352) The cuckoo suggests *Love's Labour's Lost*: "Cuckoo, cuckoo: O, word of fear, unpleasing to a married ear." Mulligan quotes this. (210) Compare the bells of St. George's. (69). The cuckoo-clock is Bloom's only time; for his watch stopped at 4.30, the hour of Boylan and Molly. (363) The Bailey light on Howth, though seen by both Bloom and Gerty, is invisible from the beach at Leahy's Terrace. That it gets dark at nine o'clock is no less remarkable, because in Ireland in June darkness falls at about 10.30 or 11.

344 : Blue, the color of Gerty's "undies," is the Virgin's color. Attentive to colors, Joyce had the first edition of *Ulysses* bound in blue and white paper. Blue and white are the colors of the Virgin, of Israel, of Greece, and, though he could not know this, of Columbia University, a center of Joycean studies.

345 : Like young Stephen, Milly, and Isabel, Gerty likes looking at herself in the mirror. "You are lovely, Gerty, it said." Cf. the Ondt before his glass. (*Finnegans Wake*, 415).

346 : For the moment, the parody of a novelette gives way to a gushing, unpunctuated stream like Mrs. Bloom's. "Lovely" Garryowen, who almost talks, (cf. 307) belongs to Gerty's grandpapa Giltrap, not to the citizen.

350 : In church the litany of "the mystical rose" and "spiritual vessel" provides a kind of counterpoint. (347-48, 352) Note "the perfume of those incense" (351) from the church.

353 : "*Tantumer gosa cramen tum*" is Gerty's version of "*Tantum ergo sacramentum*," a hymn by St. Thomas Aquinas, sung at Benediction. Bloom, already identified with the sacrament, (85) is no less misconstrued by Gerty. Cf. "*Panem de caelo*" or heavenly bread. Bloom is both serpent and man of sorrows, Satan and Jesus. Is Gerty Eve as well as Mary?

354 : Gerty the virgin blushes "a glorious rose."

357 : Gerty has a "child of Mary badge."

361 : Gerty's lameness is comparable to the imperfection of Bloom's hat.

369 : Bloom smells his unpaid-for soap. His prize titbit, "The Mystery Man of the Beach," refers to himself and to the man in the brown macintosh. Cf. "the man that was so like himself." (348)

370 : The "homerule sun," now "setting in the southeast," once rose in the northwest. (57) Boylan gets the plums, Bloom the plumstones; (cf. 146) but he still recalls those rhododendrons on Howth. (173)

372 : Bloom's "tephilim" is a "mazuza," a prayer-box at the door of a Jewish home. Note "out of the land of Egypt and into the house of bondage." Cf. pp. 121, 141, 682.

373 : Reviewing his day, Bloom finds himself victorious in his encounter with the citizen.

374 : Bloom's dream of Molly in Turkish trousers: cf. pp. 391, 432. Remember Kino's trousers. (151)

375 : Bloom's monologue disintegrates into fragments from memory (Agendath, met him pike hoses, and frillies for Raoul) as he dozes off.

CHAPTER XIV

Oxen of the Sun

At the maternity hospital, Bloom encounters Stephen, Lenehan, and a number of medical students, drinking and joking uproariously downstairs while upstairs poor Mrs. Purefoy, three days in labor, suffers. Invited to join the rioters by Dr. Dixon, who treated Bloom's bee sting at the Mater Misericordiae hospital, Bloom sits inconspicuously down with them. He is weary. They drink "number one" Bass; he drinks nothing. They mock childbirth; he alone is humane, reverent, and compassionate. In whatever company he finds himself, Bloom is always the outsider. Entering with Bannon, Milly's friend from Mullingar, Mulligan is most jovial of all. At last, occasioning further jests, the baby is born; and those revelers are suddenly off for Burke's pub. Without son of his own, Bloom decides to keep a fatherly eye on Stephen, his friend's son, who, drunk and incompetent, might get into trouble. Pausing only to send a kindly message to Mrs. Purefoy, Bloom tags along. At Burke's, where he has ginger beer and they a variety of stronger drinks, the party distintegrates. Mulligan slips irresponsibly off— to bed in the tower no doubt. Responsible Bloom follows Stephen and Lynch toward the "kips." His pursuit of these drunks is far from easy; for, however unsteady, they are quick.

This is the Homeric analogue: Ulysses and his crew disembark near the Sun's cow pasture. Ulysses falls asleep and his crew, though warned to respect these holy beasts, have them for supper.

The consequence of this impiety is spectacular. A thunderbolt, sinking ship, kills all but Ulysses; for, piously rebuking them, he detests their supper. Their disrespect of Sun and cow is a crime against fertility. Lacking reverence for creative Mrs. Beaufoy-Purefoy, the rioters of Holles Street offend fertility with jokes, their way of killing cows. "*Mort aux vaches,*" says jesting Lenehan. (392) Thunderclap and sudden shower, assuring fertility to the wasteland after long drought, interrupt their sterile revelry. Though reverent Bloom does not fall asleep, he falls into a kind of trance. In the final confusion, suggesting shipwreck, Elijah Dowie acclaims the offended Creator in a voice of thunder. Dowie and the Purefoys are Protestants and Bloom is a Jew. That, except for the busy obstetrician, these outsiders alone support fertility in Catholic Dublin is not without irony—nor altogether without hope, even in that discouraging confusion at the end; for, as a revivalist, Dowie promises revival.

The chapter is not lacking in cows. References to cows, bulls, bullocks, and oxen abound; and even the Minotaur, attended by the ghost of an artificial cow, abandons labyrinth for Holles Street. (404) The motif of cattle that began with the milkwoman, Deasy's letter, and Milly's letter from Mullingar comes to climax here. It may be that Stephen is far from "bullockbefriending" for the moment; but the man in the brown macintosh, encountered at Burke's, drinks Bovril or beef tea, denying death as he mourns his dead lady. (420) "Beef to the heels" as ever, Milly and cattle-swarming Mullingar are fittingly conspicuous. (390, 398) No less conspicuous, the cow-keeping Sun, present in the "bright one, light one" of the opening invocation, also implies "quickening and wombfruit." That oxen or gelded bulls are the titular symbols of fertility may seem curious; but Joyce liked infertile things as symbols or agents of fertility. Molly herself, less fertile, after all, than the fertility she implies, is nothing compared to Mrs. Purefoy. Bloom, whose infertile yet fertilizing bee stings him to rebuke infertility perhaps, seems to deserve this further rebuke: with what fitness, a reasonable eighteenth-century voice demands, does this man presume to rebuke others? (402) Yet, although less bee

than flower, Bloom will fertilize Stephen, bringing "quickening"
to him and to his imagination "wombfruit."

The art of this obstetrical chapter is obstetrics. The moral
"idea," said Joyce, is "the crime committed against fecundity by
sterilizing the act of coition." [1] As for the allegory: "Bloom is the
spermatozoon, the hospital the womb, the nurse the ovum, Stephen the embryo. How's that for High?" (*Letters*, 138-39) "Embryonic development," the method, is what gives most readers
most trouble. To embody the feeling and idea of development,
both embryonic and evolutionary, Joyce tells his story in a more
or less chronological sequence of parodies. Since literature shows
development and since the mind of Stephen is literary, parodies
of English literature through the years from Anglo-Saxon times to
those of Billy Sunday seem suitable. Some of these parodies are
mediocre, some brilliant—those of Swift, (393) Sterne, (399) and
Carlyle, (416) in particular. The point, however, is not their ex-
cellence as parodies but the idea of development they afford and
the idea of creation. Though identification of each parody is unnecessary, there is danger that, attempting identification and distracted by surface, we may lose track of story and underlying idea.

Joyce's ingenuity, sometimes exceeding the demands of theme,
led to further complication: a division into nine parts, corresponding to the nine months of gestation and to previous episodes
of *Ulysses*. "This procession," said Joyce of his developmental
parodies, "is also linked back at each part subtly with some fore-
going episode of the day and, besides this, with the natural
stages of development in the embryo and the periods of faunal
evolution in general." (*Letters*, 139, 141) It seems enough to keep
this subtle intention generally in mind, lest trying to find where
months begin and scouting through memories of what we have
read, we get lost entirely.[2] After all, there is a story here, a pretty

1. Contraception is implied by "Killchild," "cloak," "umbrella," the "Childs
murder" case, "French letters," and the brown macintosh itself. (387, 389,
398, 403) Consider "those Godpossibled souls that we nightly impossibilise."
(383)
2. See A. M. Klein, "The Oxen of the Sun," *Here and Now* (January, 1949),
for a full account of the nine-part structure. See Stuart Gilbert, *James Joyce's*

funny story, too; and despite the machinery designed to present it, there is also an idea: Fertilized by Bloom, embryonic Stephen may develop to the point of rebirth.

Adjusting ourselves to the terms of this prophecy, let us notice and commend emergent beauties. The invocation to the "bright one" is striking and appropriate.[3] But the fragmentary ending seems more important. A "significant form," this chaos, presenting drunkenness, the final decay of literature in American confusion, modern times in general, the nature of what has been born maybe, and a hint of renewal, invites comparison with the fragmentary ending of Eliot's *Waste Land*—and not without reason. "Agendath is a waste land," as Bloom has said. (407) "Closingtime, gents," says the curate at Burke's, (419) anticipating Eliot's "Hurry up please its time." Bloom's vision of a wasteland crowded with the ghosts of cows agrees with the theme of fertility and infertility that fascinated Joyce—and Eliot in his turn. "Mesmerised" apparently by the red triangle on a bottle of Bass, Bloom ranges the zodiac (a cycle of beasts controlled by sun and earth), pausing at the signs of Taurus and Virgo, descending to Martha-Milly. (407, 409) The fabled bull, (393-94) at once Papal, English, and Irish, is sent to Ireland by Nicholas Breakspear (Pope Adrian IV), Henry II, and Henry VIII—and "a plumper and a portlier bull . . . never shit on shamrock." [4]

A passage predicts and explains the Circe episode:

There are sins or . . . evil memories which are hidden away by man in the darkest places of the heart but they abide there and wait. . . . Yet a chance word will call them forth suddenly and they will rise up to confront him in the most various circumstances, a vision or a dream. . . . (414)

Ulysses, for identification of the parodies. The number nine, echoing the cuckoo clock, is everywhere in this chapter.

3. P. 377. "Deshil" is Gaelic for "the right side looking east." "Eamus" is Latin for "let us go." Let us go south to Holles Street. "Hoopsa, boyaboy" is what one says, dandling baby. "Horhorn" involves the name of Horne, superintendent of this hospital, and the horns of oxen.

4. Nicholas Breakspear, Henry II, and Ireland reappear in the fable of the Mookse and the Gripes, *Finnegans Wake,* 152.

377 : This unreadable confusion (what Joyce called a "Sallustian-Tacitian prelude" or what Stuart Gilbert calls "Latin written by a demented German") represents the roots of English and the unfertilized ovum. It suggests chaos before creation.

378 : "Before born babe bliss had" (alliterative Anglo-Saxon) is meant to have the heavy movement of oxen, said Joyce. The "sisters" are nurses and daughters of the Sun, guarding oxen.

379 : Bloom is moved be "ruth" or compassion. Cf. p. 382. The parody of *Everyman* (Middle English) begins.

380 : Bloom's bee sting and Dr. Dixon's invitation are reported in the language of Mandeville.

381 : Vessels "like to bubbles" are bottles of ale. The "vat of silver" is a tin of sardines. The nurse pleads in vain for reverence.

383 : Saint Foutinus is from French *foutre*. "Potency of vampire's mouth" refers to Stephen's poem. "Second month" may announce the beginning of the second month of the embryo as Stephen's theology recalls the Telemachus episode.

384 : Without manchild, Bloom grieves that his friend's son lives "so riotously." Note Stephen's preference for drink as his soul's bodiment: "Leave ye fraction of bread to them that live by bread alone." Although the liquid and solid elements of the Eucharist are identical, Stephen, like the boy in "The Sisters," rejects the solid. Cf. pp. 80, 618-19; *Portrait*, pp. 358, 514. Priest receives wine, congregation biscuit; Stephen thinks himself priest of the imagination.

385 : "Rose upon the rood of time": a poem by Yeats. "In woman's womb word is made flesh but in the spirit of the maker all flesh that passes becomes the word that shall not pass away": an analogy between female and artistic gestation, womb and creative imagination, St. Mary and the artist. "*Deiparae*": giving birth to God. "Three months" may announce the beginning of the third month.

386 : Denying he is a father (creator), Stephen ambiguously calls himself "an eternal son." Note reference to the Scylla and Charybdis episode.

387 : "Remember, Erin, thy generations . . .": a parody of the

Bible (Lamentations, 5:21; Deuteronomy, 32:15) and of the Improperia or Reproaches of the Good Friday Mass. Cf. "Improperial." (*Finnegans Wake*, 484) "Assuefaction minorates . . .": a parody of Sir Thomas Browne.

388 : "The mansion reared by dedal Jack" seems to be *Ulysses* as well as the world. Compare the thunder ("A black crack of noise in the street") with God, a shout in the street. (35) "Nobodaddy" is Blake's God. (Cf. 203) "A natural phenomenon" is scientific Bloom's god. (Cf. 299)

389 : The parody of Bunyan concerns child killing of all sorts. Cf. the passage on contraception in *Finnegans Wake*, 573-75.

391-92 : Deasy's letter on foot and mouth disease has appeared in the paper, says Lenehan. Bloom is dismayed by the slaughter of cows.

395 : Notice Mulligan's ingenious project for the relief of sterility. Ciceronian *"Talis ac tanta depravatio . . ."* is worth the pains of translating.

398 : Bannon has Milly's picture.

404 : Aristotle's "masterpiece": cf. 232. The "elegant Latin poet" on the Minotaur is Ovid.

405 : A parody of the Gothic novel recounts Haines' entrance and Mulligan's remarks. (Cf. 604) Note the association of the "black panther" with the "ghost of his own father."

406 : Bridie Kelly, the bat girl, is Bloom's first best girl. Cf. 434.

408 : Stephen proclaims himself an artist: "I, Bous Stephanoumenos, bullockbefriending bard, am lord and giver of . . . life"; (cf. *Portrait*, 428) but Lynch deflates him. A future artist maybe, this author of "light odes" is no artist yet.

409 : Lynch tells how Conmee surprised him with his girl. (221, 399) Note the theosophical interpretation of Bloom's trance. Cf. p. 407: "Alpha, a ruby and triangled sign," the emblem of Bass.

410 : Lafayette is a photographer. (Cf. 636) "Div. Scep." and the like are degrees conferred by Thomas Henry Huxley.

412 : "Pluterperfect imperturbability" is from Deasy's letter. (34)

413 : "Morbidminded esthete and embryo philosopher" is an apt description of Stephen, no artist yet.

417 : *"Per deam Partulam"*: Partula is goddess of childbirth. "Druiddrum press" and "Most beautiful book . . ." are references to Yeats. Cf. pp. 14, 213.

418 : Dixon speaks of Bloom's bee sting and of Mrs. Bloom, "none of your lean kine."

419 : "Photo's papli": Bloom is identified by Bannon as Milly's father.

420-21 : Macintosh is called "Bartle the Bread." To be sure, he eats dry bread, (251) but why Bartle? Now a lonely vagrant, he was "once a prosperous cit." Bourgeois Bloom's greatest fear is of becoming a "moribund" vagrant. (710) "The johnny in the black duds" (Bloom) "sinned against the light" (Satan) and "shall come to judge the world." (Christ) Elijah is coming. If Dowie, a revivalist promising revival, is announcing Bloom, the remedy "in his backpocket" must be potato or soap. Meanwhile, "Yooka . . . Yook . . . Ook," says someone, vomiting.

CHAPTER XV

Circe

Bella Cohen's whorehouse, to which those drunks lead Bloom, is near the corner of Mabbot and Mecklenburg Streets. A good deal happens here or in the neighborhood, but since more than half the action is interior and all things, whether outer or inner, shift and merge, it is not always easy to tell which is which, who is who or what is what. The "great technical difficulties," bad enough for Joyce, who had to rewrite the chapter six or seven times, are "worse," he said, for the reader. (*Letters*, 142)

The external action is this: Having come by rail from Westland Row to Amiens Street, Stephen and Lynch go to Bella's brothel where they talk to whores and dance to "My Girl's a Yorkshire Girl," rendered on the pianola. Suddenly Stephen lifts his stick and breaks the chandelier. Fleeing down Mecklenburg Street to Beaver Street, he meets two drunken British soldiers, who are to Stephen as the citizen to Bloom. However drunk, Stephen is harmless and reasonable; so one of the soldiers knocks him down. An exile from the society represented by these soldiers and Bloom's citizen, Stephen is a "wild goose," at least potentially. Hence Bloom's pursuit of the exile seems a "wildgoose chase." (444)

Bloom's part in the events of Mecklenburg Street is apparently less eventful than Stephen's. Near the Amiens Street station, Bloom pauses in his chase to buy chocolate, a pig's foot, and a sheep's trotter; but, losing his appetite, he feeds feet to dog as two incurious policemen on their rounds pass by. Arriving at the brothel, Bloom surrenders his potato to Zoe, a whore; for, more than normally ill at ease and out of place, he is submissive at first. Not for long, however. Recalling his mission, recovering himself, he demands and gets his potato back, bravely faces formidable Bella, and takes charge not only of Stephen's money but of his hat and stick. There Bloom stands at last, with all the responsibility and anxiety of a father, over a son supine in Beaver Street.

Stephen is plainly off his feet. Still on his, Bloom has fed feet to dog. Feet, the organs to which this chapter is devoted, are lowest of all. In the zodiac, which also includes man's organs from head to foot, feet, associated with Pisces, are the end of the cycle, which, beginning anew with the Ram, returns to the head.[1] This footy chapter is the lowest point of the day for Bloom and Stephen, the sojourn in darkness that must precede emergence into light. Like the zodiac (conspicuous in the previous chapter), they will rise from what seems an end to begin anew. That the phonograph across the way blares "The Holy City" is appropriate; for this city (from the Apocalypse) means the end of the world. But, a vision of heaven, it also means renewal.

More Apocalyptic than Homeric—indeed, more Germanic— this chapter is a kind of witches' Sabbath, a "*Walpurgisnacht*," as

---

1. Some critics have found this chapter the climax of the book. But, deceived by something "as intricate as it is long," (Joyce's own description of the chapter) those critics have confused nadir with zenith, foot with head. However attractive the confusion of these extremes, we must try to keep them apart, here.

Joyce himself agreed. Yet Homer's Circe is a kind of witch, changing men to swine by potions and brews. Fortified with "moly," an
antidote, Ulysses comes to save his men from Circe's sty. He
waves his sword, makes love, and pigs are men again. They feast
at Circe's board and drink her brew, kept harmless by their cap-
tain in her bed, until, getting up one day, Circe opens her mouth.
Go to Hades, she says.

In Joyce's parody, which is far from close, Bloom seems both
Ulysses and crew. Succumbing to the witchery of Bella Cohen, he
becomes a pig, snuffling for "truffles" (519) as his bestial lower
nature emerges to take charge. "I have been a perfect pig," he
says. (538) The sword of Ulysses is Stephen's stick. Calling it
"*Nothung*," the sword of Wagner's Siegfried, Stephen raises it to
smash Bella's chandelier. (Light is a persistent image in this dark
chapter.) But Stephen's assumption of the role of Ulysses is
momentary. Picking the abandoned ashplant up, Bloom raises it,
too. "Jesus! Don't!" screams Bella-Circe. (569) There are no beds
in her parlor nor is there feasting, unless chocolate serves as feast.
That some kind of moly is there we may be sure, but precisely
where and what were Joyce's problems as they are our own.

"*Moly* is a nut to crack," said Joyce. It can be "laughter, the
enchantment killer," chance, presence of mind, power of recu-
peration or indifference. Bloom's plant has "many leaves." (*Letters*, 142-64, 336) Nothing is likelier, but we must find the plant's
particular embodiment. Our first guess is Bloom's potato, more
conspicuous here than in the earlier chapters. Not only an Irish
seed and root, but "poor mamma's panacea," a "talisman," a
"preservative," and an "heirloom," this potato, emerging from
pocket, is hard, black, and shriveled. (428, 467, 488, 542) The
trouble with potato as moly, however, is that Bloom recovers his
manhood before he gets his surrendered potato back. Therefore,
his trouser button, suddenly breaking loose, seems a better sign.
"Bip!" says the button, (539) reminding Bloom who wears the
pants, recalling "K. 11" (151) and all its promise of renewal.

Magic is the art and hallucination the method of this chapter.
Not only changing things (making this, for example, that), magic

gives body to disembodied things, calling them down or up—the latter for the most part here. Virag, Bloom's sardonic grandfather, who is neither here nor there, becomes bird, moth, dog, the man in the brown macintosh, and Farrell with his monocle. (500 ff.) Bloom's hallucinations share the stage with Stephen's, and at several points Bloom and Stephen share a hallucination—when, for example, as both look into mirror, each sees himself as antlered Shakespeare. (553) But Bloom's hallucinations, more elaborate than Stephen's, are more fascinating.

Bloom's hallucinations, reviewing his day and all his past, put a burden on the inattentive reader; for every character, however slight, every thought, desire or fear, and almost every phrase of the book reappear, reordering themselves. Like the litany of the Daughters of Erin, (488) this chapter summarizes this book. However extensive in space, however, these hallucinations occupy little time. Asked a question, Bloom dreams for twenty pages before coming back to answer it. No more than a moment of time by the clock has passed. The occasion of most visions is a casual phrase.[2] "Do as you're bid," says Zoe, (515) and Bloom responds with suitable vision until that trouser button, snapping, snaps him out of it.

These waking dreams, projected from the subliminal self, consist of commonly buried memories, desires, and fears. Their emergence from the underworld of the mind is encouraged here by fatigue, which weakens conscious resistance to such intrusions, and by guilt. So moved and licensed, the unconscious takes charge of the conscious mind as in a dreamer's bed or in a madhouse. Bloom's nightmares include encounters with his father, his grandfather, his mother, Mrs. Breen, Gerty MacDowell, and even the Nymph on the wall of his bedroom. "A Voice," embodied and suitably dressed in Turkish trousers, reveals the presence of Molly.[3] Everyone accuses Bloom of something. His consequent arraignment and trial for "moral rottenness" take place before a

2. For Joyce too: "A catchword is enough to send me off." (*Letters*, 147)
3. P. 432. "Turkish. Wore the breeches. Suppose she does." (374) The great question in this chapter is who wears the pants? K. 11 and Bloom's tailor (487) are conspicuous.

court, which, like Kafka's, is menacing and incomprehensible.

Despite the embarrassment that attends these portents, Bloom's mind allows a vision of triumph. Becoming Lord Mayor and, like Parnell, an uncrowned king, Bloom acts magnanimously for the good of the people and answers puzzling questions. "For bladder trouble?" asks Pisser Burke. Bloom gives him a prescription. "The parallax of the subsolar ecliptic of Aldebaran?" asks Chris Callinan. "K. 11," says Bloom. Unrolling a scroll, he proclaims: "Aleph Beth Ghimel Daleth Hagadah Tephilim Kosher Yom Kippur . . . ," and Jimmy Henry reads the official translation. (477-79) Such moments of triumph are rare; for most of Bloom's phantasmagoria is masochistic.

Apparently as surrealistic or expressionistic as the rest, these masochistic fantasies are based upon Leopold von Sacher-Masoch's *Venus in Furs*, the case histories in Krafft-Ebing's *Psychopathia Sexualis*, and *Bits of Fun*, a magazine for eccentrics. Masoch, who gave masochism name, was obsessed by man's delight in being dominated by woman. The likelihood that Bloom owes his first name to the author of *Venus in Furs* is improved by Joyce's conviction that Jesus was a masochist, inviting and welcoming pain. As masochist, Leopold Jesus-Bloom, who becomes an infant in the presence of his father, becomes a woman in the presence of those terrible women he adores, while they, transvesting themselves in turn, become men. Bella becomes Bello, and Bloom, unmanned and fittingly dressed in "transparent stockings" and the frilly drawers he is devoted to, becomes Bello's willing slave. Bella-Bello is one with Turkish Molly and with all the horsy, booted, fur-wearing, whip-flourishing ladies of his delight: the Hon. Mrs. Mervyn Talboys, Mrs. Yelverton Barry, and Mrs. Bellingham, all no doubt from the Shelbourne Hotel along with Mrs. Dandrade of the black underthings. He called me "a Venus in furs," says Mrs. Bellingham. The worse the threats of these elegant Amazons, the more Bloom likes it. Being cuckolded by Molly, another pain, is another pleasure.

Not only happy cuckold, offering wife to policemen, (448) not only Dr. Dixon's specimen of "the new womanly man," (483)

Bloom is also husband and father as that trouser button reminds him. Masochistic pig no more, he becomes a man in the waking world, the responsible guardian of Stephen. Not only like Christ, Bloom is also like Ulysses; for each of us is many men or women, and Bloom would seem no queerer than most if the truth were known.

To render Bloom's nightmare Joyce chose the form of a play, complete with speech tags and stage directions—of a dream play like Strindberg's. Since dreams give objective solidity to desires, the form is suitable, far more effective than analysis and far more vivid than the stream of consciousness. Abandoning discourse, psychoanalysis becomes drama. Rising from his couch, the patient walks a stage, attended by a company as solid as he.

Since, showing Bloom up entirely, this chapter is necessarily a summary of the book, it should include the familiar motifs—and most of them, indeed, are here: not only potato, soap, hat, and stick, but Hamlet, Moses, Don Juan, macintosh, race, light, riddle, cow, rose, pot, and dog. Of these the last may serve as first example. Encountered on the way to Bella Cohen's, the dog, once protean (47) and now a victim of Circe's magic, is spaniel, terrier, bulldog, greyhound, setter, mastiff, and retriever by turns. The man in the macintosh, rising through a trapdoor to denounce Bloom, is another dog: "Shoot him! Dog of a christian! So much for M'Intosh!" (475) says Bloom, and M'Intosh disappears again. In the black mass, celebrated by Mulligan and Haines on Mrs. Purefoy's belly, god becomes dog since all is backward in matters of this kind. (583-84) All these dogs, of course, refer somehow to Stephen, the changing beast, slouching toward Eccles Street to be reborn.

Plainly stick implies creative power. Described in the first chapter as Stephen's "familiar" or attendant spirit, the stick trails impotently down the path. (21) Entering Nighttown, Stephen flourishes an ashplant Lynch calls "yellow." [4] "Take up your crutch

4. With his ashplant Stephen shatters light over the world. (425) "Time's livid final flame leaps and, in the following darkness, ruin of all space, shattered glass and toppling masonry." (567-68. Cf. 25)

and walk," says he, advising Stephen to become the artist he pretends to be. (426. Cf. 408) Idle no more, the stick puts out Bella's light, necessarily destroying the old before creating the new. Stephen abandons it. But, rescued by Bloom, the stick comes back to be put, with Bloom's help, to better use. Like moly itself, the ashplant is a tree of life.

But what of the lemon soap, climbing the sky to diffuse light and perfume? Attended by Sweny, the druggist, the soap seems rising sun at night. (433) Can it be Stephen? Your guess about soap is as good as mine. Some may contend that this chapter could do with more light, a better smell, and some cleaning up. But, after all, it is what Lynch calls "pornosophical philotheology. Metaphysics in Mecklenburg street." (425)

424-26 : Stephen's quotations from the Mass for paschal time (Easter) suggest that the whole chapter parodies a Mass, which, concerned with death, predicts rebirth. Stephen's remarks about "gesture" as "structural rhythm" involve aesthetic form. Shakespeare, Socrates, and Aristotle (the stagyrite) are men dominated by women.

428 : The "hattrick" is a dirty Irish trick: an Irishman covers a turd on the curb with his hat. Telling a policeman it is a bird, the Irishman goes off for help, asking the policeman to stand guard. Cf. p. 580.

432 : "Nebrakada," (239, 540) though part of Stephen's experience, is known to Molly and Bloom. Mind-sharing is common in this chapter—as in the collective unconscious.

433 : Compare Sweny's rising soap with soap as dawn and rising son, *Finnegans Wake*, p. 593. This would make Stephen what Dowie called the remedy in Bloom's back pocket. Stephen, like Shaun, will renew the Irish conscience.

434 : *"Ti [mi] trema . . ."* is from *"Là ci darem."* For Bridie Kelly see p. 406. Bloom's guilt evokes Gerty MacDowell.

437 : "Teapot" is a parlor guessing game. "Lemon" is the answer. (439)

441 : Chatting about the "ducky little tammy toque," Bloom becomes a woman for the first time in this chapter.

445 : The approach of two policemen occasions another hallucination. "Bloom. Of Bloom. For Bloom. Bloom" is a pig-Latin declension, ending significantly with the accusative. "Kaw kave kankury kake" is "He gave Banbury cake" in the language of gulls. (151)

446 : For Signor Maffei, the sadist, see p. 64.

448 : The "duegard of fellowcraft" and the "pass [not "past"] of Ephraim" are Masonic signs. See pp. 490, 514, 575, 581, 593 for other signs of Free Masonry.

449 : "Jim Bludso" is an American ballad about a steamboat pilot.

450 : Bloom's trial begins. Cf. Earwicker's trial in *Finnegans Wake*, pp. 85-93. For Beaufoy see p. 68. Bloom is a "soapy sneak."

451 : Bloom leads more than "a quadruple existence."

454 : Bloom's "plasterers' bucket" (cf. 442, 575) seems connected with Molly's pot and all the bowls, tubs, and pots of *Ulysses*.

455 : Notice the references to Moses. Cf. pp. 451, 458, 462.

457 : Paul de Kock's curious novel is *La Dame aux trois corsets*, 1866. Cf. p. 64. Bloom sent Mrs. Bellingham a "homegrown" potato blossom.

461 : Mocking the Benediction, Canon O'Hanlon elevates the cuckoo clock (375-76) or Bloom as Eucharist. "Jigajiga" unites the motif of the loose quoits (56) with Boylan's jaunty jingle. (264) "Gob, he organized her." (314)

462 : For Sir Frederick Falkiner see p. 180.

463-65 : Dog, Dignam, Hamlet's ghost, and rat become one. "Jacobs Vobiscuits" anticipates the verbal method of *Finnegans Wake*. Jacobs is a Dublin baker.

466 : Bloom returns to reality.

468 : "I never loved a dear gazelle" is by Tom Moore. Cf. p. 437. Bloom's vision of Oriental roses in the "womancity" is not unlike his vision of the "new Bloomusalem," (475) another utopia. "*Schorach ani . . .*" is from the Song of Solomon.

469 : Zoe's "Make a stump speech out of it" sends Bloom off into

another hallucination. The chimes of midnight, recalling Dick Whittington, make Bloom Lord Mayor of Dublin.

470 : "Pheasants and partridges," a misprint, should read "peasants and phartridges."

472 : "The wren, the wren" reappears in *Finnegans Wake*, 44.

474 : Bloom is presented with the "keys of Dublin, crossed."

475 : Higgins is the name of Zoe and of Bloom's mother.

476 : The blind stripling is Bloom's "more than Brother."

480 : All the statues of goddesses in the museum represent Venus and Molly.

481 : Bloom associates Lenehan's riddle with Molly and his tramline for cows. Mrs. Riordan, Bloom's friend, is Stephen's "Dante" in *A Portrait*.

482 : Bloom becomes Parnell or Mr. Fox, possibly one of the foxes of Stephen's riddle. Stephen is both Parnell and fox.

483 : "Hypsospadia," a misprint, should be hypospadia, a defect of the genitals.

485-86 : Bloom's line, beginning with Moses and proceeding through Christbaum and Dusty Rhodes (or Macintosh), ends with Emmanuel or Jesus. Cf. "I. H. S." (488, 531)

487 : Reuben J. Dodd and Lynch (585) are Judas.

488 : Bloom's litany, summarizing the chapters, calls attention to motifs and images we might have neglected. Bloom's hallucination ends and he resumes his conversation with Zoe.

491 : Does the "waterproof" hanging in the hall belong to Macintosh? Note the running fox with dog's eyes. Zoe (life); Kitty (animal); Flora (vegetable).

494 : Stephen's remarks about the octave, the fundamental, and the dominant suggest the artist and his image together with the relations of the lyric and the dramatic.

497 : Elijah Dowie says all are Christ: Florry, Stephen, Zoe, and Bloom. God's time, like that of Dublin, is 12.25. "Are you a god or a doggone clod?" asks Dowie, attentive to dog and God.

499 : Mananaan MacLir (A. E. from the library chapter) appears with bicycle pump. (Bloom saw A. E. wheeling a bicycle.) The pump probably means spiritual inflation. Cf. the rusty bicycle

pump in "Araby." Stephen and Bloom co-operate in this vision. Hermes Trismegistus and the twelve signs of the zodiac refer to theosophy and astrology, A. E.'s area.

507 : Philip Drunk and Philip Sober are two aspects of Stephen, "a most finished artist." Maybe they have Matthew Arnold's face to suggest Hebraism and Hellenism or Jewgreek.

510 : Virag's "Panther, the Roman centurion," said to be the father of Jesus, partly accounts for panther as His emblem.

512 : "Antisthenes, the dog sage" or cynic has been associated with Stephen. (147) As Bloom becomes Lord Mayor, Stephen becomes Cardinal, director of the cardinal sins.

513 : As a man (Boylan or Macintosh?) takes the waterproof in the hall, Bloom nervously offers chocolate to Zoe. Chocolate anticipates the cocoa offered later to Stephen.

515 : Bella's Fan says "The missus is master" and Bloom's masochistic vision gets under way. The symptoms seem symbolic rather than literal. Cf. Shem, *Finnegans Wake*, 181.

518 : "Adorer of the adulterous rump": cf. 719.

524 : As a woman, Bloom will be violated by "Signor Laci Daremo." As a man, he has been violated by "*Là ci darem*." The list of Bloom's sexual eccentricities is the product of his guilt. "Where? How? What Time?" (526) is an examination of conscience.

529 : A Rip Van Winkle motif (going away and coming back) has become apparent, pp. 370-71, 485.

534 : Molly's pot suggests Poulaphouca, a waterfall near Dublin. That her pot has "only one handle" recalls the "onehandled adulterer."

543-45 : Stephen's riddle reappears. (27)

546-47 : Broken glasses evoke Father Dolan from A *Portrait*.

548 : "Woman's hand" includes Stephen in the sexual confusion.

549 : Bloom is 38, Stephen 22, 16 years apart.

550 : The whispering of the whores (Sirens now) provokes another hallucination, this time of Boylan and Molly. Bloom's head, like Shakespeare's, is "antlered." (551, 553) The artist seems cuckold as well as deceiver.

554 : Shakespeare's "Weda seca whokilla farst" is from *Hamlet*, III, ii, 183: "None wed the second but who kill'd the first." The "grandold grossfather" who made the "first confessionbox" (artificial cow) for Pasiphaë, is Daedalus.

556-57 : Stephen's prophetic dream of the melon (47) is partly confirmed here.

557-58 : "*Pater!* Free!" refers ambiguously to Daedalus, Simon Dedalus, and Bloom. Encouraged by Simon, Stephen, the fox, flees the hunting pack. Hunt becomes Gold Cup race and Stephen the dark horse, like Swift (40) and Bloom. Mr. Deasy is last.

559 : Stephen's ashplant is an "augur's rod." Dancing with Zoe, (560) Stephen dances with life. Or is it a "dance of death?" (564) "Damn death. Long live life!" says Stephen. (576) In *Finnegans Wake* (195) Shem's creative stick is the "lifewand."

561 : For the dance of the hours see p. 69.

563 : The "*pas seul*" with hat and stick seems more suitable for Stephen.

564-67 : Stephen's mother represents the oppressive past, which, as fox, Stephen thought he had buried. Cf. "Fabled by the mothers of memory." (25, 572) Mother, history, and chandelier seem analogous. "*Non serviam!*" (cf. *Portrait*): Stephen becomes Lucifer, the rebel, a symbol of the "intellectual imagination." But Lucifer, the light bringer, puts out the light. Bloom's candle in the Ithaca episode brings light back. The "green crab" is cancer.

570 : Bloom follows Stephen with "step of a pard." (cf. 215) Corny Kelleher, the undertaker, buried Paddy Dignam.

571 : Abandoning Stephen, the hunting pack pursues Bloom, fox in his turn. Earwicker in *Finnegans Wake* (97) is also the quarry of a hunt and criminal at the bar.

573 : Cissy Caffrey, Gerty's friend, seems actually there. Not so Gerty or the Caffrey twins. (426, 434)

579-80 : Old Gummy Granny (the Poor Old Woman) is Ireland or oppressive tradition. As fox, Stephen has tried to bury his granny.

581 : "Garryowen" is a patriotic song. Stephen's encounter with the soldiers, seems another epitome of nationalistic violence.

"Hahal shalal hashbaz" (from Isaiah) means "Hurry to the spoil."
583 : For Father O'Flynn see p. 334; for the Rev. Hugh Love
see pp. 227, 241-42. Haines means hate, but Love, a grasping land-
lord, hardly means love.
584 : "Htengier Tnetopinmo Dog" is "God Omnipotent Reign-
eth" backwards. Mulligan's mock-Mass (5) celebrates dog. Juxtaposition suggests the similarity of these celebrants and the soldiers.
585 : Not reason, Stephen's stick is probably imagination. The
dog is still around, barking.
591 : That Bloom refuses a lift from the undertaker is significant.
(592) Stephen quotes Yeats' "Fergus" (cf. 11) to the "black panther vampire." The poem is associated with his mother, who
still haunts him; but Yeats has served as father-image. "Doubling
himself together," Stephen assumes foetal posture. Cf. Bloom, p.
722.
593 : Ignorant of Yeats, Bloom thinks Fergus a reference to a
Miss Ferguson. Bloom associates his dead son, Rudy, with Stephen.
That Rudy would be eleven now seems a sign of renewal. Does
the white "lambkin" mean kin of the Lamb or Jesus, the black
panther? Is Stephen the lambkin? Rudy's glass shoes suggest
Cinderella; his helmet is a warrior's; his reading of Hebrew is
scholarly and priestlike; his cane is like Stephen's stick. Bloom's
"ever conceal, never reveal" is the oath of a Mason or "secret
master."

Part III

CHAPTER XVI

Eumaeus

After dusting Stephen off and handing him hat and stick, Bloom
conducts his semi-conscious ward to the cabman's shelter near
Butt Bridge. Here the proprietor, reputed to be Skin-the-Goat,

famous for his part in the infamous affair of Phoenix Park,[1] serves customers, who include an old sailor, back from the sea. It is now one o'clock in the morning of June 17. Everyone is tired. Stephen declines the coffee and bun Bloom offers him. Gradually recovering, Stephen begins to notice Bloom, who, however absurd and ill-informed, is eager, friendly, and unoffending. He shows Stephen Molly's picture, and, since the boy is homeless, invites him home. Ill-matched and talking at cross purposes, ignorant bourgeois and aesthetic vagrant proceed toward Eccles Street, arm in arm.

When Homer's Phaeacians land Ulysses at Ithaca, Athena disguises him and sends him to the hut of Eumaeus, the noble swineherd. Fed pork by his generous host, "prudent and wily" Ulysses tells elaborate lies about himself. However dubious about these stories, Eumaeus fails to penetrate the disguise. Telemachus arrives to get news of Penelope. Ulysses, also moved by Athena, reveals himself to son, and son recognizes father after Athena increases "his bloom." Pending their return, arm in arm and armed, to Penelope, father and son plot the destruction of her suitors.

Skin-the-Goat may do for Eumaeus and Stephen for Telemachus, recognizing father at last. But the part of Ulysses seems divided between Bloom and the old sailor. Bloom plays the part of the recognized father and the sailor, telling elaborate lies, plays that of the disguised voyager. Not only Bloom's surrogate, this ancient mariner is Bloom's disguise. Telemachus is slow to recognize and accept his father. Even slower, Stephen's recognition of fatherly Bloom is less overt than that of his Homeric counterpart and less demonstrative. As the identity of Ulysses is uncertain in Homer, most identities are uncertain here. Is the proprietor Skin-the-Goat himself or the sailor what he claims to be? Plainly Stephen is not quite himself. But Bloom, however hard to recognize, is himself entirely or, better, one of his many selves.

The "ancient mariner" (who is also Sinbad the Sailor and the Flying Dutchman, 620) has much in common with many-sided Bloom. As W. B. Murphy, (608) the mariner suggests not only

1. The Phoenix Park murders and Skin-the-Goat's part in them are described by Myles Crawford, p. 134.

a potato but W. B. Yeats, one of Joyce's father-images. "Shake-speares," says Stephen, (607) "were as common as Murphies." Murphy's "green goggles," recalling the green-eyed sailor of "An Encounter," suggest Moses: "I uses goggles reading. Sand in the Red Sea done that." (643) Who but Moses, walking the bottom of that sea could get sand in the eyes there? *"For England, home and beauty"* (608) echoes the one-legged sailor's refrain. More-over, Murphy has disembarked from "the threemaster *Rosevean* from Bridgwater with bricks," Stephen's passing ship of the pre-vious morning, "a threemaster, her sails brailed up on the cross-trees, homing." (51) Crosstree suggests Christ; three masts sug-gest the trinity of Stephen, Bloom, and Molly (Christ between two thieves?); *Rosevean* seems to include Rose, Eve, and Ann, united in Molly. Bridgwater must seem promising to "a disap-pointed bridge." (26) But what of that cargo of bricks? Bricks are things for builders to build with, matter the artist needs.

Bricks and stones, constantly recurring, are among the principal matters of this chapter. Gumley, a friend of Stephen's father, guards a pile of stones; Parnell's coffin is thought filled with stones; and Molly, whose favorite exclamation is "O rocks!" comes from the Rock of Gibraltar. Asked about Gibraltar, the sailor replies: "I'm tired of all them rocks in the sea." (614) That the bun Bloom offers Stephen is "like one of our skipper's bricks" (618) unites the motif of brick and stone with that of bread, equally important in this chapter.

Offering Stephen bun and coffee, Bloom offers him commun-ion. Bread is bread after all, and coffee (a word which, as Web-ster's dictionary informs us, comes from the Arabic word for wine) does equally well for the other element of the Eucharist. (606, 618-19) The communion of Bloom and Stephen is no more than partial here, however. As Stephen, drinking Bass, has said, (384) the liquid element is his "soul's bodiment. Leave ye fraction of bread to them that live by bread alone." Faithful to this whim, he rejects Bloom's bun; but he takes one sip of coffee. Soul, says Stephen, is "a simple substance"; (618) but Bloom urges his puzzling friend in vain to partake of something more "substantial" than bad coffee. (640) It is shortly after this unsubstantial communion, however, that Stephen, looking into Bloom's eyes, discovers his identity: "*Christus* or Bloom his name is, or, after all, any other, *secundum carnem.*" [2] Any other according to the flesh seems a recognition of Bloom's humanity and humanity itself, of which bad coffee and stale bun are an appropriate sacrament—as appropriate as Cantrell and Cochrane's ginger ale (80) or Epps's cocoa. (642)

Differences of knowledge, temperament, and experience still separate those "noctambules" and imperfect communicants. The one scientific, the other theological, they are "poles apart." (618) Though looking into one another's eyes, "they didn't see eye to eye in everything." Yet "a certain analogy there somehow was"; (640) and in the end they go off together in " '*their low-backed car to be married by Father Maher.*' " The marriage or complete union of Bloom and Stephen, heralded by this quotation from "The Low-backed Car," a popular ballad, will be solemnized in the next chapter, where Stephen will receive communion.

Not unlike those of Artifoni, (225) Bloom's plans for Stephen's future subordinate writing to singing. Bloom, combining concern with concerns, will act as Stephen's manager, both in Dublin and on tour. Providing for Stephen, their connection will improve Bloom culturally and socially as well as financially. He sees Stephen, moreover, as Molly's next lover—as one who could take her mind off vulgar Boylan. (640) Showing Stephen Molly's picture, enlarging upon her already opulent *embonpoint*, and comparing her seductively with those goddesses, Bloom is offering Stephen Molly. Stephen does not understand this offering until the next chapter, where Molly's light will enlighten him.

The motif of Parnell, appearing now and again throughout *Ulysses* and *A Portrait*, is more than usually meaningful in the present chapter. Parnell's adultery, Parnell as a dead man who

2. As Stephen, the young dog, recognizes Bloom, so in Homer, the old dog of Ulysses, lying on a dungheap, recognizes his master.

may return, and the incident of the hat—all refer to Bloom, Molly, or Stephen. As Bloom has rescued and returned Parnell's hat,[3] so he has rescued and returned Stephen's.

"Narrative (old)," the method, illustrates fatigue. As the style of Gerty's monologue reveals her nature, so the style of this chapter, the condition of Stephen and Bloom. Sentences droop and trail off flabbily, nervously exhausted. (Nervous exhaustion requires nerves, the organ of this chapter.) Metaphors mix, infinitives split. All is trite, stale, and dead. "Navigation," the art, may mean dead reckoning.

598 : For the association of Ibsen and Baird see A *Portrait*, p. 436. The motif of bread begins.

599 : Lynch as Judas (cf. 585) makes Stephen Jesus. The motif of stones begins.

600 : For Gumley see p. 134. For Corley, now "on the rocks," see "Two Gallants."

601 : Homeless Stephen will not return to Mr. Deasy's school. Stephen and Corley, unemployed vagrants, are parallel for the moment. Stephen, whose name means crown, gives Corley half a crown.

603 : Boylan, serving here as Penelope's chief suitor, is suitably associated with the "bucket dredger."

606 : Still under Bella-Bello's spell, Bloom says "Bellodonna." The *"voglio"* connects Bello with Molly, the *"prima donna."* (636)

608 : For the motif of Rip Van Winkle see pp. 370-71, 529.

614 : As "a wily old customer," the sailor is "wily" Ulysses.

615-16 : The figure 16, tattooed on the sailor's chest, is puzzling. But Bloom and Stephen are 16 years apart; this is the 16th chapter; and June 16 is the day of Bloom's wanderings. Antonio, though a Greek ("ate by sharks after. Ay, ay."), suggests Shakespeare's *Tempest*. Bloom rejects this possibility. (620) "As bad as old

---

3. P. 639. Like Mr. Menton, when told of his bad hat, (114) Parnell says "Thank you," though "in a very different tone." "History repeating itself with a difference," Bloom concludes.

Antonio" is from "Has Anybody Here Seen Kelly?" For the "streetwalker" see p. 285.

618 : Note the reappearance of Bloom's "natural phenomenon" (299, 388) and his observations on Edison or Galileo. Bloom stands uncertainly for science.

619 : History, suggested by the knife, still bothers Kinch.

621 : Dante's Beatrice (Miss Portinari) as an "isoceles triangle" is enigmatic. Why not equilateral like Bass' mark? "San Tommasso Mastino" is Thomas Aquinas, the mastiff, a "dog of God." Cf. "The bulldog of Aquin." (205) "Washed in the blood of the sun" equates Lamb, sun, and son.

622 : The conversation about wrecks is fitting for a chapter on navigation.

624-28 : Bloom compares nationalistic Skin-the-Goat with the citizen. Though still opposed to violence, intolerance, and hate, Bloom is prudently silent now, publicly at least.

629 : "Ireland must be important because it belongs to me" displays Stephen's egocentricity and pride, still undiminished. If Swift, Yeats, or Joyce were to say this, it would be justifiable. No wonder Bloom is confused.

630 : Worrying about the "mad vagaries" of the aesthetes, Bloom thinks of "section two of the Criminal Law Amendment Act," under which Wilde was convicted.

631 : Rivalling Beaufoy is still Bloom's hope. Like the sailor, Bloom is "a bit of a literary cove in his own small way." (643)

631-32 : The *Telegraph* contains Mr. Deasy's letter, an account of the Gold Cup race, and Hynes' report of Dignam's funeral, attended by M'Coy, Stephen, M'Intosh, and L. Boom.

634 : Oddly, Bloom's sympathies in the Parnell case are not with the injured husband but with the suitor, "strong to the verge of weakness, falling a victim to her siren charms, and forgetting home ties." What sort of Ulysses is this?

637 : Thinking of bringing Stephen home, Bloom remembers bringing home a dog with "a lame paw." Stephen has hurt his hand—"not that the cases were either identical or the reverse."

645 : "Bid me to live and I will live thy protestant to be,"

hardly a Protestant hymn, as Bloom supposes, is a song by Robert Herrick. Bloom's ignorance is as many-sided and absurd as he. *Don Giovanni* and *Martha* reappear.

647 : "Image of his mother," is Stephen the image of Ireland, too? That he sings a song of Sirens on his way to Molly seems significant. Not only Circe, she is Siren, cause of shipwrecks, enemy "of man's reason," (649) and seaside girl.

649 : Horse and driver are suggestive. The horse creates "three smoking globes of turds" and the driver "humanely" waits "till he (or she) had ended." Is Stephen, creator of a three-part aesthetic theory, the horse, and Bloom the driver? Discussing Sirens and "usurpers" (suitors), Bloom and Stephen proceed up Gardiner Street.

CHAPTER XVII

Ithaca

A "parallel course" (650) takes Bloom and Stephen to 7 Eccles Street. Keyless (but competent) Bloom enters his home through area and basement, opens the front door to Stephen, and the two descend to the kitchen. There, where his day commenced, Bloom makes cocoa, and, while drinking it, these two talk. They get along famously together. But when Bloom, who has plans for Stephen, invites him to stay, he declines with gratitude and regret. Host accompanies departing guest to the back yard where they see the light in Molly's window. It is 2.30 A.M. by St. George's clock. Dawn, early in Ireland in June, approaches. Stephen goes off down the alley and Bloom goes into his parlor. Here he contemplates his possessions, his state, and his future. Then to bed where, as he falls asleep, Molly questions him about his day. His answers are prudently selective.

The Homeric counterpart concerns the slaughter of suitors, a problem for Joyce, who, hating hate and violence, once thought the slaughter "un-Ulyssean." (*Letters*, 160) Bloom detests all "violaters of domestic connubiality," (701) all Molly's suitors, a series of twenty-five at present, but "so on to no last term." (716) Though he destroys these intruders, their destruction is odd. Adjusting himself to what cannot be helped, and to what, after all, is better than cruelty or general disaster, he accepts things as they are, making the best of them. He destroys these intruders by "equanimity." (717-18) Not only masochistic, he is civilized and pretty reasonable, all things considered.

The killing of the suitors is the climax of Homer's *Odyssey*, but, although this chapter is the climax of *Ulysses*, as Circe is its lowest depth, Bloom's moral victory is less climactic than other things. That he asks Molly to bring him breakfast in bed (as we discover in the next chapter, 723) is a triumph—though, knowing Molly, we may ask what he asks for that for.[1] There are three (or, to be precise, four) greater elevations, however, within this climactic chapter: cocoa first, then the light in the window, and then Molly's "melons." The first two mark the goals of Stephen's quest, the last, of Bloom's.

His quest is for home. When he gets there he finds an empty pot of Plumtree's Potted Meat in the kitchen and a few flakes of the stuff in Molly's bed. (659, 716) Molly and Boylan have eaten the rest. With or without Plumtree's Potted Meat, at once complete and incomplete, Bloom's home is the best he has and there he is at last: "Weary? He rests. He has travelled." (722) Without plums for Bloom maybe, his home abounds in melons. (719) Curling up beside them, Bloom is not unlike babe in womb, Dignam in tomb, cod in pot, or potted meat itself.[2]

Stephen's unconscious quest is for charity, humanity, maturity, and self. Discovering Bloom ("Everyman or Noman," 712), Stephen discovers mankind. Joining Bloom, he becomes himself.

1. The "lightbreakfastbringer" of *Finnegans Wake*, (473) celebrating the union of Shem and Shaun, recalls the union of Stephen-Lucifer and Molly's Bloom. In *Finnegans Wake* breakfast commonly serves as symbol of renewal, associated, of course, with dawn.
2. Not of Plumtree, Bloom's disapproval centers upon the nature and placing of its advertisement. The anagrams on Plumtree suggest various ways of looking at and rendering the same thing. (668) Imitation may imply art.

"Blephen" sits down with "Stoom" (666)—not that the two elements of Blephen Stoom, the new compound, are identical. Still opposites, they are united for the moment by Bloom's love and Stephen's apprehension. Their "coincidence" (669) reveals hitherto "concealed identities." (674) Given understanding of humanity by Bloom's humanity, no longer separated by pride and childish ego from every other man, Stephen sees himself as everyman, himself grown up.[3]

If sitting down in the cabman's shelter is the rite of "atonement" (714) or of the at-oneness of Bloom and Stephen, their sitting down together in the kitchen celebrates communion or the sacramental sealing of togetherness. Stephen receives the body of his "host" (660) in the kitchen, a place for creating. Not only host but priest, officiating in a kind of Mass (and a better celebrant than Mulligan), Bloom creates the host, a "massproduct, the creature cocoa." (661) Whatever the extent of their atonement in the cabman's shelter, Stephen refuses more than a sip of coffee there. Now a better communicant, he drinks Bloom's cocoa down. Coffee, according to Webster's dictionary (as we have noticed), is Arabic wine. According to Webster, cocoa is "*theobroma*" to botanists; and *theobroma* is Greek for "god food." Receiving Bloom's god food, Stephen, the young dog pretending to be god, becomes a god. Through "creature" (or created) cocoa he puts on creative power, becoming potential creator or artist at last.[4] Communing with everyman is art's preliminary and its condition.

So prepared and conditioned, Stephen goes off to encounter

3. The statue of Narcissus, (695, 713) also brought home by Bloom, suggests an earlier, mirror-gazing Stephen. The hand of Bloom's statue is broken (751) and Stephen has hurt his hand. Molly definitely connects the statue with Stephen. (761)

4. Maybe now Stephen can realize his desire: "the eternal affirmation of the spirit of man in literature." (650) Molly's more compendious, less literary, "yes" is a similar affirmation. Cocoa, celebrating communion, may imply co-co or with-with. Cf. "cocoincidences" and "Cocoa Codinhand," (*Finnegans Wake*, 467, 597) which combines cocoa with fish and tool in the context of "our national umbloom." Cf. "coaccoackey." (*Finnegans Wake*, 516)

reality for the million and first time and to reforge that experience in the smithy of his soul. Off he goes down the lane to the sound of a "jew's harp." (689) A Jew's harp could be an Irish poet created by a Jew—Mulligan's "jew jesuit" (213) in this case. God the Father is a Jew, according to Bloom the father. The hunt for the father is over; for Blephen is the father found. That this is all as "jocoserious" (661) as Bloom's sacrament is not surprising in a book where things divine are all too human and all too human things divine.

First question: Why, becoming Bloom, does Stephen leave him? Why not? If "centrifugal departer" were to stay with "centripetal remainer," (688) that now frustrated departer would remain a simple bourgeois, not the creative coincidence of bourgeois and vagrant that Bloom has made him. Bloom has done his job, and Stephen necessarily goes off to do his. An artist, according to Joyce, is an exile from the bourgeois society that creates him. A son, reared by father, does not stay with father but goes off to rear a son.

Second question: Why do Bloom and Stephen appear to change places at the end? Stephen, the child, goes off to be a man; whereas Bloom, the man, getting into bed with a kind of mother, becomes "the childman weary, the manchild in the womb."[5] Father and son, God and Jesus, Ulysses and Telemachus, Bloom and Stephen are aspects of the same person, now the one and now the other, more or less. Child now, Bloom will be man again tomorrow. Man now, Stephen will be childish enough, often enough, God knows. Childman is manchild, as every woman knows.

Third question: Finding self and departing may constitute success for Stephen, but what sort of success is Bloom's foetal retreat? What sort of success is getting home to that home? As everyman, Bloom pursues a round, going away from home in the

5. P. 722. Bloom's position in bed, head to Molly's feet, is foetal. (Cf. Stephen, 592) Door, gate, kitchen, and Bloom's "surgical" hands suggest womb and birth. Note the "male key" in the "female lock." (688)

morning, coming back at night. Tomorrow for Bloom, like today, will be another day. But getting back, a daily success, is a
success, however unfinal.

A problem and several frustrations mar Bloom's success today.
"Who was M'Intosh?" remains a "selfinvolved enigma." Among
frustrations are failure to get tea[6] from Kernan, to get the low-
down on goddesses, and to get crossed keys for Keyes. (714)
Like all things, journey's end is mixed, like its beginning. As St.
George's bell chimes half past two, Stephen thinks again of the
dead mother he has thought himself rid of and Bloom again of
Dignam, (688-89) but that same bell heralds proximate dawn.
Thinking of death, Bloom returns to house and bed. Circum-
spectly, prudently, and reverently, he enters the bed of concep-
tion, birth, consummation, adultery, sleep, and death. (715-16)
Thinking of death, Stephen issues forth from Bloom's gate, reborn. Life and death are the reality each encounters and we are
also faced with.

Understanding Bloom and seeing himself in Bloom or Bloom
in him are only part of what departing Stephen takes along. His
final enlightenment is the sight of Molly's window, a "visible
luminous sign," a light shining in darkness.[7] Not lamp alone en-
lightens Stephen but Bloom's discourse on its meaning. "How
did he elucidate the mystery of an invisible person, his wife
Marion (Molly) Bloom, denoted by a visible splendid sign, a
lamp?" (687) By methods both descriptive and suggestive, by
adoration and affirmation. It is a credit no less to Stephen's imagination and sensibility than to Bloom's suggestive eloquence that
Stephen is able to share Bloom's vision. Understanding Bloom
has prepared the way for the fundamental and more charitable
understanding that Molly demands. What Stephen apprehends is

6. "*Thea*" to botanists, we recall, tea means goddess. As "family tea," (70)
not to be asked for in a graveyard, tea means home.

7. Molly's light reverses and brings to a climax the motif of darkness shining in
brightness, pp. 27, 29, 49. Having put out Circe's lamp, Stephen accepts
Molly's. Bloom carries a lighted candle, bringing light to the gentile; (660,
682) Stephen carries hat and stick.

revealed in the next chapter. Knowing Bloom and Molly, as every writer must, Stephen knows humanity entirely. Let him go away now and write about it.

Not only the writer's subject, Molly is his Muse, directing him, furnishing power. Looking up at her window, Bloom and Stephen make water as if, by making it, acknowledging the water of life —as if by this inconsiderable creation celebrating all creation.[8]

Fourth question: Is such celebration either suitable or seemly? This is a "jocoserious" book, remember, unlimited by middle-class decencies or habits of mind. Consider biscuit tin, bathtub, snot, and cocoa. The indecorous, the vulgar, and the commonplace reveal the higher things. If cocoa is adequate for Eucharistic wine, why not piss for this? That making water as sign of creation is not altogether adult seems a less trivial objection. But that is a matter for debate among biographers, students of comedy, arbiters of elegance, and psychologists with time on their hands.

Two parallels, one of Dante, the other of Moses, enlarge the meanings. Hinted by Stephen's rendition of the 113th Psalm, Dante's four meanings (one literal, the others allegorical) seem clues to Joyce's method.[9] That Bloom and Stephen, leaving the house, look up at the stars (683) seems another hint of Dante; for each part of his *Comedy* ends with a vision of stars. With this Dantesque preparation, the light in Molly's window seems to correspond to Dante's Paradiso, and the "concentric circles," (721) cast by Molly's lamp, to Dante's ultimate vision. His Paradise is a gigantic rose with Mary at the center. Marion (a variety of Mary) is the Rose of Castille; but what seems more

8. Compare Mrs. Bloom on pot. (755) Her going to it is the only action of the last chapter.

9. "*In exitu Israël Egypto*," the 113th Psalm in the Vulgate (114th in the King James version), is used by Dante as example of his four meanings in the epistle to Can Grande that introduces the *Paradiso*. Bloom may lead a "quadruple existence" (451) because of Joyce's Dantesque method. The stars may indicate exit from either Hell or Purgatory, probably the latter. Compare the parodies of Dante in "Grace" and *A Portrait*. The numbers 3 and 9 also suggest Dante. (e.g. 684) That Dante's journey takes place on Good Friday, Holy Saturday, and Easter Sunday may account for much of Joyce's imagery, many of his allusions.

significant, her birthday is September 8, the Nativity of the Blessed Virgin. (720) In her way, then, Marion recalls Mary, as Bloom in bed recalls the Infant Jesus. This analogy (which is not identity) serves to multiply already multiple meanings. Marion, with Dante's help, is to the Blessed Virgin as Joyce's paradise to Dante's. Joyce's paradise—and Bloom's—is not only earthly but earthy.

The 113th Psalm also suggests Moses, though not for the first or last time in this chapter. Stephen repeats his parable, "A Pisgah Sight of Palestine." (669-71) "Where," asks Bloom, "was Moses when the candle went out?" (714) Molly's melons are "redolent of milk and honey," (719) like the Promised Land, which, however near, Moses-Bloom does not enter. Yet, taking a Pisgah sight, he has pointed the way to his follower, who, as *"domus Jacob,"* seems to belong at last to the company of James.

Concerning his method and manner: they are as inhuman and objective as the theme is human and subjective. Science is the art and skeleton the organ. Form and manner are those of the catechism: questions and answers reducing all to abstraction, as science, abstracting in its turn, reduces all to matter, measure, and motion. Joyce's letters, revealing his intentions, throw some light on these "dry rock" pages, this "mathematical catechism." In Ithaca, says Joyce, "All events are resolved into their cosmic, physical . . . equivalents . . . so that the reader will know everything and know it in the baldest and coldest way." (*Letters*, 164) There seem other reasons too. A union of science and catechism in art suggests the union of Bloom (scientific) with Stephen (theological and artistic). If the highest form of art, according to Stephen's aesthetic, is the dramatic or the impersonal, the objective impersonality of this chapter seems appropriate for his aesthetic triumph—and also its parody. Stephen has gone a long way from the lyricism of the first chapters. Moreover, the reduction of humanity to inhumanity in a celebration of humanity is not only unexpected and amusing but a commentary on our times. "I like the episode myself," said Joyce, "I find it of a tranquilising spectrality." (*Letters*, 176) He told Frank Budgen that this chapter was his favorite. And I, though less of a Joycean than Joyce, find it my favorite, too.

The matter of the chapter seems more or less scientific. There are weights and measures aplenty, inches and ounces. There are passages on hydraulics, microbiology, astronomy—from Bloom's point of view. His sense of the vastness of the heavens, the insignificance of man, lost in the "cold of interstellar space," and the vanity of his concerns is not unlike Thomas Hardy's. The listing of environmental details reminds one of naturalism or literature with scientific pretensions. But actually there is almost nothing scientific here. Grotesque in diction, outrageous in manner, the construction is more Rabelaisian than Newtonian. As for naturalism: if naturalistic at all, the chapter is the reduction of naturalism, by parody, to absurdity. The details of environment that show Bloom forth again—the furnishings of his room and the contents of his drawers—are Flaubertian, reminding one of *Bouvard et Pécuchet* or of *Madame Bovary*. Scientist or householder, Bloom is pathetic and absurd, like every man—although, like everyman, not without heroism and dignity.

Suggesting science maybe, Bloom's stars are there to serve as metaphor. The correspondences are astrological. Not Copernicus, still less Newton, but rather Hermes Trismegistus or Thoth, Stephen's "god of writers," (*Portrait*, 493) presides over this affair. "As above, so below," said Hermes-Thoth, joining macrososm with microcosm, like Stephen, a declared agent of their relationship. (682) Not for astronomers, the moon is here to suggest "affinities" with Molly. (686) Cassiopeia and the collision of stars are here to suggest Stephen, Shakespeare, and Bloom. (685) A meteor, flashing from Lyra to Leo (from lyric to dramatic) also corresponds to Stephen. (688) As comet, Bloom departs and returns, in orbit around the earth; (712) and the earth is Molly. "Gea-Tellus" (721) or earth-earth, redundant, abundant, Molly is central to comet and meteor. She is the earth, the melon-bearing earth, and true Agendath. She is the Promised Land.

"*Ithaque* est très étrange," said Joyce to Valery Larbaud. (*Letters*, 175) "*Pénélope* le dernier cri."

651 : The "matutinal cloud . . . no bigger than a woman's hand" (cf. 11, 61) suggests "A Little Cloud," parallax, and Molly.

652-53 : "Golden number" and "epact," used in calculating the date of Easter, indicate the rise after Bloom's fall, and, ultimately, Stephen's Easter.

654 : Stephen's addresses are those of Joyce, but that does not make Stephen Joyce. Earwicker's addresses in *Finnegans Wake* (420-21) are also Joyce's. Kate Morkan ("The Dead") is Stephen's godmother, Gabriel's aunt. In many ways Stephen and Gabriel are parallel.

655-57 : The waterlover's meditation on water prepares for making water and rebirth. Like Mother Grogan, (14, 214) Bloom is a "watercarrier" (Aquarius in the zodiac as well as Leo). Note reference to zodiac, p. 667. As "hydrophobe," Stephen is still a dog. Lemon soap (used now for obstetrical or ritualistic washing) makes its last appearance. It was not bought 13 hours earlier. (Bloom's error or Joyce's?) Washing the hands occurs in the Mass before consecration and communion.

659-60 : Is the Gold Cup, in this context, a chalice? Bringing "Light to the gentiles" (St. Paul), especially to Stephen, is Bloom's function.

661 : "Imitation Crown Derby" involves the coincidence of hats —of Bloom's high grade ha with Stephen's crown (Stephen means crown). "Imitation" implies art or forgery. Bloom gives Stephen Molly's cream (compare the "creamfruit" Bloom has offered Stephen in a dream). Every word is loaded in this climactic passage. Three sips to one involves the three-to-one preponderance of water over land (655) and three baptisms to one. (666)

662 : "*The world is mine.*" Molly is the world.

663 : Less mathematics than mathematical fooling, but it indicates relationship. 16 is the number tattooed on the ancient mariner's chest. (615-16)

664 : Mrs. Riordan (Dante) left Stephen's home shortly after the Christmas dinner in *A Portrait*.

668-69 : "Queen's Hotel" (Molly's home?) is a "coincidence." The theme of this chapter is the coincidence of Bloom and Stephen. Do the anagrams on Plumtree, (668) parallel to those on Bloom, (662) imply that he is imitation Plumtree?

670-71 : "What to do with our wives" is Bloom's problem and every man's.

672 : Quotation of significant passages from Gaelic and Hebrew provides further evidence of union. Stephen's quotation concerns walking away and Bloom's (from the Song of Solomon) fruit or Molly. That Stephen writes Irish characters in *The Sweets of Sin* is no less significant. Jesus is the Sweet of Adam's sin.

673-74 : "*Kolod* . . ." is the anthem of Israel. To Stephen Bloom is the past (history); to Bloom Stephen is the future.

674 : "The traditional figure of hypostasis" (underlying substance) is the image of Jesus as fixed by saints and doctors.

675 : "The jew's daughter" in green suggests not only Milly but the Irish church. Stephen's Chaucerian song may function in the parody of the Mass.

676 : Not only host, Jesus-Bloom is "victim predestined." Stephen too, apparently.

678 : Milly and the cat are alike and unalike, like all analogues. Unlike Milly, the cat comes home. (682)

679-80 : Bloom dreams of Stephen's marriage to Milly after an affair with Molly. Remember that Bloom has offered Stephen a melon.

681 : The "clown in quest of paternity" is mysterious. Stephen?

682 : "Diaconal Hat": Stephen is still a deacon, not yet a priest, of the imagination. Father Bloom's candle suggests the Mass for Holy Saturday, which, centering on the Paschal Candle, celebrates new light in darkness, enlightment heralding the morrow (Easter). In this Mass (Joyce's favorite) "the light of Christ" disperses "the darkness of the whole world," as God's light guided "Moses when he went out of Egypt." A deacon assists at this preparation for renewal. Cf. Stephen's "introit for paschal time." (424)

683 : The "heaventree" is Stephen's poetic and Christian interpretation of the stars, which scientific Bloom rejects. (686)

685 : For Cassiopeia see pp. 49, 207. "The collision and amalga-

mation in incandescence" of two dark suns suggests the union of Bloom and Stephen and its result, a nova.

686 : That scientific Bloom rejects astrology as "fallacious analogy" seems ironic in this astrological and zodiacal context.

689 : The "new solar disk" implies renewal, new son.

691 : For Mulligan on green see p. 417. Bloom uses Agendath (which, having arrived in the vicinity of Molly, he needs no longer) to light the cone of incense, important in the Mass for Holy Saturday. Bloom intends fumigation, not worship. In the *Odyssey*, Ulysses fumigates his home with sulphur.

692 : Clock, tree, and owl (all defunct) seem symbols of Bloom's marriage. Is Bloom's "dwarf tree" a Plumtree? Cf. Stephen's "Heaventree." (683, 686) Like *Ulysses* itself, Bloom is "ipsorelative" (a reflexive, self-contained organization of cross references) and "aliorelative" (externally referential).

693 : Bloom's library contains several significant volumes, *The Hidden Life of Christ* (black boards), for example, and *Plain Elements of Geometry*. Geometry is measuring the earth (Molly).

695 : Trouser button and bee sting reappear.

696 : Bloom's expense account provides a review of his day.

697 : Bloom dreams of a house in the suburbs. Like all advertising men, he wants to be a commuter.

703 : Bloom's schemes for wealth are at once practical and impractical, pathetic and funny: e.g., reclaiming the wasteland as proposed by Agendath, finding a use for human excrement (immense in quantity), constructing a tramline to the cattle market— all favoring fertility. He knows, however, that few desires are realizable. (704)

705 : The list of Bloom's possessions reflects the concern of Homer's Odysseus with his possessions.

706 : The "reserved [should be "reversed"] boustrophedontic . . . cryptogram," when solved, yields Martha's name and address. Is Martha Clifford really Peggy Griffin? (448) Bloom's chest measurements are incredible. If his collar is 17, his neck is half as large as his chest. His "wonderworker" should have pleased Virginia Woolf.

709 : The ineffable "tetragrammaton" is Hebrew YHWH or Yahweh.

710 : Bloom's bourgeois fear of becoming a bum may reflect the return of Ulysses in the guise of a vagrant, vagabond or beggar.

712 : Bloom will always return—like comet, "estranged avenger" (Ulysses or Monte Cristo), "silver king" (H. A. Jones) or sleeper awaking (H. G. Wells and Rip Van Winkle).

713 : Bloom's day is recapitulated as a series of Hebrew rites.

714 : Bloom's position in bed, probably more than foetal, could refer to foot and mouth.

716 : The catalogue of lovers includes Penrose, Lenehan, Menton, Simon Dedalus, and two of Bloom's former employers, Cuffe and Hely.

717 : Bloom's "equanimity" is equivalent to Molly's "yes."

721 : Bloom has been exiled physically from Molly for ten years or so. Narrator-Listener: Homer's Ulysses tells Penelope of his adventures, keeping her awake. "Gea-Tellus": In *Finnegans Wake* (257) A. L. P. is "Gran geamatron." Bella Cohen represents the dark and terrible side of the Great Mother, Molly the benevolent.

722 : The rigmarole of Sinbad the Sailor, representing the coming of sleep, ends with dark and light (darkness shining in brightness?). A large black dot after "Where?" has been omitted in this careless edition. That dot, were it here, could imply black-out or darkness in brightness.

CHAPTER XVIII

Penelope

Ithaca, said Joyce in one of his letters, is the end of *Ulysses*; and so it is if the book is a story of a double quest, that of Bloom for home and that of Stephen, prepared by Bloom, for reality. Ithaca is the end of the action. More than an afterthought, however, Penelope is a vision of what those seekers find. For its apprehen-

sion understanding as great as theirs, as much humanity, and a
readjustment no less profound than Stephen's may be required,
but there is little need of explanation. All is evident. There great
Molly lies, evading all habits and ideas, exceeding them. There
she lies, an offering to Boylan, Bloom, and Stephen, and to our
sensibilities. To understand her is to understand all, and to understand that, as the Frenchman said, is to forgive. I accept Molly
as the American lady accepted the universe—and I should be a
fool not to. Nevertheless, born on Depot Street, reared on Main
Street, onetime scholar of two Sunday schools (one Episcopalian,
the other Congregationalist), member of a poor but decent pro-
fession, I am glad not to be married to this particular embodiment of everything. Maybe everything is good for everybody, but,
as the Englishman said, there can be too much of a good thing.
Molly's monologue is a vision of abundance—of over-abundance.
"Nevertheless," as dying Ibsen said.

Molly has the last word and that word is "Yes." Although some
critics think her yes means no, I think her yes means yes. This
word, which D. H. Lawrence tried again and again to say, is the
meaning of *Ulysses*. At once particular and general, Molly's yes is
an affirmation of life.[1]

Let Joyce describe his final chapter, the *"clou"* of his book:

It begins and ends with the female word *Yes*. It turns like the huge
earthball slowly surely and evenly round and round spinning. Its
four cardinal points being the female breasts, arse, womb and . . .
expressed by the words *because, bottom . . . woman, yes*. Though
probably more obscene than any preceding episode it seems to me
to be perfectly sane full amoral fertilisable untrustworthy engag-
ing shrewd limited prudent indifferent *Weib. Ich bin das Fleisch
das stets bejaht.*[2]

Unflattering word perhaps, *Weib* recalls Goethe's *"ewig Wei-*

1. "I did say yes," says Father G. M. Hopkins, who means what Molly means.
The "wee follyo" of *Finnegans Wake* (197) is at once Anna Livia and *Ulysses*.
"Wee" means small and *oui* or yes. Cf. *Finnegans Wake* (604): "Oyes! Oyeses!
Oyesesyeses!" On p. 425 of *Finnegans Wake Ulysses* is called a "trifolium
librotto, the authordux Book of Lief."
2. *Letters*, 170. The fourth of Joyce's cardinal points was suppressed by Stuart
Gilbert, editor of the *Letters*, in the interests of delicacy.

bliche" or female principle. More than individual woman, more than everywoman, Molly is woman's essence.

All the women of the book—Milly, Martha, Gerty, Miss Douce, Mrs. Purefoy, Mrs. Breen, and Bella Cohen—all those seaside girls—are aspects of Molly. Like most women, she dislikes most women. Impatient with Milly, she is catty about Mrs. Breen. As for Kathleen Kearney, a rival in song, Kathleen is a "sparrowfart."

Though Molly likes most men, she is to men as being is to becoming, a little contemptuous. Seeking, thinking, and fretting about this or that, men come and go, worrying about syntax, but she, making men seem peripheral and all their concerns irrelevant, goes on forever, as constant as the inconstant moon. The little cloud no bigger than a woman's hand, observed by Stephen and Bloom, has filled the sky, come down in shower, become a stream—not only the stream of Molly's consciousness but her more commodious stream. Mother Grogan's tea and water pot of the first chapter has become Molly's in the last. Potted Molly likes Plumtree's Potted Meat; for, great-rooted bloomer, she is pot, plum, and meat, without which home is incomplete.[3] (How can we know the potted from the pot?) Meat or flesh, she is flesh for the skeleton of Ithaca.

Not only flesh, pot, tree, cloud, water, and moon, she is "flower of the mountain," [4] whether that mountain is Gibraltar or Howth. She is the force that drives the flower through its green fuse. ("Yes we are flowers all a womans body yes." 767) She is the flowering, fruitful earth, and melons are her hemispheres. Beyond good and evil, at once artless and creative, she unites the ignominy and glory of creation. "Its only nature," as she says. (762) "Like it or lump it." (730)

Whether collective or essential, Molly as voice of nature seems one of those residues of racial experience that haunt the darkness of our minds to emerge in dream or literature with hints of all but unspeakable significance. Among such archetypes (that include

3. P. 726. Homerically, Molly's Plumtree corresponds to the olive tree that grows from the center of Penelope's bed. Homer calls Penelope "steadfast." Molly is bedsteadfast.
4. Or in the words of Father Hopkins, "bole and bloom together."

the circle, the voyage, death and rebirth) is the great figure of the Woman—for Jung the *Anima* and for anthropologists the Great Mother, who preceded and created gods and tried to manage them. Acclaiming her in *The White Goddess*, Robert Graves laments her displacement by the masculine divinities she bore. Incredibly ancient, she is earth, creative principle, and life force. Venus is one of her vestigial embodiments in classical times, the Virgin Mary another in the Christian era. Gods of a sort, Bloom and Stephen walk the earth. Bloom adores a stony Venus in the museum, and Stephen, despite his repeated preference for father, adores the Virgin Mary still—"the figure of woman as she appears in the liturgy of the church." (*Portrait*, 515) Looking up at Molly's window, Blephen apprehends Venus-Mary-Molly. As Molly, she is "human all-too-human" but as *Anima* or Great Mother, she is "prehuman and presumably posthuman." (*"Letters*, 160, 180)

To render this archetype, Joyce chose another: the circle, without beginning or end, turning from yes to yes and turning again —the very form he was to choose for *Finnegans Wake*. Here as there, the circle is divided into parts. The "unpunctuated monologue" of Penelope revolves in "eight sentences." (*Letters*, 170, 206) Whether these "sentences" differ from one another in theme or character I am unable to say. Someone someday may prove that the first four correspond to Molly's four cardinal points and that the second four correspond to these points over again. The cardinal points are certainly there, lost in the great confusion. But that some structure underlies apparent flux is what we should expect of Joyce. Why eight sentences? I have no idea but I can try: Molly was born on the eighth (the Virgin's day), Stephen is fascinated by the octave, and the system of Giambattista Vico (used in Nestor and *Finnegans Wake*) is a cycle of four recurring parts. In *Finnegans Wake*, the eighth chapter, devoted to Anna Livia Plurabelle, another Molly, celebrates renewal. Eight lying down (as Mrs. Bloom commonly is) is a sign of infinity.

Apparent incoherence and lack of punctuation suggest Molly's absence of mind. With neither art nor mind, she seems formal

Stephen's opposite. Yet there are signs of coherence in her monologue. "Love's Old Sweet Song" and "In Old Madrid," constantly recurring, serve as motifs. And whatever the straying of her thought (if one can call it that), it always returns to Bloom,[5] who seems not only comet in orbit around her, but the axis on which she turns. Her speculations about Stephen and her designs upon him are no more than the attention we give to meteors.

Bloom to her is man in all his aspects: infant, Byronic lover, sympathetic understander, responsible husband, cuckold, and an odd one, "mad on the subject of drawers." He is "beyond everything." Once he "wanted to milk me into the tea." "If I only could remember the one half of the things and write a book out of it." (739) Plainly, she inspired someone else to do that.

723 : *Yes, because, woman,* and *bottom,* the four key words, occur on the first page. Molly's monologue begins and ends with yes and Bloom. The reference of the pronoun "he" is usually indefinite and uncertain since men are man to her.

724 : Mr. Menton is the first suitor to be mentioned, but almost all listed in the catalogue (716) appear, even Father Corrigan. In Homer the spirits of the slaughtered suitors appear in the fields of asphodel. Molly is both field and flower though hardly flower of death.

726 : The thunder (natural phenomenon to Bloom, terror for Stephen) woke Molly up, suggesting God, in whom she firmly believes.

728 : Bloom "knows a lot of mixed up things especially about the body." Molly seduced Bloom as Ann Hathaway seduced Shakespeare. (189, 194)

729 : The second sentence begins. Not quite sentence maybe, but still less paragraph.

732 : Bloom sent her eight poppies for her birthday, the eighth.

736 : Bloom gave her Rabelais to read, shocking her.

5. Homer's Penelope, though slow to recognize Ulysses, prefers him to the suitors. Molly's obsessive return to Bloom may imply Penelope's belated recognition of Ulysses.

738 : The third sentence begins. The fourth begins on p. 739, the fifth on p. 744, the sixth on p. 748, and the seventh on p. 755.

744 : Notice Don Miguel de la Flora and "there is a flower that bloometh." (Cf. 506)

746 : She thinks bloomers named after Bloom.

749 : Cat, bee, and Gold Cup reappear.

751 : Milly broke the hand of Bloom's Narcissus. Molly had it mended. The poet's hand?

753 : Stephen and the dog are reunited.

756 : Bloom lies in bed like a Hindu god "with his big square feet up in his wifes mouth."

759 : The meditation on Stephen begins.

760-61 : Stephen is a poet and "they all write about some woman in their poetry well I suppose he wont find many like me." Stephen is like Narcissus, like a god. She will read a book, the better to seduce him. She can "teach him the other part," and he will write a book about her. Boylan "doesnt know poetry from a cabbage." The period at the end of the seventh sentence is a misprint.

763 : Molly's Bloom is "the great Suggester." Ours too.

764-65 : Molly on women: "We are a dreadful lot of bitches." She is willing to bring Stephen breakfast in bed and provide room for his "scribbling." But let Bloom bring breakfast to Molly and Stephen. She would get red Turkish slippers. "Masetto" (Bloom) is the last appearance of the Don Giovanni parallel.

766 : The time is now 3.15. "I love flowers," says Molly, the rose, "Id love to have the whole place swimming in roses God of heaven."

767 : Praise of God, nature, and all abundance: wheat, cattle, flowers, sea, river. Beginning with Gibraltar, her meditation ends at Howth, among Bloom's rhododendrons. (Cf. 173) According to Webster's dictionary, rhododendron means rose tree, as suitable for Molly as Plumtree—suitable too for Henry Flower or Bloom in his capacity of Jesus. Molly's "O rocks!" (64) includes Gibraltar and Howth. For more of Howth, turn now to *Finnegans Wake*.

Finnegans Wake

Finnegans Wake is about *Finnegans Wake*. That is this: not only about everything, the book is about putting everything down in records and interpreting them. Such records, their writing, and their reading compose the book or, at least, a great part of it. To say, then, that *Finnegans Wake* is about itself is to say that, including our reality, *Finnegans Wake* is about our ideas about it and they are *Finnegans Wake*. Turning in upon itself yet including all our troubles, it is a great thing entirely.

A trouble is that something in which everything involves everything else demands notice of everything at once. This demand, to which Joyce was equal, is plainly beyond his readers. Yet, however formidable, *Finnegans Wake* is less formidable than it seems on first looking into. However unfamiliar it seems, there is much that should be familiar to readers of *Ulysses* and the earlier works; for *Finnegans Wake* is their consequence and their logical development in theme and method alike. Anyone who can read *Ulysses* will find *Finnegans Wake* readable enough. Anyone who enjoys *Ulysses* will have lots of fun at Finnegan's wake.

What puts one off at first, seeming to defer that fun, is the verbal extravagance, which, however, is only an elaboration of verbal methods met here and there in *Ulysses*. "Poached eyes on

ghost" (162) combines Parnell's brother, Parnell, and food as
the context demands. Mr. Bloom's "menagerer" (433) condenses
manager, ménage, Mrs. Bloom, and Blazes Boylan in one brilliant
word. These punning concentrates, both witty and efficient, anticipate the general method of *Finnegans Wake*, in which verbal
distortions—like the Croppy Boy's "Horhot ho hray ho rhother's
hest" (578)—become no less general. But what is easy to take
met here and there, as in *Ulysses*, may prove harder to take in
the dizzy abundance of *Finnegans Wake*. The reader, like Finnegan himself, must become a "gaylabouring" man, (6)[1] as full of
knowledge as falling Adam, alert as the rising son.

Another thing to put one off is lack of customary surface. In a
novel—though *Finnegans Wake* is hardly that—we expect an
overt narrative, which, leading us along, holds parts together while
it offers them and fixes our attention while the other elements
work. In *Ulysses* the story of Stephen and Mr. Bloom threads the
maze of their day. But what of this "nightmaze"? (411) Lacking
overt narrative, *Finnegans Wake* seems a buzzing as well as a
blooming confusion. We lose the wood from sight for all those
trees. "You is feeling like you was lost in the bush, boy?" asks the
genial supervisor of records and commentaries. Without the
"poultriest notions what the forest he all means," you call it "a
puling sample jungle of woods." (112) So any reader for whom
the surface that habit requires has yielded to a surface of sound,
rhythm, and multiple suggestions. He suspects, moreover, an in-
terplay between something elusive and something hidden.

To proceed from *Ulysses* to *Finnegans Wake* is like proceeding
from a picture by Cézanne to a recent abstraction. In the absence of identifiable surface, we must make what we can of blots,
blurs, and scratches, patiently awaiting the emergence of an order
which, though there maybe, is not immediately visible. But this
analogy is inaccurate; for *Finnegans Wake*, calling for reading
aloud, appeals to ear, not eye. Let us begin again. To proceed

---

1. Hereafter, unless otherwise specified, numbers in parentheses refer to pages
in *Finnegans Wake*, New York, The Viking Press, or London, Faber and
Faber. The paperback has the same pagination.

from *Ulysses* to *Finnegans Wake* is like proceeding from Bach to Bartok. But this analogy is also inaccurate; for, like a poem by Dylan Thomas, *Finnegans Wake* is composed of words and words, though valuable in themselves, are referential by nature. A thing of words, however free from customary order and however harmonious, can never approach the autonomy or abstraction of a thing of sounds or a thing of colors. But our analogies of painting and music are not altogether wild; for, like any composition, *Finnegans Wake* is an arrangement of its proper materials. These are words. Whatever its apparent abstraction and autonomy, I repeat, a thing of words always refers to other things. Autonomous only in the sense of placing value on its materials, presenting itself, and of being separate from what surrounds it, as any work of art must be, *Finnegans Wake* refers with understanding and compassion to our deepest concerns. Literature, not music, *Finnegans Wake* not only is but says. No more private than autonomous, this radiant embodiment is merely difficult.

The "Tunc" page of *The Book of Kells*,[2] which seems to have served Joyce as model, looks like an intricate and empty design. But playing around—partly for its own sake maybe—is also playing upon. The arabesques conceal, embellish, and reveal a page of gospel. Things of beauty, *The Book of Kells* and *Finnegans Wake* are designs which, at once formal and moral, bring news of man's condition. When, not so long ago, a publishing house asked its readers to name ten books that best "embody the wisdom, good humor, love, and conscience of the human race," many must have named the Bible. Few could have named *Finnegans Wake*, for few have read it; but not even the scriptures displayed in *The Book of Kells* are better qualified for nomination.

Though plainly a work of literature and, according to the judgment of its readers, as plainly one of those ten shining books, *Finnegans Wake* is hard to classify. It has the expansive abundance of the novel, the texture, rhythm, and density of the poem,

2. *The Book of Kells* is an illuminated manuscript of the gospels, on display in the library of Trinity College, Dublin. For references to the "Tunc" page and its arabesques see *Finnegans Wake*, pp. 107, 119, 122, 298, 611.

yet it is neither one nor the other. Nor is it a play for all its characters, conflicts, falls, and triumphs. *Finnegans Wake* is itself alone—among books the very Phoenix.

Birdwatchers many—for many people nowadays keep a copy on the parlor table as curiosity or cultural object—but readers few. I know someone who has written an essay on *Finnegans Wake,* commending it to respectful multitudes, without having read it. But I know a reader or two, too: a housewife in Texas, a lawyer in Evanston, and the proprietor of a gallery in Provincetown. These read little else; for all seems trivial after this. And there is Thornton Wilder, who counts none with less than a thousand hours of reading as veritable reader. This rare man has spent those hours going forward and backward through the text, noting connections among parts, proceeding from parts to whole and from whole to parts until able to grope his way around with some, but not much, assurance. But even those this side that happy man can find delight and the sharpened awareness of father, daughter, wife, son (and who else is there except mother-in-law?) that *Finnegans Wake* offers all but the most casual reader. A hundred hours or even less should get you into the circle.

Once within this circle and the larger circle of the work, which, though broken like Molly's monologue, is like it in having neither beginning nor end,[3] you may share Joyce's compassionate vision of humanity, as clear and charitable as that of *Ulysses* and even gayer. But there is resignation in the gaiety. This, Joyce says, is what we are stuck with. He impartially displays our ignominies and discomforts, our fortitude and all our little triumphs. Comprehending all, he forgives as he accepts; and that acceptance is genial. *Finnegans Wake* is an arabesque on Molly's "yes."

This design is so vast and intricate that no attempt to trace it can be altogether adequate. The ordinary reader need not despair, for, after a suitable novitiate, his reading may be almost as

3. The first sentence of *Finnegans Wake* meets the last, which, ending in the middle, resumes in the middle of the first, completing the circle. The greatest gap in the circle is the omission of mother-in-law, of whom Joyce had no experience.

good as the expert's. A college of critics, comparing words, contributing facts, and tirelessly reading aloud to one another in a confusion of tongues, might produce something as long as the *Encyclopedia Britannica* or longer. Indeed, I know a fifty-page study of one paragraph. Even such commentaries, however, are or would be inadequate. My brief commentary here (and what matter if brief or tediously copious?) can be no more than a wave of the hand. But the pointing teacher, crying encouragement, is also a beckoner. "Let us leave theories there," however, "and return to here's here. Now hear." (76)

At the center of the nightmaze is a family consisting of father, mother, and three children. These Dubliners live in Chapelizod, an outlying district of the city, at the edge of Phoenix Park beside the river Liffey. H. C. Earwicker, the father, is the host of a pub called the Mullingar or, sometimes, the Bristol.[4] His wife, Anna, is mother of Isabel and of twin sons, Kevin and Jerry, better known as Shaun and Shem. Old Joe is the handyman or bouncer at the pub and old Kate is the maid of allwork. Twelve customers of the pub are usually around until closing time, together with other characters who may or may not be actually there: four old men, sometimes included among the twelve, and twenty-eight girls who, if actual, are children of the neighborhood. Just over the hill, in the bushes of Phoenix Park, are two girls and three soldiers. Corresponding to the five members of Earwicker's family, these seem less actual than the rest, though pretty important in the cast of characters.

Although it is never easy to determine the actual and though, as I have said, there is no overt narrative, the ghost of a plot, emerging here and there, gradually appears. This plot—if, indeed, it can be called that—is something like that of a story in *Dubliners*, as slight apparently, yet substantial and endlessly suggestive. Here is a guess at the "actual" action—a guess because everything is un-

4. This pub, still serving Jameson, Power, and Guinness, is still called the Mullingar. The present host has never heard of Joyce or Earwicker. Bristol, a word derived from bridge, may refer to the bridge across the Liffey at Chapelizod. The pub on the south bank is called the Bridge Inn. Maybe divided Earwicker and his pub occupy both banks, Shem's and Shaun's.

certain here: "all these events they are probably as like those which may have taken place as any others which never took person at all are ever likely to be." (110)

Beginning in the evening, the story ends at dawn; for this is the story of a Dublin night as *Ulysses* of a Dublin day. At dusk, as the animals in the zoo in the Park curl up for sleep, the three children play outside the pub with the little girls of the neighborhood. During their games, Shem and Shaun become rivals for the favor of the girls. Shaun is their natural selection. (Chapter IX, 219-59) After supper, the three children go upstairs to do their homework, which includes a lesson in geometry. The rivalry of the twins continues, but Isabel remains constant—to herself. (Chapter X, 260-308) Downstairs, serving drinks to the customers and telling stories while the radio blares, Earwicker presides over his pub. (Chapter XI, 309-382) After closing time when all the customers have gone, Earwicker, already drunk, drinks the dregs, impartially, whether of Jameson's whisky or Guinness' porter. (380-82) Meanwhile someone, pounding for admission on the closed door, abuses the host. (70-73) Aroused by the noise, Kate hurries down in her shift to find Himself, his "clookey in his fisstball . . . the whites of his pious eyebulbs swering her to silence." Apparently naked, he collapses on the floor or slumps to "throne." (382, 556-57) And so to bed, where Earwicker and Anna make, or try to make, love. She gets up to comfort a whimpering child. Isabel sleeps on, but those twins seem to have been peeping at their parents. (Chapter XVI, 555-590) Dawn comes. Another day begins, and Anna, who always sees her husband plain, sees through him again. (Chapter XVII, 593-628) Earwicker's night has been as quotidian as Bloom's day.

As the story of Bloom, going away and coming home, is the story of every man, so that of Earwicker, sinner and victim of gossip, falling on the floor, going to sleep and waking up to start another day. If their stories are common and vulgar, as Virginia Woolf complained, we must try to adjust ourselves. Everyman, after all, is common and vulgar by definition. As for the pub: a pub is a public place, open to any drinker—old boys of Harrow, too, or even of Eton. Chapelizod, like the rest of Dublin, is everywhere, everywhen. Thinking ourselves in Dublin now, we find ourselves in "Edenberry, Dubblenn, W. C.," (66) a place that combines three cities and, with the help of Eden, two times. Earwicker's family, becoming archetypal, includes the people of the world. The action, such as it is, suggests all action at any time. The tensions within the family, the changing relationship among sons, father, daughter, and mother—the family process, in short— is the process of history. As Joyce, making particulars general, made *Ulysses* everybody's story, so he made this story of a man and his family in a remote part of Dublin that of all men at all times, their action all history, their conflicts all wars and debates. All myth, all literature, all time and space—our general sto v emerges from this local.

This, briefly, is the family process: the father begets twin sons, who quarrel. Uniting at last against father, they replace him as he falls. The rising son (a union of the quarreling twins) becomes father in his turn and begets two sons, who quarrel, unite, and, after his fall, become father. Tempting him and attracting the divided sons, the daughter is a cause of contention and fall; for Earwicker's family, like Freud's, is more or less incestuous. But the daughter becomes the mother, who gathers the pieces after war and fall in order to put them together again. The father rises and falls, divides and unites; but the mother, appeasing and renewing, is constant. This process, which is that of any family, suggests problems that have fascinated philosophers and theologians: the one and the many, the creator and his descent into creation, the happy or creative fall, relativity, recurrence, permanence and change, fall and renewal. Moreover, this domestic process, embodying our ideas of reality, is also the pattern to which trousers, organs, bricks, and dynasties conform: "Gricks may rise and Troysirs fall (there being two sights for ever a picture) for in the byways of high improvidence that's what makes lifework leaving." (11-12)

To make his family general and place it in time and times, Joyce used analogy and parallel as he had in *Ulysses*. There Homer, adding general meaning to particular Bloom, provides the structure of his day. So here, Joyce called upon the system of Giambattista Vico, an eighteenth-century philosopher, who found history cyclical. Each revolution of his cycle consists of four ages, eternally repeated: a divine age, a heroic age, a human age, and a period of confusion, at once the end of the old cycle and the beginning of the new. The divine age, peculiar for religion and marked by fables and hieroglyphs, is primitive. This is the period of Genesis. The heroic age, notable for marriage, conflict, and metaphor, is the age of the Trojan war or of King Arthur's knights. The human age, characterized by burial, democracy, and abstract language, is that of Pericles, declining Rome, and modern times. The *"ricorso"* or the age of confusion that heralds renewal is represented by the dark period which, after the fall of Rome, preceded the triumph of Christianity or the new divine age.[5] The creative father, the quarreling sons, and the renovating mother of Earwicker's household fit this pattern nicely—or, rather, Vico's pattern nicely fits Earwicker's family process; for, after all, Vico is but parallel or analogy to enlarge the meaning of an all but suburban home and give it temporal dimension. The process is general, particularly in Dublin.

"The Vico road goes round and round to meet where terms begin. Still onappealed to by the cycles and unappalled by the recoursers we feel all serene, never you fret. . . ." (452) For the successful union of the local with the universal it is fortunate that Dalkey, just south of Dublin, has a Vico Road and that Dublin itself has a bookshop called Browne and Nolan, which brings us to Bruno of Nola, whose philosophy supplements Vico's.

For Joyce, Giordano Bruno meant the one and the many, the relationship of maximum with minimum, and, above all, the reconciliation of contending opposites. "A kind of dualism," Joyce said (*Letters*, 224-25) of Bruno's system: "Every power in nature must evolve an opposite in order to realize itself and opposition brings reunion." Plainly this idea proved handy for enlarging the contention of father with son and of son with son in Earwicker's family. "I would not pay overmuch attention to these theories,"

5. "Ragnar rocks" (19 and *passim*) is Ragnarok, the Norse twilight of the gods or Vico's *ricorso*.

said Joyce (*Letters*, 241) "beyond using them for all they are worth." For *Finnegans Wake* they are worth not only enlarging parallel but structure.[6]

Like Vico's history, Joyce's *Wake* is divided into four large parts, which represent the divine age, the heroic age, the human age, and the period of renewal. But within these four parts are seventeen chapters, each of which corresponds to one of Vico's ages. The eight chapters of Part I compose two subcycles. Two more revolve within Parts II and III, which have four chapters each. Part IV, with its single chapter, is the general *ricorso*. After that we turn back and begin the book again. A circle composed of smaller circles, *Finnegans Wake* has the shape of a great wheel, a "Wheel of Fortune," (405) a "millwheeling vicociclometer," (614) a "corso in curso on coarser again." (89) "The old order changeth and lasts like the first." (486) All "moves in vicous cicles yet remews the same"; (134) yet, according to Joyce (*Letters*, 251) his great wheel is "square." This is confusing; but on, on—"we must grope on." (107) Implying the four aspects of Vico's wheel maybe, Joyce's square wheel, bumping along to no end, may also imply the four old men, always around, peeping. These four are annalists or historians, representatives and recorders of tradition, authors of Irish history. As "mamalujo," (397) they are Matthew, Mark, Luke, and John, authors of the four gospels. Your guess about the donkey that follows John is as good as mine.[7] But we can be sure that, observing, judging, gossiping, and "repeating themselves," these four preside over the Viconian process and the affairs of Earwicker. John lags a little behind the synoptic three as a recourser must. "Auld Lang Syne," the favorite song of these fourbottle men, implies the end of an old year and the beginning

6. For more elaborate accounts of Vico and Bruno see Samuel Beckett's essay in *Our Exagmination*. Elements of Nicholas of Cusa (49) are also present. Among the innumerable references to Vico and Bruno in *Finnegans Wake* see pp. 131, 287, 481, 599, 614. The word "Silence" or "Silent" implies the end of a cycle. A recurrent word of a hundred letters (e.g. p. 3) signifies not only Earwicker's fall but the thunder that begins Vico's divine age. See Vico, *The New Science*, translated by Thomas Bergin, 1948.

7. My guess is that Shaun-Joyce or Ireland is the donkey. The four men are also the four provinces, the four directions.

of a new—amid barrels of Guinness and bottles of Jameson and a tear or two for the old ones.

Under the eyes of these inspectors, H. C. Earwicker becomes Viconian man: "A human pest cycling (pist!) and recycling (past!) . . . here he was (pust!) again!" (99) General man, his nickname is Here Comes Everybody; (32) for, like us all, he is "human, erring and condonable." (58) That he is present everywhere and everywhen under a variety of names is shown by the recurrence (as here) of his initials. His presence in our times, for example, is proved by "Heinz cans everywhere." (581) A multitude of analogies and allusions affirms the omnipresence of that "patternmind," our "forebeer." As creator, H. C. E. is "the Great Sommboddy within the Omniboss." (415) Like Frazer's dying and reviving god, he is at home with holly, ivy, and mistletoe. As faller, he is Adam, Humpty Dumpty, and Ibsen's master builder. As riser, he is Christ. As host of a pub, he is the Host or the Eucharist. Not only the thunderfish, he is whale, insect, goat, and holy tree. As famous man, he is Cromwell, Noah, Isaac, King Mark, and the Pope (a pontifex or bridge builder). He is sailor and tailor and Russian general. Outlander and invading Dane or Englishman, he is also King Rory O'Conor and Finn MacCool, the whiteheaded boy of Tara. As Arthur, H. C. E. unites Sir Arthur Wellesley or the Duke of Wellington, King Arthur of the suitably round table, and Sir Arthur Guinness, who also had two sons, Lords Iveagh and Ardilaun. "Arise, sir Pompkey Dompkey!" (568) As an individual in Chapelizod now, Mr. Earwicker is somewhat deaf, a little humpbacked and henpecked; and since, as a victim of gossip (on trial at his bar) he feels a little guilty, he stutters. In short, he is everybody entirely. "Your Ominence," those four men shout, acclaiming him, "Your Imminence." (504) Is it yourself? we cry.

Now, old Coppinger or Oglethorpe (or whatever you want to call him) has two sons, Shem and Shaun (or whatever you want to call them), who give him trouble. These twins are rivals or equal opposites like Bruno's contending elements in search of the Monad. Shem is outsider, introvert, artist, and failure. Shaun is insider, extrovert, bourgeois, and success. Shem is tree and Shaun stone. Shem is baker, Shaun butcher. Shem drinks, Shaun eats—"stenk and kitteney phie in a hashhoush," (59) for example. Their incompatibility produces conflict to end all conflicts: those of Jacob and Esau (or "castor and porridge," 489), of Cain and Abel ("I cain but are you able?" 287; am I "your bloater's kipper?" 305), of Mutt and Jeff, and of the ant and the grasshopper. Mark that these twain are Tom Sawyer and Huck Finn, Michael and Satan (or Mick and Nick), Peter and Paul, Tweedledum and Tweedledee, Romulus and Remus, St. Thomas Beckett and St. Lawrence O'Toole, St. Patrick and Bishop Berkeley. Their contention produces all battles, particularly Clontarf, Waterloo, and Balaclava, Joyce's favorites. In them "Battleshore and Deaddleconchs" (390) wield Milton's "twohangled warpon." (615) Their contention is that of being with becoming and of ear with eye or of time with space. Yet neither is hero, neither villain, neither altogether good or evil; for both are aspects of every man— principles rather than people. Joyce treats them both with irony and compassion, impartially, preferring neither. Detached again, he keeps his distance, by "gemini!"

Shem or James is another Stephen, egocentric and literary, author of *Ulysses* and Joyce's other works. Shaun or John is another Mulligan or Cranly. But Bruno Nowlan and Nolan Browne (152, 159) can change in the "twinngling of an aye." (620) "Swapsons" or "changelings," (87, 206) they are inconstant. Successful Shem becomes Shaun and failing Shaun, Shem. It is true that Joyce applies details of his own career to Shem and that he associates Shaun with T. S. Eliot,[8] John McCormack, Wyndham Lewis, Stanislaus Joyce, Oliver Gogarty, Frank O'Connor, and a host of others. But when Shem, as author of *Ulysses*, is

---

8. T. S. Eliot figures throughout *Finnegans Wake*. "Shaunti! Shaunti! Shaunti!" an echo of the end of *The Waste Land*, becomes a motif for Shaun: pp. 235, 305, 408, 454, 528, 593, 605. Echoing the first part of *The Waste Land*, Shaun calls Shem "my shemblable! My freer!" (489) See Joyce's parody of *The Waste Land* in *Letters*, p. 231. *The Waste Land* may be a parody of *Ulysses*, as Joyce contends; but in another sense *Finnegans Wake* is a parody of *The Waste Land*.

applauded by Irishmen, he is Shaun. Elsewhere Joyce and Eliot swap places. As son, Joyce is either Shem or Shaun as circumstances and the principle of relativity demand; but he is always H. C. E. That Joyce used details of his own life for Shem, H. C. E., and sometimes Shaun, is far from odd; for the artist, using his own image, always projects himself. Himself is handiest and most familiar. Yet for one who knows himself as Joyce knew Joyce, his own experience must be that of anyone. Etonian and Bowery bum are brothers under the skim since every man is everyman.

Shaun the Ondt, having become as much of a poet as Shem the Gracehoper, poetically sings of his brother and himself: *"These twain are the twins that tick* Homo Vulgaris." Yet "precondamned," they must quarrel *"Till Nolans go volants and Bruneyes come Blue* . . . In the name of the former and of the latter and of their holocaust. Allmen." (418-19)

As Bruno presides over the contention of these identical opposites, so, together with Hegel,[9] he presides over their eventual union in H. C. E., who is the sum of Shem and Shaun or those two "amallgamated." (308) Their father, Anna tells her sons, is "you all over"; (620) for *isce* and *ille*, those "equals of opposites," evolved by the one power, *iste*, return to him. (92) "Dialytically," thesis and antithesis become synthesis. (614) Outwardly resembling bourgeois Shaun, the great composite is Shem within. Not only Arthur Guinness Sons and Company, Limited ("Awful Grimmest Sunshat Cromwelly. Looted," 9), H. C. E. is John Jameson and Son, Limited. If Shem is time or ear and Shaun space or eye, H. C. E. is spacetime as his name implies. Earwicker (meaning earwig, an insect like any man however great and also dweller in Eire) combines "ear" or time with "wick" or place. "Time, please!" in his pub becomes "Time, place!" (546) If Joyce is anybody in *Finnegans Wake*, he is Earwicker—and so is anybody or, at least, any man of good will, and who else would be reading this at all?

Like Wagner's Isolde, who lived at Chapelizod and gave her

9. Hegel may also help explain the structure of *Ulysses*: Part I could be thesis, Part II antithesis, and Part III synthesis.

name to the place, Joyce's Isabel is the cause of rivalry between the old man and the young, between King Mark-Earwicker and Tristan-Shaun. This temptress is also a cause of contention between rival sons. Since Isabel always turns to the rising son (Shaun), her flower is the heliotrope. The twenty-eight flower girls who surround her, composing a month and four rainbows, seem her extensions. As the twenty-ninth girl, she represents leap year. This "flickerflapper" is always sitting at the dressing table, admiring her bonehead in the mirror. (527, 561) "Miss Yiss, you fascinator." (398) When she is around, the rhythm and diction, aping those of a noveletta, become "strip teasy." In shorts, this "linkingclass girl" is another Gerty MacDowell or Milly Bloom, that other girl from Mullingar. However ironic, Joyce treats Isabel with understanding and sympathy; for this girl is our hope for the future.

Mrs. Earwicker or Anna Livia Plurabelle (the initials A. L. P. reveal her omnipresence) presides over Vico's *ricorso* as agent and principle of renewal. With 1001 children, Abha na Lifé (496) is "Bringer of Plurabilities." (104) Jung's "annyma" (426) or the great female figure that haunts our dreams, she is also the red triangle on a bottle of Bass. As "Mistress of Arths" (112) she is the artist's Muse as well as Guinevere. Not only a "poule" (a hen, a whore, and a puddle), she is also "wee" (small, *oui*, and wee-wee or urine; for as H. C. E. is associated with creative defecation, so she with making water). She is Eve, the Virgin Mary, Pandora, Noah's wife, Napoleon's Josephine, and the Moon, ruling those twenty-eight monthly girls and their rainbows. The "Rejaneyjailey," (64) she is at once Queen of Heaven and the Regina Coeli jail in Rome. As H. C. E. is Alpha, she is Omega. (196) Treating her with a mixture of tenderness and contempt, Joyce adapts his rhythms to her presence and nature. Either tripping or softly flowing, these rhythms, embodying A. L. P., are the lady herself.

As H. C. E. is the sum of his sons and of Joe, the bouncer (old H. C. E.), so A. L. P. is the sum of young Isabel, Mrs. Earwicker, and old Kate. "Anna was, Livia is, Plurabelle's to be." (215)

Here under the nose of Robert Graves—too close for notice maybe—is his triple goddess, the Great Mother of the ancients and another Molly Bloom. All the women of *Finnegans Wake*, under whatever names they are disguised, are aspects of A. L. P., as all the men, whatever their names, are H. C. E. There are only two characters in *Finnegans Wake*. "Gammer and gaffer we're all their gangsters." (215) Isabel may be called Lettucia, Margareena, Sylvia Silence, Mildew Lisa (after Tristan's *"mild und leise"*), or Nuvoletta, but she remains Isabel, and this girl is young A. L. P. The "wastepacket Sittons," an actress at her mirror, gossiping about H. C. E., (58-59) is an evident union of mother and daughter. "A L I K E" (165) means Anna Livia Isabel Kate Earwicker. So with Shaun. Whether disguised for the moment as Philly Thurnston, Peter Cloran, Jones, or Yawn, he is always the outward part of H. C. E.

Geographical metaphors improve the generality of Joyce's Adam and Eve. As a sleeping giant with his head at Howth, his feet at the magazine in Phoenix Park (his feet are sons), H. C. E. is one with the landscape. Since Howth is one hill and the magazine is atop another, he unites the "two mounds." As he is hills, so she the river. A. L. P. is the river Liffey from its source in Wicklow to Island Bridge, just below Chapelizod, where she meets her tide. The river is time and life. As the "Brook of Life," (263) flowing through its "microchasm," (229) A. L. P. furnishes water for Guinness and Jameson, and up her course the salmon leap. A little cloud, Isabel drops as rain into the upper Liffey. The dirty, tired old river flows with Kate to sea, to be sucked up into cloud again, again to fall as rain into the upper Liffey—as if Vico's cycle in hydraulic terms. The banks of the Liffey are the rivals (Latin *rivae*) or Shem and Shaun. Meanwhile, washerwomen on those banks, washing dirty clothes, make things new, "wasching the walters of, the weltering walters off. Whyte," (64) for it all comes out in the wash.

The movement of washing is up and down. This, aside from cycling, is the general movement of *Finnegans Wake*, which goes round and round, up and down, ceaselessly, like some great engine—though this comparison, while faithful to all the clicking and meshing and reciprocating, is otherwise alien to so humane an intricacy. The rhythm of falling and rising is announced at the beginning of Chapter I, the first book of "guenneses," by the ballad of "Finnegan's Wake," to which the book owes its name. Tim Finnegan, a hodcarrier, climbs his ladder one thirsty morning, "tippling full. His howd feeled heavy, his hoddit did shake. (There was a wall of course in erection) Dimb! He stottered from the latter. Damb! he was dud. Dumb! Mastabatoom. . . ." (6) So they lay him out at his wake with a bottle of Jameson at his feet and a barrel of Guinness' at his head. One of H. C. E.'s most congenial surrogates, Finnegan has a fine name, recalling that of Finn MacCool himself. "Wake," a fine word too, means celebrating death and waking up or resurrection. Finn no more, like any sinner, will be Finn again. When a mourner at the wake throws a keg of spirits across the room "with the shoutmost shoviality," the sprinkled corpse revives. "Do you think I'm dead?" asks Finnagain. There is no apostrophe in *Finnegans Wake* since Finnegan, like H. C. E., is at once possessive and plural.

"Lead, kindly fowl!" (112) This parody of Newman implies that A. L. P., "original hen" and "parody's bird," will make a new man out of H. C. E. It is she who, picking her fallen husband up, "waked him widowt sparing and gave him keen and made him able." (102) That he has fallen is sure, but why and how remain uncertain. Maybe his fall, like those of Adam, Oscar Wilde, or any jerrybuilder, was "due to a collupsus of his back promises." (5) That he feels as guilty as others find him is sure. But gossips try in vain to pin that sinner down; in vain the efforts of the court—despite four old judges, twelve jurors, a multitude of witnesses, and a keen attorney for the defense. This sin remains as debatable as Adam's in a liberal seminary, as indefinite as that of the "smugging" boys in Clongowes Wood. Both the certainty and uncertainty of Earwicker's sin, however, conspire to make it seem every sin of every man—his sin our best endeavor; for, as Alfred Hitchcock says, there is some good in the best of us. Whatever the sin of H. C. E., it seems to involve three encounters: with two girls and three soldiers in the Park; with a Cad in the Park; and with the floor of the Mullingar at the edge of the Park. Phoenix Park is central.

At once his Eden and a kind of dump, Phoenix Park is where the "foenix culprit" (23) falls. But as its name implies, Phoenix Park is where he rises, too.[10] When the foenix culprit jumps out of his frying pan into the pyre, his sin becomes the *"felix culpa"* or happy fault of the Mass for Holy Saturday, preceding Easter. Adam's fall was fortunate ("O fortunous casualitas!" 175) in the sense that, promising our renewal in Christ, it sent us out, the world before us, to sweat for our living and, sweating, to create. From sin came Son and the wonders of civilization—"a pretty nice kettle of fruit." (Forbidden fruit, redeeming fish, and the general mess of things unite in this radiant phrase. 11) The happy faller, our "very phoenix," builds the city of Dublin and New York City, too. Creative H. C. E., our general maker, becomes Haveth Childers Everywhere.

But back to "Phornix Park" (80) and those three encounters, now. Lotta Crabtree and Pomona Evelyn or Lupita Lorette and Luperca Latouche (or whatever you want to call them), the two girls, "gigglibly temptatrix" in the bushes near the magazine, strip "teasily" while Earwicker peeps or exhibits himself. "He fell for them." It is plain that drawers, peeping, making water, and exposure are involved in his fall; for those who "bare whiteness" against him are "pairadrawsing . . . under the threes" while "(peep!) meeting waters most improper (peepette!). . . . trickle trickle triss." (52, 67, 79, 96, 379) Meanwhile the three soldiers are around, peeping at the peeper maybe or rejecting his advances, according to another story. "Sam, him and Moffat" (or whatever their names), these sons of Noah also bear witness against the sinner. As "Tap and pat and tapatagain," (58) they include the blind stripling of *Ulysses*, St. Patrick, the reversal of

---

10. One of the hundred-lettered words announcing H. C. E.'s fall includes "humpadump" and ends with "turnup." (314) A reference to Mr. Micawber (131) implies waiting for something to turn up.

Bruno's contraries, and the cycle of Vico. Yet these Refuseleers seem to be Earwicker and his sons. ("There were three men in him." 113) The two girls seem A. L. P. and Isabel as well as Eve and Lilith. The sin is a family affair—and no man is without dishonor in his own company.

Not far away in the Park, near the Wellington Monument ("where obelisk rises when odalisks fall," 335), Earwicker meets a Cad, who asks the time of day. (35) This apparently harmless encounter of young man with old, of son with father, arouses Earwicker's guilt.[11] Stuttering, he defends himself unnecessarily, protesting innocence. His third encounter—with the floor, drunk and shameless—is spectacular. It is a fall.

We know from *Ulysses* that thirty-two is the number for falling and eleven the number for rising. We know that Joyce was fascinated with numerology. 1132, the central number of *Finnegans Wake*, includes not only rise and fall; it is all-inclusive. Ireland is there with its thirty-two counties and so is the public family. When the digits are added, 1132 amounts to seven or the members of the household at the Mullingar. 1132 is the number of father and sons together: eleven for rising Shaun or Kevin (K is the eleventh letter), thirty-two for falling Earwicker, and twenty-one, their difference, for Shem. As Jerry (J is the tenth letter), Shem is also ten, the Kabalistic number of completeness; and so is H. C. E. as creator. 566, the number for women, is half 1132, the better half, no doubt. 1132, 566, (Silent), 566, 1132, a sequence composing a Viconian cycle, (13-14) includes the history of this rising, falling family. A. L. P. herself has other numbers: 40 from Noah's forty days and forty nights of rain; 54 from LIV; and 111 or 1001 for renewal and creation. *The One Thousand and One Nights' Entertainment*, inspired by this Muse, is *Finnegans Wake*.

Numbers, the Cad, the girls and soldiers all become motifs. There is no chapter, indeed, there is hardly a page, without some

---

11. Variants on "Fieluhr? Filou!" (213) become a motif for this encounter. Answering German "What time?" by French "pickpocket" or "cheat" is an example of a misinterpreted question from World War I.

reference to these girls and soldiers or without some hint of the
verbal tags that attend them: "By the mausolime wall. Fimfim
fimfim" and "Up guards, and at 'em." So obsessively recurrent
these motifs and a few others that *Finnegans Wake* seems a vast
arrangement of limited materials, repeated again and again with
small variations—like Bloom's "neverchanging everchanging"
water. But what is life but that, and what the *Wake* but its very
image?

Among lesser motifs are fog, tree, and clothing. The fog, recalling the "London particular" of *Bleak House*, (62) and no
less pervasive and significant, makes it difficult to identify the
individual or even to gossip with assurance about him. (48, 51,
403, 502, 555, 593) The tree is the tree of life, the "blomster-
bohm" in Phoenix Park, (55) the tree of knowledge or the "ab-
falltree," (88) the Norse ashtree or "beingstalk," (509) and the
family tree. H. C. E. is "Yggdrasselman," his children are
"bloomkins," and his wife is a leaf: "I am leafy speaking," says the
Liffey, as if a book. (88, 505-06, 600, 619) Shem is an elm or
willow beside her, Shaun a stone: "Polled with pietrous. Sierre
but saule." (159) The theme of clothing, which involves tailor
and washerwomen, is supported by references to Carlyle's *Sartor
Resartus* and Swift's *Tale of a Tub*. As envelope to letter, so
clothing, an outer husk, to body: an external manifestation depending upon time and place. "One Life One Suit" (63, 109)
maybe, but drawers suit H. C. E., Bloom, and Joyce, as they suit
that "pair of sycopanties" (94) among the fig leaves.

Hat, stick, race, hunt, and tea, carried over from *Ulysses*, join
the complex of motifs. In *Finnegans Wake*, however, despite
pervasive fogginess, these inherited images seem more nearly
definite than in *Ulysses*, as if general uncertainty were the product of many little certainties. Take the hat. Mr. Bloom's hat,
which invites our speculation, becomes the half a hat that
Willingdone hangs on the backside of his big white harse. That
this misplaced, defective hat, the property of Lipoleum, is three-
cornered suggests the three soldiers, and half this hat, half their

sum or one of the twins. The four old men have half a hat among them. A whole hat seems the sign of individual identity, maturity, adequacy or union. H. C. E. bets half his crown on each of his sons. Changing identities, Mutt and Jute "swop hats" as if waiting for Godot. (10, 16, 390, 610) The stick, Shem's property here as it was Stephen's once, becomes a "lifewand." When Shem lifts this creative tool, the "dumb speak." (195) The race, on which H. C. E. bets two half crowns, is plainly the Viconian cycle ("from spark to phoenish") and the human race. (13, 322) Compared to this steeplechase, the Gold Cup race is obscure. The fox hunt, in which John Peel and "Ramrod the meaty hunter" ride, has guilty H. C. E. for quarry (96) instead of the Stephen or Bloom of the Circe episode. As for Bloom's "family tea," it becomes "tea for two" or marriage here. Sometimes H. C. E. is unable to wet the tea. Sometimes, however, he makes "infusion more infused." But tea (*thea*) is commonly the beverage of Ann Lynch: "Houseanna. Tea is the Highest!" Her letter is significantly teastained at the Boston Tea Party in the new world. (111, 406, 542, 585)[12]

Verbal motifs, sometimes familiar or unfamiliar tags and sometimes single words, also complicate the great design, carrying, depositing, and connecting part with part. Reminiscences or distortions of popular songs and poems, no less recurrent, add meaning to, or take it from, each context.[13]

12. References to the new world (Australia, New Zealand, and the United States) mean renewal. Shaun points the "deathbone," (193) but since death-bones are Australian, the meaning is not altogether deathly.
13. Sample motifs: "The hearsomeness of the burger . . ." (23) parodies the motto of Dublin. "*Securus iudicat* . . ." (96) may be found in Webster. "There's the Belle for Sexaloitez! And Concepta de Send-us-pray!" (213) distorts the Angelus (in French) and *Sechseläuten*, the spring festival of Zurich. "Mishe mishe" (Gaelic "I am") and "tauftauf" (German "baptize") are motifs for Shem (being) and Shaun (pious doing). "Pass the kish for crawsake" (7) implies the Eucharist. Recurrent passages of Pidgin English, generally associated with businesslike Shaun, may mean that every man has "a chink in his conscience." (486) There are also recurrent metaphors of the theater, the movies, and games. As for songs, nursery rhymes, and popular poems, they are everywhere: e.g. "Op. 2 Phil Adolphus" (93) is "Off to Philadelphia," the city of brotherly love.

But back to the Park again. Here, atop its mound, is the magazine, which, having once provided Swift with matter for art,[14] now
does more for Joyce. Swift's magazine, haunted by those two
girls and scene, therefore, of Earwicker's sin and fall, unites in
Finnegans Wake with the Wellington Monument, scene of Earwicker's encounter with the Cad, to become the museum.
Whether you take this composite as magazine, museum or barrow, the "museomound" contains fragments and records of the
past, all the materials of history and literature, and works of art
like the Ardagh Chalice and *The Book of Kells*. At once tomb
and womb, container of the past and creator of the future, the
"Museyroom" is also home of the Muses, daughters of Memory.
Welcoming Burke, Shaw, and Yeats, old Kate may condescend
to take us through; for, as curator and janitor, she has charge of
the "waxworks," and for a tip, is willing to display them. (8, 113,
303)

But "tip," a verbal motif for the museum, also means dump.
The museum is not only a burial mound or barrow but a "midden" in which a "horde of orts" is terracooking in its juices until
ripe. In the "middenst" of this accumulation, "dump for short,"
are "droppings of biddies, stinkend pusshies, moggies' duggies,
rotten witchawubbles, festering rubbages . . . if not worse . . .
(Tiptiptip!)" from the "mistridden past." (*Mist* is German for
manure.) But also containing "olives, beets, kimmells, dollies"
(the Hebrew alphabet), this "timeplace" is an "allaphbed," a
"claybook" which "he who runes may rede" on all fours. So "if
you are abcedminded, you must stoop." "Please stoop" becomes
the motif for those who, like the four old men, are willing to
undertake "midden research." Not only the festering matter of
the prehistoric past, this ort is art or man's attempt to record his
origin, career, and surroundings in runes, hieroglyphs, type, and
bits of paper.

The magazine, as haunt of the three soldiers, has military

14. For a parody of Swift's epigram see pp. 12-13: "Behove this sound of Irish
sense." Swift is everywhere. As an old man with two girls, Stella and Vanessa,
he is H.C.E. As a man of letters he is Shem, and as a cleric, Shaun. Yeats continues to serve as father-image.

associations. The Wellington museum, therefore, is also the field of Waterloo or of Clontarf, littered with the debris of battle. As scavenger, Kate-A. L. P. picks the pieces up in "nabsack" or "whillbarrow." Victim of conflict and of fall, H. C. E. "dumptied the wholeborrow of rubbages" here. Place of sin, fall, conflict, renewal, the dump is Eden, Phoenix Park, and dear, dirty "dumplan." Being everything, this heap of "rubsh" is also *Finnegans Wake*.[15]

Tim Finnegan fell from a "latter." From latter comes "litter" and from the litter the letter. It all works out. Found in the dump by a hen, the letter litters "as human a little story as paper could well carry." Essence of dump, it is "artifact" and "chaosmos" as well, concentrating all the muddled affairs of Earwicker's family, from alpha to omega, in a page. Not only involved in it, the members of his family are involved in its writing, finding, and attempted delivery; for this letter is "carried of Shaun, son of Hek, written of Shem, brother of Shaun, uttered for Alp, mother of Shem, for Hek, father of Shaun." A. L. P., as Muse, inspires and finds it. Shem the Penman writes it. (Its "gist is the gist of Shaun"; its hand "the hand of Sameas.") Shaun the Post, who claims credit for finding the letter, is unable to read or deliver it; for H. C. E. has moved from every known address, and the letter is Greek to the postman. Therefore, he condemns what he carries: far from "nice," this confusion of "clerical horrors" is nothing but "a pinch of scribble . . . puffedly offal tosh."

We can sympathize with bourgeois Shaun; for, whatever its apparent paucity of substance, this letter is so difficult to interpret that all the scholars guess in vain. This is what it means, say some, and some say that. "However basically English," the puzzling document seems written in "anythongue athall." Moreover, it seems to be shifting continually under our eyes. Though by no means the "miseffectual . . . riot of blots and blurs . . . and hoops and wriggles and juxtaposed jottings" that it seems, the letter, uniting "soundsense and sensesound," seems con-

---

15. For the dump see pp. 11, 15-20, 69, 79, 80, 93, 110, 111, 113, 261, 272-73, 307, 350, 352, 476, 595. "Hump to dump": his dump is also defecation.

demned, nevertheless, "to be nuzzled over . . . for ever and a
night till his noddle sink or swim by that ideal reader suffering
from an ideal insomnia." As with *The Book of Kells*, another
recovered document confused by arabesques, one may doubt the
"whole sense of the lot, the interpretation of any phrase in the
whole, the meaning of every word of a phrase so far deciphered
out of it," but not "its genuine authorship and holusbolus au-
thoritativeness." "An illegible downfumbed by an unelgible," the
letter seems the very image of life, with which it shares "adomic
structure." But, we ask, is it art? Plainly this formidable gospel,
like the dump from which it comes, is *Finnegans Wake*. Mainly
about itself, this book is everywhere in this book. Hosty's ballad
about H. C. E., for example, is another epitome of the book that
contains it and another account of its author.[16]

Indeed, the writing, method, nature, and reception of *Finnegans Wake* seem the principal concern of *Finnegans Wake*; but
these from innumerable examples must suffice: Coming home
drunk one night and making a "belzey babble" as of foreign
instruments, H. C. E. incurs the wrath of Maurice Behan (Shaun,
Joe, and Stanislaus Joyce), of Isabel, and of the old "liffopota-
mus." (63-64) This "belzey babble" is *Finnegans Wake*. "Jocax"
and "blind pig," H. C. E., its author, is plainly Joyce. When
Shem-Joyce is dominant in H. C. E., he is author, and when
Shaun-Joyce is dominant, he is audience, if any. After his trial,
H. C. E., the "Parish Poser" with a "blink patch" over his eye,
murders the King's English. "You and your gift of your gaft of
your garbage abaht our Farvver!" say the twenty-eight girls.
"Shun the Punman!" (93-94) Drinking the dregs in his pub,
H. C. E. is writing *Finnegans Wake* again. Belching, breaking
wind, singing, and muttering to himself in divers tongues, he sops
up the leavings of drink and literature. (381) Shem, the literary
side of H. C. E., having made ink out of his excrement, writes on
his own skin "till by its corrosive sublimation one continuous
present tense integument slowly unfolded all . . . cyclewheeling

16. For the letter see pp. 11, 66, 93-94, 107-22, 393, 419-21, 424-25, 482, 483,
495, 615-19, 623-24. For Hosty's ballad see pp. 44-47.

history (thereby, he said, reflecting from his own individual person life unlivable, transaccidentated through the slow fires of consciousness into a dividual chaos . . . common to allflesh, human only . . ." (185-86) Building the tower of Babel with its 1001 stories and its confusion of tongues, Finnegan, the master builder, is constructing *Finnegans Wake*. (4-5) Not language "at any sense of the world," (83) but the babble of Babel [17] and the product of its fall, the language of *Finnegans Wake* consists of "the sibspeeches of all mankind . . . foliated . . . from the root of some funner's stotter." (96) "Fabulafigured," (596) the "monomyth" (581) proceeds "seriolcosmically." (263) When, a success at last, the author of *Finnegans Wake* accepts the applause of Ireland, he is Shaun. "Brave footsore Haun!" they cry in Dublin. "Work your progress!" (473) It must be almost plain by now that *Finnegans Wake* is about *Finnegans Wake* or almost.

An example of "wordsharping," (422) this book is "the hoax that joke bilked" (511) or a fraud. "You'll have loss of fame from Wimmegame's fake." (375) Even the letter is a forgery, and Shaun's claim to its discovery is "counterfeit." (421, 483) The theme of forging and forgery that we encountered on the last page of A *Portrait* comes to climax here, where literary creation is fake in two senses: first, in the Aristotelian sense of imitation; second, by popular estimate. Not only a story or something made, a fiction is a lie. The public of our time—even such eminent representatives as Oliver Gogarty and Frank O'Connor—is convinced that Joyce's art is fraud. The ordinary reader is sure his leg is pulled. Therefore H. C. E. and Shem, as authors of *Finnegans Wake*, are the "masterbilker" (111) and the "littlebilker." (37) Like Daedalus himself, H. C. E. is a "neoliffic smith." (576) As Shaun's "fakesimilar," Shem is a "sham," expert in "jerrybuilding." (170, 181, 484) Another "jameymock farceson" (faker of *Ossian*), Shem is an "ambitrickster." (423) Jim the Penman, from whom Shem takes his name, was a notorious forger: "Forge away, Sunny Sim." (307) The *"fecit"* of this

17. The tower of Babel is the tower of Balbus (cf. *Portrait*, 287): "Blabus was razing his wall." (552) "Balbulus" (4) is the master builder as stutterer.

creator means faked. (185) But H. C. E. as God, the creator of heaven and earth, "forged himself ahead like a blazing urban-orb." (589) It is hardly surprising, then, that when the members of Earwicker's family sacramentally devour His body, they partake of "fraudstuff." (7)

The verbal motif for forgery is "hesitency," a word made famous at the trial of Richard Pigott for forging letters to implicate Parnell in the Phoenix Park murders. Occurring appropriately during the encounter with the Cad in Phoenix Park, (35) "hesitency" becomes associated with both Shem and "HeCitEncy" in their capacity of creators, and even with Shaun. (187, 305, 421, 483) "He prophets most who bilks the best," (305) says Joyce's Ancient Mariner.

About the language, which we noticed briefly sometime back: a multitude of examples must have made it plain by now that, as Joyce affirms, *Finnegans Wake* is composed of "a jetsam of litterage," of "lapsus langways," of "falsemeaning adamelegy," of "lowquacity," of "any way words all in one soluble," of "counterpoint words"—puns, in short, or doublin talk and a variety of distortions. (77, 292, 299, 424, 482, 485) "Saint Calembaurnus," (240) the patron of puns, presides over this confusion and condensation, as over Freud's wit and dream or over Lewis Carroll's "Jabberwocky" with its "portemanteau" (240) words.[18] This language, at once efficient, meaningful, and funny, is the only medium Joyce could have chosen for all he had to do. Made of many languages, it is universal. A concord of discords like a seventeenth-century "conceit," this language is witty in a way John Donne would have applauded and Dr. Johnson deplored. If condensation is a literary virtue, as some say, here is the most virtuous of works.

Let us notice once again some beauties we have noticed and

18. That Joyce was familiar with Freud is proved by many references in the text and by two passages: the story of Wellington (8) is based on a joke in Freud's book on wit (Modern Library edition, p. 673); and the story of Burrus-Casseous, (161) told by Professor Jones, is based on a passage in Ernest Jones' essay on *Hamlet* (Anchor edition p. 139). Joyce discovered Lewis Carroll late, while writing *Finnegans Wake*, yet there are many references to him.

some more. Take "goddinpotty." (59) This witty condensation
includes the garden party of Eden or Adam's fall and the Eucharist in chalice or Jesus; summarizing fall and redemption, this
complex brings Plumtree's Potted Meat back to mind. On the
face of it, "goddinpotty" is as absurd and portentous as those
occupied ash cans in Samuel Beckett's *Endgame*. On the same
page of *Finnegans Wake* is "homelette," a condensation of ome-
lette and home, implying the broken egg of Humpty Dumpty's
fall and cooking or bringing together and renewal, the happy or
creative fall that makes the family. The "Wet Pinter" (92) is a
West Pointer and a drunk. This concentration, suitably applied
to the Cad or cadet, implies the new world or renewal and the
decline of the old in disorder. "Doubleviewed seeds," (296)
viewed in its context of domestic geometry (constructing triangle A L P or mamma is the problem), means that viewed by
peeping doubles or twins, angle P of the maternal triangle unites
W. C. or the place for urinating with seeds or sex. Never were
two words less decorous or more efficient.

Advancing now from word or two to words in phrase or sentence, let us notice these—and this our first example: "Behose
our handmades for the lured," (239) an obvious play on "Behold the handmaid of the Lord" from the Angelus. Implying the
Virgin, this mixture combines handmades or drawers with peeping and those two girls. The "lured" is H. C. E., their victim and
our father. This is simple, but consider: "Reeve Gootch was
right and Reeve Drughad was sinistrous!" (197) Taken in the
context of the Liffey, Reeve Gootch and Reeve Drughad are
plainly the Rive Gauche of the river Seine, the Latin or artists'
quarter, and the Rive Droite or that of the bourgeoisie. Since the
twins are rivals, they are banks of any river. "Gootch" is corrupt
French for left. "Drughad" is Gaelic for right; so that we have a
conflict of Parisian exile and artist with conventional Dubliner.
But Gootch or left is "right," and "Drughad" or right is "sinistrous" or, in Latin, left. Therefore these opposites, swapping
places, become one another. Our third example is funnier: "Are
we speachin d'anglas landage or are you sprakin sea Djoytsch?"

(485) This question, which involves French and German, land and sea, English and Joyce's joyous improvement on it, and the conflict of all twins, is that of every reader.

The first sentence of *Finnegans Wake* (or, to be accurate, the half a sentence that serves as opening) is as crowded with meaning as any of Joyce's openings: "riverrun, past Eve and Adam's, from swerve of shore to bend of bay, brings us by a commodius vicus of recirculation back to Howth Castle and Environs." The first and most important word, "riverrun," is almost the key to the book; for A. L. P. is the river of time and life as H. C. E., whose initials appear in the last three words, is the hill. This great, inclusive sentence unites Dublin or particular reality in our time with general reality in time past. "Eve and Adam's" [19] is not only a Dublin church near the Liffey, opposite the court house, but the Eden of our general parents. Not only Dublin Bay, the bay is Killiney Bay, to the south, along which runs the "vicus" or Vico Road. Howth Castle at the foot of its hill marks the northern extremity of Dublin. "Recirculation" and "vicus" plainly announce Vico and his system; but "commodius" is tricky. A commode is a chamber pot or jordan (another river); and the first name of Bruno, Vico's twin, is Giordano or Jordan. As *Ulysses* ends with one commode, so *Finnegans Wake*, celebrating the same flow, begins with another.

Proceeding for example from sentence to paragraph and thence to page seems almost too much for here and now; for, Joyce tells us "how every word will be bound over to carry three score and ten toptypical readings throughout the book of Doublends Jined." (20) Time and space are lacking for the examination this demands. Anyway, Joyce explained a page or

---

19. "Eve and Adam's" is a reversal of Adam and Eve's, the actual name of the church. Such reversals, occurring throughout, imply renewal (by woman), as here, or else the changing relationship of the twins, who swap places in the middle of Chapter X. "Kram of Llawnroc" (388) is Mark of Cornwall; "Elin" (364) is Nile; "Titep Notep" and "Aruc-Ituc" (237) are *Petit Peton* and Cuticura; the twins are Roma and Amor, (487) Anol and Nobru (490) or Bruno and Nolan. "Pu Noseht" (593) is The Sun Up. That many of the reversals are Egyptian implies *The Book of the Dead* or the book of coming forth by day, an account of death and resurrection.

two himself, (*Letters,* 247-48, 263-64, 273-74) and his disciples explained page after page in *Our Exagmination.* Every subsequent critic has exagmined more and more. These examples should be exemplary. Even my words and sentences should be enough. You get the idea. Explain a page or two yourself or, better, sit down and read as you would read another book; for, as Joyce assures us, *Finnegans Wake,* though "from tubb to buttom all falsetissues," is "readable to int from and." (48) Enjoy what you can follow, and if you do not understand it all, be comforted; for you are one at last with all the scholars, one with all but Joyce, who understood everything, even himself. "Wipe your glosses with what you know," (304) as Isabel advises, or yourself with you know what.

A language based in part on Freud and corroborated by "Jabberwocky," a dream poem, is suitable to dream. Joyce's vision of the dark side of man, the night of his soul, before his coming forth by day,[20] is an enormous dream, like Dante's vision. Fog and verbal obscurity are to be expected in this "traumaturgid" (496) area; for dreaming in our night, if not in Dante's, attempts to conceal what it reveals, and with good reason. Stephen's dreams and the Circe episode, a dream play anticipating the "drema" or "drame" (69, 302) before us, prove long preoccupation with night thoughts. Indeed, a manuscript now at Cornell includes records and analyses of Joyce's own dreams. Replacing Joyce here, the four old men examine "irrmages" from the mind of sleeping Yawn, supine on mound instead of couch (Chapter XV); for by such analysis we can hope to get at the heart of man and all his motives. "How culious an epiphany!" (508) say those four analysts.

The principal dreamer, however, is probably H. C. E. *Finnegans Wake* tells "how our mysterbilder his tullen aslip . . . and bares his sobconscious inklings." (377) The voice we hear is that of this "traumconductor." If his learning and linguistic accomplishment seem beyond those of an ordinary publican, we

20. Not only Freud but *The Dark Night of the Soul* by St. John of the Cross and (as we have noticed) *The Book of the Dead* determine Earwicker's dream.

must remember that H. C. E. is also everybody (including Joyce)
and his dream the dream of all men. Our ears pricked to hear his
"sleeptalking," our eyes intent upon his "traumscrapt," (459,
623) we follow him as we can "durk the thicket of slumbwhere,"
(580) feeling like "narcolepts on the lakes of Coma." (395)
There is nothing "supernoctural" about "feeling aslip and wauk-
ing up." (597-98) It is our natural rhythm; and, closing the book
of sleep, we shall wake from our "foggy doze" (367) at dawn, for
"Dies is Dorminus master." (609) [21] "You mean to see," we ask,
"we have been hadding a sound night's sleep?" (597)

In our encounter through dream with all of man's experience
we have also encountered the feeling of experiencing and the
feeling of trying to interpret our experience and its record.
Finnegans Wake is cunningly designed to give us these two feelings: that of encountering life and that of reading its record. In
this book, as in our daily lives, we can interpret some things
easily. Others yield at last to deeper investigation; but some continue to baffle us. If Joyce is to give us the feeling of reality and of
our attempts at it, *Finnegans Wake* must be easy, difficult, and
impenetrable by turns. The mixed feeling of small triumphs and
of ultimate frustration is part of the fun. Could the book be
understood entirely, it would lack its intended effect. *Finnegans
Wake* is an imitation of life. Undiscouraged by what is beyond us
in life or in this book of life, we must keep on trying, doing our
best like Samuel Beckett's bums. Some things will yield some
meaning somehow sometime. *Finnegans Wake*, then, is the record of reality, of man's attempt to explain it, and an invitation to
explain. *Finnegans Wake* is about *Finnegans Wake*.

The public may enter Earwicker's pub with assurance. There is
God's plenty of entertainment here for any man until closing
time.

The following pages provide brief and general views of the
seventeen chapters. Knowing something of structure and of some

21. See *Letters*, 406: This phrase, which alludes to *Dominus noster*, means
day is lord over sleep.

of the parts may help with other parts and with the whole. No account can be adequate, but some account may help. The descriptive titles for parts and chapters are mine.

A danger to guard against is free-wheeling interpretation. Your guesses about the meaning of any word or phrase must be justified by both immediate and general context. The text limits its interpretation. Not only idea but tone and movement (gay or resigned, tripping or heavy) can serve as limiting context.

Part I

THE FALL OF MAN
(*Eight chapters. Vico's divine age.*)

CHAPTER I

The Fall of Man
(*Pp. 3-29. Vico's divine age.*)

Although the book is circular, this chapter is general introduction as the last is summary. Centered in the first period of Vico's cycle, the first chapter concerns the primitive and the religious, as references to Genesis, anthropology, archaeology, and puns in Hebrew and Arabic imply. Fable and hieroglyph are suitable method. But since each period contains the others, substance and method alike involve other periods, too. The tower of Babel easily becomes the Woolworth Building and the fall of man the fall of stocks in Wall Street. All things and times are neighbors here and all man's languages.

Chapter I falls into five parts: the first, after an allusive view of all the themes (see *Letters*, 247-48), concerns man's fall and wake; (3-7) the second presents the magazine in the Park, the battle of Waterloo, and the family-centered process of history; (7-14) the third includes the story of Mutt and Jute, the battle of Clontarf, and the dump; (15-20) the fourth is the story of the

Prankquean; (21-23) the last, an address to the dead. (24-29) All these matters are important, but most readers are fascinated most by the three fables: Willingdone and Lipoleum, Mutt and Jute, and the Prankquean.

Announced by the hundred-lettered word, (3) the story of the fall begins with Tim Finnegan (H. C. E.), the "bygmester" or Ibsen's master builder. Building a tower, he falls from his ladder. His wake, attended by friends and relatives, and his revival proceed according to the ballad. Builder dead becomes a sleeping giant, extending from Howth to the magazine. A salmon, he is sacramentally devoured by his survivors; for this "brontoichthyan form" is a thunderfish or Jesus-God. Adam, Jesus, faller and creator, Finnegan will be Finnagain. (4-7)

The magazine, to which the sleeping giant's clay feet extend, is the haunt of three soldiers and two tempting girls, "so gigglesomes minxt [Latin *mingo*] the follyages, the prettilees!" Wellminxt, the countryside is "waterloose." Joining the Wellington Monument, the magazine becomes the museum, through which Kate, the janitrix, conducts us. "Tip" means that the museum is a dump. (7-8)

Kate's conducted tour amounts to the history of Waterloo. Willingdone-H. C. E., speaking German, defeats French-speaking Lipoleum, a composite of the two girls ("jinnies") and the three soldiers or the members of Earwicker's family. (German generally implies father and French implies mother.) References to many battles and a game of football, accompanying the action, enlarge this family conflict. Father thinks he wins. (8-10) After the battle, a bird (A. L. P.) picks the pieces up to renew them. From the litter of battle comes the hen's letter. (10-13) This process of conflict and renewal is that of all history from 1132 A. D. to 566 and then from 566 A. D. to 1132. History is centered in Earwicker's family from A. D. ("antediluvious") to A. D. ("annadominant"). Peace follows conflict, (13-15) and after peace comes another conflict, that of Mutt and Jute on the battlefield of Clontarf, where Brian Boru defeated the invading Danes.

Mutt and Jute (Shem and Shaun, Irishman and Danish invader) are so primitive that communication is difficult. Mutt (ear-time) and Jute (eye-space) fail to say ear to eye. No wonder Jute is "astoneaged" by Mutt's poetic discussion of the dump, which, equivalent to the museum, is tomb and repository. An "allaphbed," the dump is literature, which, coming from debris of conflict like the letter, is debris itself. "Futhorc" (18) is the runic alphabet. (15-20)

The story of the Prankquean (21-23) is that of family conflict from A. L. P.'s point of view. She baffles Jarl van Hoother (H. C. E. as Earl of Howth) with her riddle[1] and defeats him. Coming and going three times, as in a fairy story, this trickster steals Earwicker's twin sons to convert them to their opposites. Hilary (gay Shem) becomes Tristopher (sad Shaun) and Tristopher becomes Hilary. The "dummy" or Isabel remains the same. Making her wit (wet) against Earwicker's door, the Prankquean takes three soundings of the river. The presence of Mark Twain marks her as Muse and patron of wits. Indeed, the result of her tricks and soundings is "porthery" (a union of poetry, pot, and porter). Baffled Earwicker ordures in his pub and falls, but from the happy fall of this "foenix culprit" comes the city of Dublin with its motto. References to the legends of Dermot and Grania and Grace O'Malley and to the conflict of Catholic with Protestant generalize this familiar story.

An address to dead Finnegan concludes the chapter. (24-29) Rest easy, "Finn no more." Your family is happy without you, say all the mourners at Finnegan's wake.

---

1. The Prankquean's riddle, "Why do I am alook alike a poss of porterpease?" confuses Earwicker because it is so close to home. Porter and Piesporter are drinks, and the twins of whom he is composed are as alike as two peas. Porter is Earwicker himself, "peacisely." The poss is A. L. P., the "potmother," (11) or what the peas are stewed in.

Riddles abound in *Finnegans Wake*, itself a riddle: e.g. pp. 170, 219, 223, 231, 253, 324, 607. Sometimes that of the Sphinx, the riddle is more often that of the universe or of the "anniverse." Stephen's riddles in *A Portrait* and *Ulysses* were but "the first rattle of his juniverse." Joyce, who admitted adding "puzzles," (*Letters*, 228, 250) expected readers to solve them. H. G. Wells accused Joyce of turning his back on common man to elaborate "vast riddles." (*Letters*, 274)

CHAPTER II

The Cad

(*Pp.* 30-47. *Vico's heroic age.*)

Joyce called this the "H. C. E. chapter." Its central episode, the
encounter of H. C. E. with the Cad and their heroic conflict,
is "the basis of my book," said Joyce. (*Letters,* 396)

The origin of Earwig's name and gossip about his alleged mis-
demeanor with the two girls in the Park (Eden) compose the
opening section. As capable of any enormity as Oscar Wilde,
H. C. E. is a "big white caterpillar." (31-34) In the Park, near
the Wellington Monument and not far from the magazine,
guilty Earwicker meets a Cad with a pipe, who asks him the time
of day. (35) H. C. E. is old and the Cad (Cadet or Shem. Cf.
"kidscad," 3) is young.[1] When a young man asks an old man the
time of day, the question, implying time to retire, can be sinister.[2]
Taking the question for accusation, stuttering Earwicker, "carrying his overgoat under his schulder [German, "guilt"], sheepside
out," unnecessarily protests his innocence; and the astonished
Cad goes home to his wife, Bareniece Maxwelton—Annie Laurie
or A. L. P. (38) Evidently, through this encounter with his
father, the young man has taken his father's place. This is the
old story of father, son, and father again.

Gossip spreads the story of the significant encounter. Philly
Thurnston, Winny Widger (a tipster at the races), Treacle Tom,
Frisky Shorty, Peter Cloran, O'Mara, Mildew Lisa, and the rest,

1. The encounter of young man with old has literary parallels. H. C. E. is old
Yeats accosted by caddish young Joyce. Later, H. C. E. is old Joyce, accosted
and imitated by young Eliot. "Bhagafat gaiters" (35) and "I have met with
you . . . too late" (37) or Joyce's legendary remark to the celebrated poet,
establish Yeats. "Ildiot" with his "secondmouth language," appropriating the
"bigtimer's verbaten words," (37) establishes Eliot. All is relative and changing: as Joyce to Yeats, so Eliot to Joyce.
2. Cf. "Quote awhore?" (154) "whose o'cloak," (155) and "embouscher"
(156) in The Mookse and the Gripes, another conflict of time and space. That
the time is twelve (35) implies the end of an old cycle (the father's) and the
beginning of the new.

who shift and merge in a bewildering manner, are only members of the family, disguised by other names. (38-40) Hosty and two companions, inspired by gossip, cross the city (all cities) to be joined by "a decent sort" or H. C. E. himself. They compose a ballad or "rann" about the fall of H. C. E. "The rann, the rann, the king of all ranns" (Cf. *Ulysses,* 472) combines this ballad with the wren ritually sacrificed on St. Stephen's Day. Literary references prove the ballad literature as well as music. (41-44)

The hundred-lettered word for fall that announces this creation implies defecation. "It's cumming, it's brumming," (44) referring to *le mot de Cambronne,* means that the ballad—indeed, all literature—is *merde,* even Sophocles, Shakespeare, Dante, and Moses. (47) All droppings are fertile as all falls are creative; but the queasy reader, all at sea, may suffer from *mal de merde.*

Hosty, the composer, is host (of pub), *hostie* (French for Eucharist), and *hostis* (Latin for enemy or Satan). In a word, Hosty is the union of father and son, of H. C. E. and Shem,[3] who replaces father by joining him. The union of bourgeois and exiled poet, as of Bloom with Stephen, is creative. Earwicker-Shem composes and sings the ballad about Earwicker. "The Ballad of Persse O'Reilly" (*perce-oreille* is French for earwig), one of the best accounts of H. C. E.'s nature, fall, and renewal, is an epitome of *Finnegans Wake,* but so is almost everything else in *Finnegans Wake.*

CHAPTER III

Gossip and the Knocking at the Gate

(*Pp.* 48-74. *Vico's human age.*)

The fog, particularly dense around here, makes it difficult to identify the "individuone," Earwicker in particular. "Who was he to whom? . . . Whose are the placewheres?" (56) But references to Nicholas of Cusa and Bruno, (49-50) introducing the

3. Cf. Osti-Fosti, tenor and minor poet, or pure Shem. (48)

coincidence of contraries, provide a clue. As Archdeacon F. X. Preserved Coppinger, (55) Earwicker is the coincidence of Catholic and Protestant—in short, a *"Cainandabler."* (71) "Biografiends" and "factferreters" find it hard to place him. Indeed, this "Dyas in his machina" seems at once in a theater and riding round the Park in a jaunting car throughout the introductory section. (48-57) One thing alone is clear: "The house of Atreox is fallen indeedust (Ilyam, Ilyum! . . .)." (55) [1] Two girls and three soldiers are somehow involved in this collupsus.

But, in the human age now, we may expect democratic action or talk. The second part of this chapter (57-62) is devoted to gossip about Earwicker's sin and fall. (For Joyce as victim of gossip see *Letters*, 165-66.) The three soldiers guess that Lilith "souped him." A "wastepacket Sittons" (Isabel), Missioner Wombwell (a revivalist or A. L. P.), and Sylvia Silence, the girl detective (Isabel) contribute their opinions; and there are many other speculators. Nothing, however, is more indefinite than the nature of Earwicker's sin.

The third part of this chapter consists of two versions of trouble at the gate of the pub. According to the first story, Earwicker is waylaid by Whenn with a revolver (the Cad again) in a fog. These two compose the "fender," one the defender, the other the offender. Arriving drunk and disorderly at his door, the fender raises such a row that Maurice Behan (Joe and Stanislaus Joyce) and the rest of the family pile indignantly downstairs to see what the matter is. (63-64) According to the second story, Earwicker, the "heeltapper," is besieged in his pub by some intruder, who, hammering on the door, demands drink after closing time and shouts abuse in "mooksed metaphors." [2] Herr Betreffender (the man in question) is not only the reporter of

1. "Ilyam" and "Ilyum" are appropriately in the accusative case; the first is feminine, the second masculine; one is of the first declension, the other of the second. Women fall first and we fall for them. Consider Helen of Troy. Accused, we decline and fall in grammar as in life.
2. The intruder (another Cad) is the young man, knocking at the door. The old man's fear and guilt are apparent. Cf. "knock out in the park." (4) Shaun, as postman, always knocks twice

Adam's fall for a Wasteland "payrodicule" but the offender and the defender. At once outside and inside his pub, Earwicker is outsider and insider, Shem and Shaun, father and son. (67-74) Plainly the "hypostasised" (55) pantriarch is the union of two natures. Yet for this compromised compromiser there is promise of renewal after fall. Like Arthur, he will come back, saying "Add some," with father Abraham. (73-74)

The interlude of Daddy (H. C. E.) with his two peaches (64-65) is the most amusing part of the chapter. Presented in terms of popular songs and movies, this story of the old man with two girls parallels that of old Swift with his Stella and Vanessa. Deep in our hollywood, we "roll away the reel world," confusing real with fake.

CHAPTER IV

The Trial

(Pp. 75-103. Vico's ricorso.)

Dreaming of the Cad and the two girls who caused his fall, H. C. E. lies buried in his coffin under a lake or in the dump. Kate, the scavenger, is in charge of this museum piece. Tip. (75-85)

After this sepulchral opening, the trial of Festy King (H. C. E.) before his bar at the Old Bailey begins. There are four judges, twelve jurymen, and a multitude of witnesses and advocates. (85-91) An eye, ear, nose, and throat witness (Shaun-Gogarty) gives evidence against him. The cross-examining attorney seems Shem. The evidence concerns the Cad, the two girls, the three soldiers, and the twins or the two sides of H. C. E. Accused by one son, he is defended by the other. At last, like Bloom on a similar occasion, King testifies unintelligibly in his own defense. Amid general laughter, the twenty-eight advocatesses, joined by a "leapgirl," (Isabel) gather around Shaun, the eye, ear, nose, and throat witness, praising him and "stincking thyacinths through his curls," as if they were Lady Chatterley herself. The four old men render a verdict of Nolans Brumans, the only possible one for a criminal so shifty; and two-faced King goes off scotfree. (93)

With his Shem side out, the great man, about whom nothing can be proved, is scorned by the twenty-nine girls as the author of *Finnegans Wake*: "Shun the Punman!" they cry. The dump and the letter recur by easy association. Fully described as art and life, the letter, like *Finnegans Wake*, is Alpha and Omega. (93-94)

Meanwhile the four judges, gossiping about H. C. E., agree that he stinks like the breeze off a "manure works." (94-96)

Free but hounded by slander, H. C. E., like Stephen and Bloom before him, becomes a fox, hunted by the pack. His Shem side still out, he flees into exile; yet as the Pope, he displays his Shaun side too. (96-100)

Every fourth chapter ends with A. L. P., who, as principle of renewal, must preside over each *ricorso*. It is she who, forgiving buried H. C. E., guards his grave, and it is she who will wake him. (101-03) The poem that concludes this inconclusive chapter does for A. L. P. what the poem at the end of Chapter II does for H. C. E. A parody of "At Trinity Church I Met My Doom," a music-hall song, the poem celebrates her as river, him as fish—and a poor one, too. The great mother of many children washes the washed-up up. Let Noman laugh at Jordan.

CHAPTER V

The Letter
(*Pp. 104-25. Vico's divine age.*)

The first cycle of four chapters ends scripturally with the river. The second cycle, meeting the first, begins with the river, scripturally. As this sentence recalls the first sentence of Chapter I, so the last sentence of Chapter IV predicts the last sentence of the book. Chapter V, says Joyce, (*Letters*, 104) is generally considered the "easiest" part of *Finnegans Wake;* and this judgment of the world seems secure enough.

The second cycle, which moves like the first within the great age of the father's fall, seems less concerned with father than with members of his family, his wife and children. But fallen Earwicker is a family man and here is what surrounds him. Here is what causes his fall.

A parody of the Lord's prayer, the opening sentence is the Lady's prayer; for as Muse and life force and mistress of plurabilities, she is as important as he and no less venerable. As Lord and Lady are united in this reverent parody, so are Christian and Moslem; for "In the name of Annah the Allmaziful" is a Moslem formula for beginning something. All is suitable here to another divine age, even the titles for the "untitled mamafesta," which serve as a kind of litany. (104-07) A. L. P.'s manifesto or the letter itself provides another summary of *Finnegans Wake.* Each title is one of its aspects.

A scholar, lecturing on the letter, finds it a "proteiform graph" or a "polyhedron of scripture," like the Rosetta stone. Who, he asks with professorial informality, "wrote the durn thing anyhow?" Was it "a too pained whittlewit laden with the loot of learning"—someone like spectacled Joyce? Consideration of the missing envelope suggests that, as drawers should not be contemplated apart from what they cover, so a text should not be judged apart from context. (107-09)

A hen dug the letter up in the dump. But Kevin, a bantling, takes credit for finding it. In the sense of always "euchring" credit for what others have done, Shaun is as much a fake as Shem. (110)

Though apparently simple, the text of the letter (111) is far from clear. We know that, sent from Boston on January 31 to a nameless person, it is signed by a spot of tea. Long residence in the dump has injured the text. Apparently about Father Michael, Maggy, the twins, cakes, and Van Houten's cocoa, the letter leaves us in some doubt about what it is about.

This combination of simplicity and obscurity is a challenge

to scholars, who, for the rest of the chapter, attempt to solve the riddle by a variety of disciplines. There are Freudians (115) and Marxists, (116) paleographers, epigraphists, linguists, and probably epistlemologists. Each attempt on the document is sound and each inadequate. Some compare it to the "Tunc" page of *The Book of Kells*. Plainly, since these learned men are not unlike those who attempt explanations of *Finnegans Wake*, Joyce is mocking his critics.

Distance and freedom from preconception give common readers an advantage here. We gather that the letter concerns the Earwicker family. Father Michael is H. C. E. and the four "crosskisses" at the end may be Vico's system. Dictated by A. L. P. and addressed to H. C. E., the letter was written by Shem the Penman and carried by Shaun the Post. The letter, we gather, is an epitome of *Finnegans Wake* and, like it, is at once simple and baffling. But so, apparently, is the universe, where we get along as we are able.

CHAPTER VI

The Quiz
(*Pp. 126-68. Vico's heroic age.*)

Another summary of *Finnegans Wake*, this chapter presents the matter as a quiz set by Jockit (Shem) for Shaun, lettercarrier for Jhon Jhamieson and Song, or the creative company of father, sons, and spirit. That there are twelve questions suggests the co-operation of the "twelve apostrophes" of the jury, apostles now. Naturally these questions include Dublin and the members of the family as well as the book itself. The riddling questions provoke riddling or ambiguous answers.

Question 1, (126-39) which concerns H. C. E. or Finn MacCool, provides another description of one who, like Atlas, Dan O'Connell, and Richard Crookback, is "larger than life." Our "supreme mytherector," he is our "maximost bridgesmaker" or Adam.

Question 2 (139) describes A. L. P. in suitable rhythm.

Question 3 (139-40) : The sign on the pub is the motto of Dublin.

Question 4 (140-41) is a riddle about Dublin.

Question 5 (141) : An advertisement for a handyman or curate is answered by Joe.

Question 6 (141) concerns Kate and her "midden name." Tip.

Question 7 (142) introduces the twelve customers or apostles, as their names imply. Words ending in "tion" are the sign of the twelve.

Question 8 (142-43) is about the "maggies" or the twenty-eight girls.

Question 9, (143) on the "panorama of all flores of speech," is a description of *Finnegans Wake*, that "collideorscape."

Question 10, (143-48) on Isabel, is improved by references to Swift, Tristan, and the *New Free Woman* "with novel inside" (or the *Egoist*, where *A Portrait* was published). She has twenty-eight classmates. Her interest, like her father's, is in "wonderwearlds" or underwear. "I'm only any girl," she says.

Question 11 (148-68) provokes a long and fascinating answer. Shem's question, a rhymed parody of "The Exile of Erin," is answered by Shaun in the guise of Professor Jones, the eminent "spatialist." Trying to prove space superior to time, he presents his argument abstractly first, then by parable, and by example from history at last.

Formidably learned, the lecturer cites Winestain (Einstein), Bitchson (Bergson), space-adoring Wyndham Lewis, Lévy-Brühl, the anthropologist, and the quantum theory to establish his side of the *talis* and *qualis* (such and as) controversy. "Myrrdin aloer!" he finally exclaims with old Cambronne. To reach such "muddlecrass" pupils he must descend from abstraction to parable. But the fable of the Mookse and the Gripes (152-59) proves no less unsatisfactory; for, like any work of art, it exceeds the artist's intention. Designed to demonstrate the victory of Mookse-space over Gripes-time, the fable ends with the victory of space-time or the union of these shifty antagonists. Later (472) their union is the "grand continuum" of the physicists.

"Eins within a space," the first sentence, parodies that of *A Portrait of the Artist.* Even here "Eins" unites time with space. The following story of Pope Adrian IV (Nicholas Breakspear) and the Irish recalls the fable of the bull in the hospital scene of *Ulysses.* The Mookse (a fox in search of grapes) is the Pope; Peter is a stone; and Rome is *raum* or German space. As the frog who would a-wooing go, the Mookse sets out for Ireland, where he finds the sour Gripes hanging from his tree.[1] The heroic contention of these antagonists is any between Shaun and Shem. That the grapes become the fox at times is no more than we might expect; for both antagonists are parts of H. C. E., who, as fox, is both hunter and quarry—this, that, or anything.

Nuvoletta, the little cloud, failing to make peace, falls as a tear into the river "whose muddied name was Missisliffi"; for Isabel is a "leaptear." Mookse and Gripes, having become washing on the banks, are gathered up by the washerwomen to end in the same basket. Only an elm and a stone and the river remain, for these go on forever. That Bruno, patron of quarreling opposites and of their reconciliation, presides over this affair is proved by a listening pupil. Bruno Nowlan at the beginning, he is Nolan Browne at the end.

The dissatisfied professor, still intent on his "cashdime" problem (time is money), turns to history now for fitting analogue. The history of Burrus and Caseous (161-67) renews the quarrel of Shaun and Shem in terms of politics, geometry, and food (Burrus is butter, Caseous cheese). After having killed their father

1. References to the Aurignacian, Mousterian, Tardenoisian, and Robenhausian cultures of paleolithic or neolithic times make the conflict seem very primitive, like that of Mutt and Jute; but, after all, Part I, whatever the chapter, is Vico's divine age. There are references to St. Malachi's prophecy to Adrian IV. Conflicts of orthodox and heretic, of English with Irish are also suggested. The "zozzymusses" in their "robenhauses" (154) refer to Zozimus, a blind, nineteenth-century Irish singer. The Mookse is Stephen's moocow. Since *Mukke* is Danish for "gripe," the Mookse gripes.

(Caesar), Brutus and Cassius (the sons) begin to quarrel. Their sister, Margareena, Nuvoletta's successful successor, brings peace by introducing Anthony, who makes a triangle out of the "isocelating biangle" of B and C by adding A. Triangle A B C, a triumvirate of soldiers, is equivalent to H. C. E. or spacetime again. The two girls enjoy peace for a short space of time.

A petulant letter from Merus Genius (pure, unchanging Shaun) to Careous Caseous (decaying, changing Shem) asserts creative ability. Shaun knows the "rite words by the rote order." (167)

Question 12 (168) and its answer are in ambiguous Latin. "*Esto?*" is at once imperative and interrogative. "*Sacer*" means either accursed or sacred. "*Semus sumus,*" at once singular and plural, means we are the same or we are Shem. This answer introduces the next chapter.

CHAPTER VII

Shem

(Pp. 169-95. Vico's human age.)

Commonly ironic about Shem and Shaun, Joyce is heavily jocular in this elaborate portrait of Shem as a young man—as if the effort required for distancing were almost too formidable for ease. Joyce does his best; but the quiet irony of *A Portrait* is more agreeable.

This chapter reveals another Stephen Dedalus. Taking himself in his "art of arts" for "some god in the manger," (188) Shem also refuses to serve. Like Stephen, he is prig, sponger, and victim of pride. "Self exiled in upon his ego," (184) this heretical outlaw, abandoning the four masters who brought him up, scribbles "inartistic portraits of himself" in "monolook interyrear." (182) These portraits of "telemac" (176) include *Dubliners* (186-87)[1]

1. There are references here to "The Boarding House," "A Painful Case," "Clay," "Two Gallants," and "The Dead." "Telemac" seems to unite Telemachus with macintosh. In Chapter XIV (473) Shaun or Shaun-Shem is the author of *Dubliners*.

Ulysses, "his usylessly unreadable Blue Book of Eccles," (179) and *Finnegans Wake* or those "quashed quotatoes" and "messes of mottage" (183) for which he has sold his birthright. Written in ink made of his own excrement on his own thin skin, these forgeries are "obscene matter" unprotected by "copriright." (185)

This wild goose teaches in the Berlitz School, and, like Joyce, is half blind. But details of Joyce's life do not make Shem Joyce. Shem is that side of Joyce which must unite with his Shaun side in order to make Bloom or H. C. E. Joyce was a bourgeois as well as an artist. It is only after uniting with H. C. E. (179) that Shem is able to write *Ulysses.* Moreover, Shem's *Finnegans Wake,* like Joyce's, rises from the personal to the universal, from his own skin to what is "common to allflesh." (186)

Shem is less Joyce's view of Joyce than Shaun's view or that of the world. Embodying it, Constable Sistersen (a union of Joe, Shaun, and Stanislaus) appoints himself his brother's keeper. (186) Becoming Justius, Shaun rebukes his brother, Mercius. (187-93) "Let us pry," says Shaun Stanislaus Justius. Waving his "deathbone," this censor represents the great "No." (193) Lifting his "lifewand" or creator's rod, Shem utters the "Yes" that seems implied by the sudden intrusion of A. L. P. (194-95) "Sonnies had a scrap," she tolerantly observes, knowing that these scrappers must unite in H. C. E.

The emphasis on personality seems appropriate to Vico's human age. That Shem is civilized is proved by his preference of "tinned" salmon to the real thing. (170) H. C. E., the great salmon of the Liffey, sacramentally consumed by his survivors, is the thing itself, and *Finnegans Wake* is his fish story. Maybe, of course, *Finnegans Wake,* both tin and fish, is also the tinning of fish and the fishing. Consider Plumtree's Potted Meat.

CHAPTER VIII

A. L. P.
(*Pp.* 196-216. *Vico's* ricorso.)

This is one of the most pleasing chapters of *Finnegans Wake.* That it is also one of the most familiar may be due to Joyce's recording of the last few pages, (213-16) which prove the book an arrangement of sounds as well as senses. It must be read aloud, preferably by Joyce.

A. L. P. is back again for another *ricorso.* "O," the opening word, set apart from the rest, is the Omega with which she answers H. C. E.'s Alpha. Female O, she is the brook of life. From bank to bank of the Liffey at Chapelizod the two washerwomen who picked the Mookse and Gripes up gossip about H. C. E. as they wash his dirty linen in public ("A catchword is enough to set me off," said Joyce. *Letters,* 147.) "Tell me all about. . . ," says one gossip to the other, and the other says, "Tell me more." Earwicker's sins and domestic affairs occupy their tongues and ears as their hands restore the whiteness of his underpants. On opposite banks, these rivals seem Shem and Shaun, tree and stone. Names of rivers embellish their chatter. He gave her "the tigris eye," they say. Look, they say, holding Earwicker's wash up, at "the mouldaw stains. And the dneepers of wet and the gangres of sin in it." Not only the Liffey, A. L. P. is all the rivers of the world.[1]

The washerwomen's account of the relations of A. L. P. and H. C. E. follows the course of the Liffey from Wicklow to the sea, where "there's Zambosy waiting for me." (207) There, like Adam and Danish invader, he shoots up the river "in this wet of his prow." (198)[2] Their legend finds parallel in that of Petrarch and

---

1. "Hundreds of river names are woven into the text. I think it moves." (*Letters,* 259) Later Joyce added 152 more rivers. (*Letters,* 261)
2. That much of A. L. P.'s chapter is concerned with H. C. E. is not surprising. He is her center as she his. Mrs. Bloom's monologue is largely concerned with Bloom.

Laura or stone and tree. (103-04) From A. L. P.'s capacious "zak-bag" come gifts for all her children: "a collera morbous for Mann in the Cloack" (the Thomas Mann of *Death in Venice*), and no less appropriate gifts for Swift, Yeats, Gogarty, Shaw, and James Stephens, not to mention a "Congoswood cross" for "Sunny Twimjim" or Joyce as the union of twins. (211) "That's what you may call a tale of a tub."(212)

Gradually turning into tree and stone, these gossips hear the Angelus, childishly remember nursery rhymes, and think they see the great Finnleader in their mist, but it is only the ass of those four men. With darkness comes confusion: "Fieluhr? Filou!" They pray to the Virgin as Gerty's bats flit overhead. "Can't hear with the waters of." (215) Nothing remains at last but blind stone, deaf tree, and the "hitherandthithering waters of. Night!" But all is new again, however dark and dumb: "Wring out the clothes! Wring in the dew!" (213)

Part II

CONFLICT

(*Four chapters. Vico's heroic age.*)

CHAPTER IX

Children at Play

(*Pp. 219-59. Vico's divine age.*)

This gay and genial chapter "came out like drops of blood." (*Letters,* 295) Like Mozart, Joyce was most cheerful in art when in life most troubled.

Literally, this chapter tells of children at play in the road out-side the pub. Their game is an old one called Angels, Devils, and Colors. It is twilight. Soon the lamplighter comes, the animals in the zoo in Phoenix Park lie down, and all grows dark in the "fun-naminal world." (244) The "childergarten" is dismissed when fa ther, coming to the door of the pub, where he is entertaining twelve customers, calls the children in for supper, homework, and bed. (253, 256) "Grant sleep in hour's time, O Loud!" (259)

Glugg (Shem), Chuff (Shaun), Isabel, and the Floras or Maggies, her twenty-eight friends from St. Bride's School, are the players. Chuff is the angel (Mick), Glugg is the devil (Nick), and the girls are all the colors of the rainbow, "four themes over." These girls ask the devil to solve a riddle. The answer is "heliotrope," but the devil, black as sin, is "off colour." (230) Twice Glugg tries and twice he fails while, mocking him, the heliotropic girls dance in a ring around Chuff, the son or sun. Chuff's "inners even. All's rice with their whorl." (225) Baffled Glugg, recalling H. C. E. teased by the Prankquean and her riddle, runs away twice to exile in "visible disgrace." He "don't know whose hue." (227)

Author of *Chamber Music*, Glugg displays his "pricoxity" to the girls; "he make peace in his preaches and play with esteem." (224-25) These girls are not amused. During his consequent exile, he writes *Ulysses*, his "farced epistol to the hibruws." (228-29) (He is Paul-Saul-*saule* as Chuff is Peter-stone.) "Ipsey Secumbe" now, himself alone, Glugg weeps tears "such as engines weep." "Was liffe worth leaving?" he wonders. (230) Called home by letter, he tries again, fails again, and is off again: "Hark to his wily geeses goosling by." (233)

Meanwhile, the "twentynines of bloomers," expert beyond "punns and reedles," dance round Chuff in "heliolatry," screaming "Xanthos! Xanthos! Xanthos!" as if acclaiming a popular poet. (234-35, 239, 249) Poor Glugg, a poor poet, is "dense floppens mugurdy." (231)

This chapter begins and ends in a theater where *The Mime of Mick, Nick, and the Maggies* is presented by an impressive cast. The curtain falls to loud applause. But this theater is only a metaphor for "at play." Vico is the producer, the applause mimics his cycle, and the riddle is that of the universe. (255-59) The world is stage; games are a metaphor for living. Children at play involve everything in *Finnegans Wake* or everything.

Echoes of nursery rhymes and fairy stories are what the children's hour demands. (223, 224, 227, 235-36, 242) Larger references to Tristan, (232) *Don Quixote*, (234) *Huckleberry Finn* ("Jempson's weed" and "Jacqueson's Island," 245), and a parody of Edgar Quinet (236) enlarge the meanings. Memories of the Mookse and the Gripes, the Prankquean, and the Cad provide connection and parallel. When Father emerges from his thundercloud to summon the children "enthreatingly," (246) he is not unlike God the Father.

CHAPTER X

Homework

(*Pp.* 260-308. *Vico's heroic age.*)

However formidable this chapter, its action is simple: The children prepare their lessons. Shem and Shaun (called Dolph and Kev) quarrel as usual while Isabel looks on without concern. Assuming a suitably academic form, the chapter is a text with marginal comments and footnotes. To the right at first, Shaun's professorial marginalia are abstract and general. Shem's marginalia, to the left at first, are playful and irreverent. But, responsive to Bruno, the twins change sides in the middle. Shem's comments move to the right, Shaun's to the left. Isabel's footnotes, embodying woman's view of man's affairs, remain at the bottom, where they belong. She, at least, is constant. If the text is taken as life or as *Finnegans Wake*, marginalia and footnotes are attempts at interpretation. A difficult chapter, as Joyce concedes, (*Letters*, 406) yet not so difficult as it seems.

The dense and philosophical introduction (261-65) concerns H. C. E. as creator. "More mob than man" (261) and an "archetypt," (263) he is also Ainsoph or the God of the Kabala, who, descending in nine emanations, creates all things. His number is ten, the number of completeness; or, looked at another way, "the decemt man" is one and his creative partner, A. L. P., is his "zeroine." The numbers three and four are also important. Representing the trivium and quadrivium of mediaeval studies, these numbers are also traditional signs of the above and the below. Under Hermetic auspices, the corrrespondence of above and below is also creative. (263) However you look at him, father is creator. "GNOSIS OF PRECREATE DETERMINATION" says marginal Shaun. "Dig him in the rubsh," says marginal Shem. "Groupname for grapejuice," says Isabel, bringing it down to a footnote. (261-62) Not there for its own sake or to make an occult point, this philosophical machinery is no more than another analogy. H. C. E. is like Kabalistic God; and the relations of H. C. E. with his creation are like those celebrated by Hermes Trismegistus or Thoth, Stephen's god of writers and libraries.

Naturally and unnaturally, H. C. E. is at once above and below. Below in the pub, he is making "tin for ten" or money before closing time. Above, his children, representing him, open grammars. (266-70) Her knowledge inherited from "gramma's grammar," Isabel needs no books; for hers is the "law of the jungerl." (268) She sits and knits, bringing things together, while the twins bicker over Browne and Nolan's divisional tables.

History, the next lesson, (271-81) reviews conflict and peace, sin and fall, and all the affairs of Sire Jeallyous Seizer with his "duo of druidesses" and the "tryonforit of Oxthievious, Lapidous and Malthouse Anthemy." (271) Wellington, magazine, dump, and letter reappear under Viconian auspices. History, as always, is family history and the same old things again. Edgar Quinet, parodied in Chapter IX, reappears in French: the flowers persist, he says, whatever the horrors of conflict. (281)

Geometry next. (286-99) The problem, first in Casey's Euclid, is to construct triangle A L P.(293) Dolph's "loose carollaries" (294) attend a demonstration of his "geomater," an ideal delta, whose muddy delta is her "safety vulve." (297)[1] Dolph's

---

1. Her triangle, like Mrs. Bloom's, is also that on a bottle of Bass, as Shem's marginal comment implies. (286) Twins peeping at parents, the sins of H. C. E., and the creative cycle are all involved in this geometrical demonstration. Fig leaves figure, along with pubic forest, apron, Dublin's landscape, defecation (H. C. E.) and urination (A. L. P.). Geometry, after all. is measurement of the earth.

Q. E. D. establishes another metaphor, another epitome.

Preceding this dream demonstration (in the manner of Lewis Carroll) and this familiar application of Euclid, a passage without marginal notes marks the changing of sides. (287-92) A Latin account of Bruno and Vico, of river, dump, and rival banks announces the machinery of process and reversal. What follows concerns H. C. E. as invader, Joyce and his critics, and the affairs of Tristan, Isolde, and Mark.

Dolph's Euclidian competence and his indecorous exposure of mother annoy Kev in spite of Dolph's efforts to teach his brother the use of pen. "Wreathed with his pother," as Cain with Abel, Kev knocks Dolph down. After conflict, however, comes the rainbow of reconciliation and renewal. (301-04) "Forge away," says Shaun or Kev. No less benign to his "bloater's kipper," Shem hails his popular antithesis. "We've had our day at triv and quad," (306) the twins agree. Three and four make seven or the family; but the number ten, which opens the tenth chapter, closes it as the children go down to supper. Their nightletter conveys new year's greetings to father and mother.

Isabel's ambiguous hieroglyph of "skool and crossbuns" (308) recalls her signs for the Doodles family. (299) See *Letters* (213) for their meaning. Her thumbed nose (308) is woman's opinion of eggheads—readers of Joyce, maybe.

CHAPTER XI

The Tale of a Pub
(*Pp.* 309-82. *Vico's human age.*)

Open to the public and more or less democratic, a pub is a good place for the human age. In the Mullingar at Chapelizod a twelve-tube "daildialler" broadcasts news and weather reports. Maybe an actual radio, this machine is certainly a metaphor for the twelve patrons of the bar, who, drinking Bass' ale with its red triangle, gossip about Earwicker, "host of a bottlefilled." (309-10,

324) As he gives them their "beerings," (321) they spread ru-
mors about the affair of the two girls, the three soldiers, the magazine, and the fall from the magazine wall. (314) Breaking now
and again into song, the twelve customers render "John Peel,"
"Casey Jones," and "wather parted from the say," (317-22, 368,
371-72) another version of Hosty's ballad.

"John Peel" may have been suggested by a glossy picture of
this huntsman, which, hanging on the wall, advertises Adam Findlater, the Dublin grocer. (334)[1] Another picture on the wall—this
one of the charge of the Light Brigade—may have suggested Earwicker's story of the Russian general. Trying like any host to en-
tertain his guests, he tells them stories while serving drinks. His
story of the Russian general is preceded by that of the sailor and
the tailor. These hospitable yarns are the central materials of a
long and difficult chapter.

Earwicker's story of the sailor and the tailor, (311-33) which
echoes the legend of the Prankquean and seems no less archetypal, is the story of Earwicker's marriage. The Norwegian sailor
orders a suit for which, on his visits to port, he refuses to pay.
But he marries the tailor's daughter. A tailor making clothes
("sartor's risorted," 314) is a creator; and a sailor is a rover. As
"ship's husband," or master, Earwicker is sailor, but he seems both
sailor and tailor. Their conflict is another of those civil wars that
divide and ultimately unite the great composite. One side sits
creating while the other comes and goes like the Viconian Prankquean. His "baffling yarn sailed in circles." (320) Those who
think the sailor "down to the button of his seat" with McGinty
(316) are deceived; for back to port comes porter. A "blondblub-
ber" at last, caught and caged by Nanny Ni Sheeres, the tailor's
daughter, the sailor roves no more. (328-29) As Earwicker finishes
this pathetic story, Mrs. Earwicker sends Kate down with a message: "Come to bed," says A. L. P. "This is time for my tubble,"

---

1. Findlater involves Finnleader, Finnlater (or Finnagain), as well as ladder,
litter, and letter. Findlater, "our grocerest churcher," built Dublin a church,
known as Findlater's "fire escape." (Cf. 558, 619) John Peel, like H. C. E.,
goes forth in the morning.

reflects Mr. Gladstone Browne, despairing of home rule. "Dip."
(333-34)

Not yet the time for tub or other tubbles; for other duties detain the decent man downstairs. He must serve the clamoring customers drinks and tell another story. "How Buckley Shot the Russian General," a tale within a tale, is the climax of a debate between Taff or Shaun and Butt or Shem. For those unruly drinkers at the bar "drouth is stronger than faction." (334-58)

Earwicker's first "hostory" concerns his marriage and his second its consequences. Children mean quarreling sons, who follow the usual pattern. Knocked down by Taff, (344) Butt forgives his brother, and the twins agree. Sooner or later, however, the quarrel of son with son becomes the quarrel of son with father, whose place the son usurps. Buckley is another Cad. Like Buck Mulligan, Buckley owes his name to Gaelic *bouchal* or *bouchaleen*, boy or buck. (314) The Crimea, where Buckley shoots the Czar's general, implies crime; and a general is far from particular. But which of the twins is Buckley?

Like Synge's playboy, called to mind by rhythm and diction, (344)[2] Butt kills the "aged monad" (Bruno's Monad) because he has to. "Hump to dump," says he. Taff's immediate reaction is favorable: "Bullyclaver of ye . . . you were shutter reshottus and sieger besieged." (344, 352) Thinking it over, however, he disapproves; for the killing of the "mangoat" involves general confusion, even atomic disintegration. (353) But thinking it over again, Taff is pleased. It may be that Butt has shot the old man, but Taff gets credit for the deed. Ironically, Taff is Buckley—or, since Taff and Butt are "now one and the same person," (354) Buckley is composite son or father again. "I am, I am," (358) says falling and rising Earwicker, ending his story.

It is closing time: "Tids, genmen, plays." (371) The twelve reluctant customers and the four old men go home, each in his own direction. Alone in his pub, Rory O'Conor Earwicker drinks the dregs and falls. However ignominious, his fall is creative, equivalent to writing *Finnegans Wake* and putting out to sea

2. Cf. Shem's "Western playboyish world," p. 183.

(380-82) We are all at sea in the next chapter. Faugh MacHugh O'Bawlar or Ford Madox Ford is at the wheel (*Letters*, 405) because he published an early version of this voyage in the *Transatlantic Review*.

(Shooting the general with his pants down seems unsporting; but, wiping himself with a sod of turf, he has insulted Ireland, 333.)

CHAPTER XII

Tristan

(*Pp.* 383-99. Vico's ricorso.)

The four old men observe the affairs of Tristan, Isolde, and King Mark. Conflict of young and old resuming, the young man takes the old man's girl away. Mark is H. C. E., Tristan is Shaun, and Isolde is Isabel. During the voyage of Tristan and Isolde from Chapelizod to Cornwall, the four old gossips sigh and look, sigh and look, sigh and look, and sigh again. Seabirds or scavengers are their metaphor. (383)

As becomes authors of four gospels, the first three of which are synoptic, these peepers tell the same story from four points of view, but not in the usual order. John, Mark, Luke, and Matthew is the order here. The first three of these are now synoptic, the last no better than optic. Reversal of the usual order implies renewal. The waters of the sea, to which the Liffey flows, imply renewal—so too young lovers, and so the matters of these gospels.

A repeated "up" is plain enough; but what of repeated references to Trinity College, Protestantism, the new world, wrecks, and auctions? A little thinking makes these no less plain. A college is a gathering and an auction a dispersal. Death by water means emergence from it. Protestantism and the new world mean renovation of old orders: "Runtable's Reincorporated" or "regnumrockery roundup." (387-88) "Repeating themselves" (394) like Vico's ages, the synoptic annalists preserve the past "in spirits of time," (394) while announcing the future. Taking John's place, Matthew celebrates renewal with a little difference.

"Pass the teeth for choke sake, Amensch," say Mamalujo, repeating the formula of the Eucharist. (397) This sacrament, made possible by death, means life and Son; and Son introduces three chapters on Shaun as son. Isabel, the boneheaded princess with "bedroom eyes," is his darling.

Note the reversal (suitable to a recorso) of words, names, sexes, and identities in this chapter.

Part III

HUMANITY

(Four chapters. Vico's human age.)

CHAPTER XIII

Shaun the Post

(Pp. 403-28. Vico's divine age.)

This chapter opens a three-chapter celebration of Shaun as beloved son and human being—"the most purely human being that ever was called man." (431) Beginning in the manner of a mediaeval vision, this chapter becomes an interrogation of Shaun by the four old men and their ass. The tone is genial. Everybody applauds the "beamish" postman, whose lamp shines through our fog, despite his sins of gluttony, envy, and pride; for these, after all, are human. "Shaunti and shaunti and shaunti again!" (408) we cry from our wasteland.

Shaun's fable of the Ondt and the Gracehoper, (414-19) recalling the fables of Mutt and Jute, the Mookse and the Gripes, and the Prankquean, parodies La Fontaine, not "Esaup." Here too the conflict of the twins is of space with time, of prudence with improvidence. The "foibler" is another Jones. His hero, the Ondt (Danish for evil), says "Nixnixundnix" to the irresponsible Gracehoper, whose virtue is a "smetterling of entymology." But the prudent Ondt gets his reward. Basking with his four insectuous girls on the Libido, he smokes "a spatial brunt of Hosana cigals." (417) The poem that brings the fable to a close sums up the

conflict between artist and bourgeois: "*Your genus its worldwide*,"
says the defeated Gracehoper, "*your spacest sublime.*" (419) The
Gracehoper's dancing and singing (art) amount to Finnegan's
Wake, hence to *Finnegans Wake*, dismissed by the Ondt with a
"Ptuh!" (415) References to Soviet Russia, implying a society of
ants or bees, establish Shaun's ideal. References to philosophers,
I "spinooze," fourmish conflicting ideas of reality. References to
Egypt, evoking *The Book of the Dead*, imply death and renewal.
In short, an epitome of *Finnegan* again.

After this agreeable entertainment, the four interviewers question the postman about the letter he carries (on His Majesty's or
H. C. E.'s service), cannot read, and tries in vain to deliver. (419-
25) The addresses of H. C. E. on the envelope are Joyce's own.
(420-21) If the letter is *Finnegans Wake*, Joyce addressed it to
himself, either to his early self, as the Dublin addresses imply, or
to a later self, implied by H. C. E. Not even he receives it. But
thinking Shem the writer, Shaun claims credit, as usual, for his
brother's work: "What Sim sobs todie I'll reeve tomorry." (408)
The letter, says Shaun, is his in part. Indeed, Shem stole the entire document from Shaun; (422-24) for, at this point, he is clearly
Stanislaus Joyce. The sympathetic interviewers, ignoring this
claim, suggest that Shaun could write as well as Shem, maybe
better, if he took the time and trouble. Shaun cheerfully agrees;
but taking that trouble is beneath him.

Not only a postman, Shaun is a Guinness barrel floating down
the Liffey with the corks and other refuse. (414, 419, 426-27;
Letters, 214) Leaving us and promising return, he is also Jesus
Christ.

During this triumphal progress down the river, he is associated
not only with Stanislaus Joyce but with Gogarty, Wyndham Lewis,
De Valera, John McCormack, Lord Ardilaun, and Swift. That
Shaun also resembles Frank O'Connor is hinted by references to
"ghuest of innation." (414, 426) In the next chapter Shaun is
Synge, Joyce, and Christ again. "Turn your coat, strong character," we cry. (428) Good luck to "your bunghole."

CHAPTER XIV

Jaun's Sermon

(*Pp.* 429-73. *Vico's heroic age.*)

Rolling down the Liffey, the barrel pauses at St. Bride's school, where the twenty-nine girls, sitting on the bank, paddle their fifty-eight feet in the water. Versed in "lithurgy" like a "poorish priced," (432) Jaun addresses these girls from the barrel. Either the barrel serves him as pulpit or else his voice is a voice from the bung. Jaun's Lenten sermon is sententious and didactic: "Look before you leak, dears"; observe "as many as probable" of the Ten Commandments; make a "hopesome's choice" of the saints in the "colander." (432-33) A colander, of course, is as holy as a saint. The piety of preaching Shaun is not unlike that of Father Purdon or of Father Coffey.

As "brotherkeeper," Jaun soon comes to Shem, his "altar's ego," (443, 463) against whom he warns Isabel and her companions. Full of "novel ideas," and having jilted "three female bribes" (religion, country, and mother), Shem is only an "illstarred punster." (465, 467)

About to ascend to heaven, Jaun leaves the Eucharist as memento. He is glad to take off. We come "touch and go, from atoms and ifs," he says, and nothing is certain down here; but in heaven all is "dead certain." (455) That Jaun is Jesus is also implied by his progress through the Stations of the Cross.[1] Taking half a glass of Juan Jaimesan, the "export stout fellow" departs while the sorrowing girls, waving handkerchiefs, recite a Maronite liturgy. Their twenty-nine names are words for peace in twenty-nine languages. (470-71) Jaun's return will be the Second Coming.

1. Or so Joyce assures us. (*Letters*, 214) In the text the fourteen Stations of the Cross (which begin in Chapter XIII) are obscure, but I have been able to identify a few: the carrying of the cross, (430-31) falling with the cross, (433-34) the vinegar and gall, (456) Veronica, (458) the body taken from the cross. (470) Shaun's hat with "reinforced crown" (430) seems a crown of thorns. His sermon parodies a Mass.

As exile, however, Shaun will be Shem. Coming home to "Shamrogueshire" from his "French evolution," a worldly success at last, Shem will be Shaun. Indeed, the Johnny who comes marching home is Shaun-Shem, with Shaun on top. Walker and Waltzer at once, he is cock of the morning, awaking all by a Wake. The mixture of tones in our "*Va faotre!*" fits this triumphant mixture as the sense of our advice fits this self-begetting Phoenix. (472-73) We must take the singular bird at his own estimate, or almost.[2] But Joyce's estimate (at once ironic and sentimental, self-involved and distant) is hard to estimate.

Celebrated by Ireland, Joyce would be Shaun—and so he is today. Being Shaun is more of a thing than some think.

"Va faotre" is also "My Son" in Breton.

CHAPTER XV

Yawn

(Pp. 474-554. Vico's human age.)

Worn out on his "cruxway," (478) the "salve a tour" (409) becomes Yawn. There he lies on a mound in the Park, replacing H. C. E. as sleeping giant. The mound is barrow, magazine or dump. The four old men, snooping as usual, approach the "slipping beauty" (477) with "exagmination" (497) in mind. Analysts rather than annalists now, the four "psychomorers" (476) dig in the dump to uncover the "soul's groupography." (476) Since Yawn as son is Earwicker renewed, his sleeping mind holds everything. That is what those four old men are after. Everything is H. C. E., the father-image lying deep in Yawn's unconscious. The task is arduous; for, although buried H. C. E., as Yawn says, is "the person whomin I now am," (484) Yawn's an-

---

2. As "lightbreakfastbringer" the great composite recalls the union of Stephen-Lucifer and Bloom. As "champion docile" with his "high bouncing gait" Shaun is Stephen of *A Portrait*, trained by Mike Flynn. Minding us of "the withering of our ways," or paralysis, Shaun is author of *Dubliners*. References to "devil era" or De Valera remind us that the civil war is over, that the age of Lucifer has begun. (473) This is one of the most important pages of *Finnegans Wake*.

swers are evasive or obscure—in the attempt, no doubt, to defend his hidden, essential self.

Everything in *Finnegans Wake* includes everything in *Finnegans Wake*. The minimum is the maximum and every part the whole's epitome. What these inquirers dig up, therefore, is all the matters of the book, all the characters, all the themes, and all the motifs. The Cad is here again, along with the two girls, the letter, and Buckley. These and all the rest are what Yawn's mind is made of. "I'm not meself at all," says all-inclusive Yawn.

Not to be put off, taking deeper "soundings," (501) fishing for the greatest fish, (525) the four analysts succeed in bringing up A. L. P., who defends her sinning husband. (492-96) Next they come to Isabel, who, though still before her mirror, is somewhere in Yawn. (527-28) But such approximations of the real thing only increase their effort. Becoming a "braintrust," (529) the four analysts arrive at Kate, (530) who brings them to the deepest layer, where H. C. E. is lurking. "Arise, sir ghostus!" (532) Less psychoanalysis now than séance, the exagmination achieves its end. H. C. E., "the Real Absence," (536) evoked from Yawn, speaks through Yawn, who becomes the Real Presence or father himself.

H. C. E.'s monologue (532-54) is at once a defense and a boast. Guiltless of the sins imputed to him, even when detected, he is the great builder. It was he who founded the city, and, as Ibsen's master builder (540) or Balbus, (552) constructed towers, domes, bridges, and zoo. Modern Dublin, which with the aid of references to London, New York, Paris, and Rome becomes all the cities of the world, is his achievement and his pride. References to *Ulysses* (542) imply both city and creation.

This vision of the city is a vision of the human age, the age of "gossipocracy." (476) Human Earwicker is its creator and human Yawn, whose language suitably degenerates, is its embodiment and its authentic voice. *Finnegans Wake* is its document. "Gags be plebsed," (485) cries the voice from the dump.

CHAPTER XVI

The Bedroom

(*Pp.* 555-90. *Vico's ricorso.*)

Up from pub, the publican lies bedded with wife. In another room Saintette (*sans tête*) Isabel is sleeping, soothed by the rhythms of Gerty MacDowell. (556, 561-62) She dreams of mirrors. In another room Kate lies dreaming how she went downstairs to find H. C. E. with his "clookey" in his hand and his "pious eyebulbs" imploring silence. (556-57) In another room the twins are sleeping. Kevin or "Father Quinn again," will be off to "Amorica" someday, with Tristan, for a "cashy" job. Jerry, having wet the bed with his "foundingpen," is crying in his sleep, dreaming of father. (562-63) So surrounded, Victoria and Albert lie, doing their best, in their "bed of trial." (558)

Those four old men are back again, peeping. Matthew, Mark, Luke, and John, four bedposts now, offer their versions of this bedroom scene. Whether they report interruptions of Earwicker's dream or parts of it remains uncertain. What seems actual may be dream and what dream, actual.

Hearing Jerry crying, A. L. P. gets out of bed to comfort him. His dream of father, she says, was nothing but "phanthares." (565) Later, after she returns to bed, the twins appear to be peeping at their parents, with those old men, but Isabel is "peerless." (566, 587-88) Metaphors suggest parental activity. (567-71)

Proving inadequate for that, metaphor yields to abstraction. A Latin-legal-pathological synopsis reviews family relationships. Depravities, no longer hinted, are displayed. The point of view is Kinsey's or a lawyer's, if not worse. (572-73) This discouraging view of complicated incest is followed by an account, no less discouraging, of H. C. E.'s failure to satisfy his "couchmare." (584-85)

Yet, let us pray for this man and this woman. God guide them through their "labyrinth"—guide us too. (576-77) Such as they are, they are our parents, who "met and mated and bedded and buckled and got and gave and reared and raised . . . and bequeathed us their ills." (579)

Serving as a *ricorso*, this chapter, nevertheless, seems better adapted to the human age. It is all too human. Made parallel to the story of Tristan, an earlier *ricorso*, by the presence of the four reporters, this chapter seems degenerate *ricorso*, if *ricorso* at all. Indeed, after the first, each renewal seems less hopeful than the last. We must remember, however, that the renewal of the present subcycle is within the human age of the larger cycle. A small *ricorso* within a human age must be human, more or less. Yet dawn is breaking, and the great *ricorso* of a larger cycle awaits us in the final chapter.

Part IV

RENEWAL

(*One chapter. Vico's ricorso.*)

CHAPTER XVII

New Day

(*Pp. 593-628. Vico's ricorso.*)

Renewal begins with T. S. Eliot's formula for Shaun. The "latterman" (603) is our hope for the future his mother creates; so he and she are hero and heroine of the final chapter. "Calling all downs" means calling all downs up.

"Whithr a clonk?" (599) the Cad's question, is answered by the "ricocoursing" (609) cock. It is cock's time. Having cooked in his pot awhile, the Phoenix is climbing out. "O rally, O rally, O rally!" (593) At his wake, Finn is waking up.

As the first chapter is an introduction, so this is summary. All the themes and motifs reappear, time and space and all the characters. The twenty-nine "heliotrollops" and even the "dubbledecoys" dance in "prayfulness" around Schoen the Puzt. "Oyes! Oyeses! Oyesesyeses!" they scream. "I yam as I yam," replies this divine potato from the new world. (603-04) References to Oriental philosophy, lacking profound intention, are here to indicate Orient and rising sun.

After these generalities, the ruly chapter, falling into four parts, rises to its climax. A saint's legend, another debate of Mutt and Jute, bringing the first chapter back, and a review of the letter precede the final monologue of A. L. P.

The legend of Saint Kevin of Glendalough (604-06) celebrates Kevin-Shaun, the son. Sailing to Yeats' lake isle of Innisfree in his portable bathtub-altar, the holy boy sits down in the water. His "Yee" echoes Mrs. Bloom's "Yes"; for the waters of birth and baptism, renewing him, have given him being and identity: "Messy messy . . . douche douche." Bloom was a waterlover. So Saint Kevin Hydrophilos, whose legend is another tale of a tub. Glendalough, not far from the meeting of the waters at Avoca, has seven churches. Maybe this is why Joyce's legend of Kevin involves the seven virtues, the seven ecclesiastical orders, the seven canonical hours, and the seven sacraments. Nine orders of angels, also present by the aid of puns, violate this numerical harmony a little—but no matter. That the seven sins are nowhere to be found in this sunny fable is encouraging.

Mutt and Jute reappear as Muta and Juva. Still divided by language, invader and native debate as before. Juva, the invader, is Saint Patrick now, speaking pig Latin and Nippon English to Muta (change), who speaks the vulgar tongue and Pidgin English. Muta is an Irish druid and Bishop Berkeley, somehow united with Buckley. Their debate is an attack upon, and a defense of, *Finnegans Wake*. Muta, the "Irisman," supports the manycolored veil of appearance, the world of dream, imagination, and symbol. Practical Juva supports discourse, fact, and the white light of common sense. Defeated by Patrick and the light of the sun, the druid Berkeley falls, "Thud." Art falls victim again to utility and fact.

A new version of the letter from A. L. P. to H. C. E. (615-19) reviews the themes of *Finnegans Wake:* the Cad, the two girls, the sin, and all the gossip. She forgives him his trespasses.

The final monologue of A. L. P. (619-28) corresponds to that of Mrs. Bloom. Both, seeing their husbands plain, find them inescapable. Maybe to A. L. P. her "Cooloosus" is Cinderella's "bumpkin," yet he is also husband, son, and father, "darkly roaring." An old woman now, she flows out to her father's sea, with the Guinness barrel, to be supplanted in father's affection by a "daughterwife"; for as son replaces father, so daughter mother. Lonely and sad, she is "passing out." Her farewell, poetic and tender, is purest *schmalz.* Whatever our tough convictions, however, there is little wrong with a little *schmalz* in the right place at the right time. Whatever our tough convictions, we are human, after all, or ought to be. Sad, lonely Anna-Kate, passing out to sea, is not without hope; for she knows there will be "Finn again." (628) Turn back to the first page, now, and see for yourself.

bibliography

Dubliners, 1914.

> GHISELIN, BREWSTER, "The Unity of Joyce's *Dubliners*," *Accent*, XVI (Spring and Summer, 1956).

> LEVIN, RICHARD and CHARLES SHATTUCK, "First Flight to Ithaca," *Accent* (1944).

A Portrait of the Artist as a Young Man, 1916.

> ANDERSON, CHESTER, "The Sacrificial Butter," *Accent*, XII (Winter, 1952).

> KENNER, HUGH, "The Portrait in Perspective," in SEON GIVENS, editor, *Two Decades of Criticism*, 1948.

> SULLIVAN, KEVIN, *Joyce Among the Jesuits*, 1958.

Stephen Hero, 1944. Edited by Theodore Spencer. Editions since 1956 contain a newly discovered fragment.

> ANDERSON, CHESTER, *Word Index to Stephen Hero*, 1958.

Exiles, 1918. The Viking Press edition of 1951 contains Joyce's Notes on *Exiles*.

> FERGUSSON, FRANCIS, "A Reading of *Exiles*," in *Exiles*, New Directions, 1945.

> AITKEN, D. J. F., "Dramatic Archetypes in Joyce's *Exiles*," *Modern Fiction Studies*, IV (Spring, 1958).

Ulysses, 1922. The Odyssey Press edition, second printing, 1933, is the most nearly accurate text. The John Lane text is good.

BUDGEN, FRANK, *James Joyce and the Making of Ulysses,* 1934.

GILBERT, STUART, *James Joyce's Ulysses,* 1930.

HANLEY, MILES, *Word Index to James Joyce's Ulysses,* 1937.

STANFORD, W. B., *The Ulysses Theme,* 1954.

ALBERT, LEONARD, "Ulysses . . . and Freemasons," *A.D.,* II (1951).

DAMON, S. FOSTER, "The Odyssey in Dublin," in Givens, ed., *Two Decades of Criticism.*

HALL, VERNON, "Joyce's Use of . . . *Don Giovanni,*" PMLA, LXVI (March, 1951).

KLEIN, A. M., "The Oxen of the Sun," *Here and Now,* I (1949). "The Black Panther," *Accent,* X (Spring, 1950). "A Shout in the Street," *New Directions,* XIII (1951).

TINDALL, W. Y., "Dante and Mrs. Bloom," *Accent,* XI (Spring, 1951). Reprinted in Tindall, *The Literary Symbol,* 1955.

Finnegans Wake, 1939. Recent printings embody textual corrections.

BECKETT, SAMUEL, Stuart Gilbert, Eugene Jolas, *et al., Our Exagmination,* 1929. Reprinted as *An Exagmination.*

CAMPBELL, JOSEPH and HENRY MORTON ROBINSON, *A Skeleton Key to Finnegans Wake,* 1944.

HALPER, NATHAN, "The 'Most Eyeful Hoyth' of *Finnegans Wake,*" *New Republic,* CXXIV (May 7, 1951). "James Joyce and the Russian General," *Partisan Review,* XVIII (July, 1951).

HAYMAN, DAVID, "From *Finnegans Wake:* A Sentence in Progress," PMLA, LXXIII (March, 1958).

WILSON, EDMUND, "The Dream of H. C. Earwicker," in Wilson, *The Wound and the Bow,* 1947.

Aside from the major works of Joyce, these are of interest:

Chamber Music, 1907. Edited by W. Y. Tindall, 1954.

Critical Writings, 1959. Edited by Ellsworth Mason and Richard Ellmann. Contains essays, speeches, and verse.

Epiphanies, 1956. Edited by O. A. Silverman.

Letters, 1957. Edited by Stuart Gilbert.
Bibliographies:
> SLOCUM, JOHN and HERBERT CAHOON, A *Bibliography of Joyce,*
> 1953.
> BEEBE, MAURICE and WALTON LITZ, "Criticism of James Joyce,"
> *Modern Fiction Studies,* IV (Spring, 1958).
> MAGALANER, MARVIN and RICHARD M. KAIN, *Joyce, the Man, the*
> *Work, and the Reputation,* 1956. Contains a valuable
> survey of the criticism.

Criticism of special areas:
> HOFFMAN, FREDERICK, *Freudianism and the Literary Mind,*
> 1945.
> MORSE, J. MITCHELL, *The Sympathetic Alien: Joyce and Ca-*
> *tholicism,* 1959.
> NOON, WILLIAM, S. J., *Joyce and Aquinas,* 1957.
> SCHUTTE, WILLIAM J., *Joyce and Shakespeare,* 1957.
> TINDALL, W. Y., "James Joyce and the Hermetic Tradition,"
> *Journal of the History of Ideas,* XV (January, 1954).

Biographies:
> GORMAN, HERBERT, *James Joyce,* 1939.
> ELLMANN, RICHARD, *James Joyce,* 1959.

Memoirs:
> BYRNE, J. F. (Stephen's Cranly), *Silent Years,* 1953.
> GOGARTY, OLIVER ST. JOHN (Stephen's Mulligan), *Mourning*
> *Became Mrs. Spendlove,* 1948. "They Think They
> Know Joyce," *Saturday Review of Literature,* XXXIII
> (March 18, 1950). *It Isn't This Time of Year at All!*
> 1954.
> JOYCE, STANISLAUS, *My Brother's Keeper,* 1958.

Pictures:
> TINDALL, W. Y., *The Joyce Country,* 1960. Photographs of
> Joyce's settings, e.g., Stephen's tower, Bloom's house.

selective index